THE TESTAMENTS OF THE TWELVE PATRIARCHS

INSIGHTs

S.N.Strutt

ISBN 978-1-78222-964-3

CREDITS: R.H.Charles translated the 'Testaments of the Twelve Patriarchs' from Latin into English in 1917]
The original Hebrew version was translated into Latin in the 13th century by the bishop of Lincoln - Robert Grosseteste, who stated that he believed that the Testaments were a genuine work written by the Twelve Patriarchs - the sons of Jacob.

Artwork: front cover by Susanne Strutt
www.suzannestruttartist/instagram.com
www.suzannestruttartist/facebook.com

Book design, layout and production management by Into Print
www.intoprint.net
+44 (0)1604 832149

DEDICATION

This book is dedicated to all the faithful writers or scribes throughout history, who have brought the scriptures to light and made them available for us. Without their dedication and sacrifice we would not have the Word of God so freely available to us in these modern times. It is also dedicated to all those who take the time to diligently study what has been said by God in the Bible and the Apocryphal Books.

– S.N.Strutt (Author)

PREFACE

This book is Based on the Apocryphal Book of the '**Testaments of the Twelve Patriarchs',** which were originally written around the 16-17 Century BC or around 3700 years ago, by the 12 sons of Jacob, who himself was also known as 'Israel'.

This book covers the whole panorama of the nation of Israel from Abraham to the Messiah and on to Eternity.

I would like to state that the 'Testaments of the Twelve Patriarchs' is one of the most important ancient manuscripts that I have ever read, because of the amazing content.

The 'Testaments of the Twelve Patriarchs' do state that one day the Nation of Israel would embrace their Messiah as mentioned in the Book of Zechariah after the infamous Bible verse of the 'Time of Jacob's Trouble'.

From that time onwards Israel would be a righteous nation forevermore.

The 'Testaments of the Twelve Patriarchs' were apparently re-written between 107 and 137 B.C. from much older manuscripts.

Until 1885 many of the apocryphal books used to be in the KJV of the Bible. Many of the apocryphal books can still be found in the Catholic and Orthodox Bibles to this day.

- Stephen Nigel Strutt

CONTENTS

Credits   2
Dedication   3
Preface   4
Contents: 5
Format of this book   7
Introduction   8
The Front Cover Art   9

THE TESTAMENTS OF THE TWELVE PATRIARCHS *INSIGHTS*   13
  THE TESTAMENT OF REUBEN - 1st born to Jacob and Leah   15
  CHAPTER 1 (1) Lecture against Fornication   16
  CHAPTER 2 (2) A prophecy about the Messiah   24
  THE TESTAMENT OF SIMEON - 2nd son of Jacob and Leah   35
  CHAPTER 1 (3) Youthful Plot against Joseph   36
  CHAPTER 2 (4) Envy   40
  CHAPTER 3 (5) The Messiah   44
  THE TESTAMENT OF LEVI - 3rd son of Jacob and Leah   49
  CHAPTER 1 (6) Teaches Humility   50
  CHAPTER 2 (7) Mystic and prophet - Shechem   60
  CHAPTER 3 (8) Visions and Rewards   63
  CHAPTER 4 (9) Israel corrupted   76
  CHAPTER 5 (10) Messiah   83
  THE TESTAMENT OF JUDAH - 4th son of Jacob and Leah   95
  CHAPTER 1 (11) Lion-hearted   96
  CHAPTER 2 (12) Giant and Warrior - Siege   104
  CHAPTER 3 (13) Tamar   112
  CHAPTER 4 (14) Priesthood to Levi - Kingdom to Judah 123
  THE TESTAMENT OF ISSACHAR - 5th son to Jacob and Leah 131
  CHAPTER 1 (15) Mandrakes   132
  CHAPTER 2 (16) 'Backslidden' Israel   142
  THE TESTAMENT OF ZEBULUN - 6th son of Jacob and Leah 147
  CHAPTER 1 (17) Inventor and Philanthropist   148
  CHAPTER 2 (18) 'Love your neighbour'   153

THE TESTAMENT OF DAN - 7th son of Jacob and Bilhah   159

    CHAPTER 1 (19) Thesis on Anger   160

    CHAPTER 2 (20) Prophecy and Restitution   165

THE TESTAMENT OF NAPHTALI - 8th son of Jacob and Bilhah   171

    CHAPTER 1 (21) 'Swift as an eagle'   172

    CHAPTER 2 (22) Vision of Mount of Olives   179

THE TESTAMENT OF GAD - 9th son of Jacob and Zilpah   187

    CHAPTER 1 (23) Strong Man and shepherd   188

    CHAPTER 2 (24) Story of Joseph   194

THE TESTAMENT OF ASHER - 10th son of Jacob and Zilpah   199

    CHAPTER 1 (25) Lecture of Dual-Personality   200

THE TESTAMENT OF JOSEPH - 11th son of Jacob and Rachel   209

    CHAPTER 1 (26) Joseph the 'Beloved'   210

    CHAPTER 2 (27) Memphian woman temptress   225

THE TESTAMENT OF BENJAMIN- 12th son of Jacob and Rachel 239

    CHAPTER 1 (28) Philosopher   240

    CHAPTER 2 (29) 'Salvation for the Gentiles'   249

*(29) Overall total number of chapters.

APPENDICES

APPENDIX 1 'Credits'   261

APPENDIX 2 Meaning of 'Israel'   261

APPENDIX 3 Moses   261

APPENDIX 4 Abraham   261

APPENDIX 5 Pharisees   261

APPENDIX 6 Warrior King Priests   262

APPENDIX 7 The Oppressors   262

APPENDIX 8 Living Waters   262

APPENDIX 9 Books   262

APPENDIX 10 The Maccabees   263

APPENDIX 11 Melchizedek   263

APPENDIX 12 The Twelve Testaments   264

APPENDIX 13 Alexandria   266

APPENDIX 14 The Patriarchs & Heaven   267

APPENDIX 15 The Throne of God   268

APPENDIX 16 The future?   269

APPENDIX 17 Holy Spirit   269

APPENDIX 18 The Messiah   270

APPENDIX 19 Self-Works   273

My 7 Insights Books   277

THE FORMAT OF THIS BOOK

i) The original text from the '**Testaments of The Twelve Patriarchs'** will be surrounded by boxes.

ii) I have typed a chapter of the 'The Testaments of the Twelve Patriarchs' and included in each chapter my commentaries, which are just that: inspiration gleaned from much study of the subject matter, as well as my opinions and speculations. My hope is simply that others by doing further investigations will prove the things that I have written to their own satisfaction.

iii) I have also put cross-references to the Bible, and other Apocryphal books where appropriate.

iv) Details: The first 'comment' in each chapter, will be noted as being 'Comment:1' & then C.2, C.3, etC. I have done this to make it easier as a study book to find the different comments and information. In some chapters I have made a lot of comments, and in others I have made few or no comments. Some of the time the story just speaks for itself.

v) The original text from the 'The Testaments of the Twelve Patriarchs' is in slightly larger text than either the 'comments' or 'Bible verses.

vi) Three different types of writing are used. One for the original text, and another type of writing for my comments, and yet another for the Bible verses.

vii) The longest commentaries and conclusions are in the 'Appendices' of this book.

viii) The KJV of the Bible is what is quoted most of the time in this book

INTRODUCTION

The Patriarchs were very wise, as many of them confessed their own sins and mistakes to their relatives, as they died, or as we would now say they were 'on their 'deathbeds" and admonished them to worship and obey God and to not to make the same mistakes as they had done.

1 John 1.9 If we confess our sins God is faithful and just to forgive us our sins and to cleanse us from all unrighteousness.

Six of the twelve Patriarchs mentioned and quoted from the Book of Enoch.

Enoch prophesied about the coming of Abraham and Israel in Enoch Chapter 93: 'After that in the 3rd Week at its close, a man shall be elected as the 'Plant of righteous judgment; and his posterity shall become the plant of righteousness forevermore.'

The Patriarchs also mentioned visions and dreams that they had had. These are often confirmed in the Book of Jasher and Jubilees.

Wonderfully, the Twelve Patriarchs mentioned the coming of the Messiah 'Yeshua Messias'.

The Twelve Patriarchs mention the coming waywardness and rebellion of the nation of Israel and how that they would be overthrown by their enemies, time and time again. They actually described in detail how that the Messiah would be betrayed by his own people.

In studying the texts, I think that the Twelve Patriarchs were themselves inspired by God to write down their own Testaments, which were unfortunately added to at a much later date such as 100 BCE to try and make the Pharisee political party popular. [See my article about the history of the Pharisees in the APPENDIX]

Apparently, the people in general in Israel did not like the Pharisees according to Dr Charles who got his information from the ancient Jewish Historian Josephus who wrote the 'Antiquities of the Jews' circa 100 AD.

The Front Cover Art

The picture of Joseph and three of his brethren about him, which were Reuben, Judah and Levi on the front cover is just perfect, because Joseph was not born a great leader, but he was made into a great leader by the hands of the Almighty, by all the terrible things that he had to endure for 13 years.

As is famously stated 'Leaders are not born but made', which is a true saying in the case of Joseph. All the trials that Joseph had to go through, as well as temptations in order to make him into the gold that he became, ended up with him becoming Pharaoh for a season when the next Pharoah was too young to rule.

Joseph became the mentor of the young Pharoah whilst Joseph ruled as Pharaoh for a season. In the Testaments of The Twelve Patriarchs, they all spoke very highly of their brother Joseph. Whilst they also confessed their heinous sins against Joseph whilst he was yet only 17 years old, when most of them wanted to kill him because he was very arrogant and sassy. They sold Joseph into slavery into Egypt by the hand of the Ishmaelites when he was only 17 years old.

The book rotates around Joseph as the great deliverer of both His people Israel and of the nations, who would have faced starvation without Joseph's godly policies of preparation for the great Famine.

In spite of Joseph having had so many trials, tribulation and temptations for 13 years he did not become bitter or resentful, but his own brethren stated that he was a kind and loving person, who forgave his brothers for their iniquity against himself, stating that it had 'all been part of God's greater plan' to save his whole family from the 7 years of famine that later ensued.

Genesis 45 ⁴And Joseph said unto his brethren, 'Come near to me, I pray you. And they came near. And he said, 'I am Joseph your brother, whom ye sold into Egypt'. 'Now therefore be not grieved, nor angry with yourselves, that ye sold me hither: for God did send me before you to preserve life'. 'For these two years hath the famine been in the land: and yet there are five years, in the which there shall neither be earing nor harvest'.

Amazing prophecy about the 12 PATRIARCHS:

Rebecca, the wife of Isaac prophesied over Jacob her son the father of the Patriarchs when he was yet 'young' and unmarried that he would have 12 sons and that they would be born under the '**12 different star signs**' in the book of **Jubilees** Chapter 25.

Rebecca's Prayer and Prophecy for Jacob & his 'Future Sons' The 12 Patriarchs: Book of Jubilees 25.11-23

11 'And thereupon she lifted up her face to heaven and extended the fingers of her hands and opened her mouth and blessed the Most High God, who had created the heaven and the earth, and she gave Him thanks and praise.

12 And she said: 'Blessed be the Lord God, and may His holy name be blessed for ever and ever, who has given me Jacob as a pure son and a holy seed; for he is Thine, and Thine shall his seed be continually and throughout all the generations for evermore.

13 Bless him, O Lord, and place in my mouth the blessing of righteousness, that I may bless him.'

14 And at that hour, when the spirit of righteousness descended into her mouth, she placed both her hands on the head of Jacob, and said:

15 Blessed art thou, Lord of righteousness and God of the ages and may He bless thee beyond all the generations of men. May He give thee, my son, the path of righteousness, and reveal righteousness to thy seed.

16 And may He make thy sons many during thy life, and may they arise according to the number of the months of the year. And may their sons become many and great beyond the stars of heaven, and their numbers be more than the sand of the sea.

17 And may He give them this goodly land - as He said He would give it to Abraham and to his seed after him always - And may they hold it as a possession for ever.

18 And may I see (born) unto thee, my son, blessed children during my life, and a blessed and holy seed may all thy seed be.

19 And as thou hast refreshed thy mother's spirit during her life, The womb of her that bare thee blesses thee thus, (My affection) and my breasts bless thee and my mouth and my tongue praise thee greatly.

20 Increase and spread over the earth, and may thy seed be perfect in the joy of heaven and earth for ever; And may thy seed rejoice. And on the great day of peace may it have peace.

21 And may thy name and thy seed endure to all the ages, and may the Most High God be their God, And may the God of righteousness dwell with them, And by them may His sanctuary be built unto all the ages.

22 Blessed be he that blesses thee, and all flesh that curses thee falsely, may it be cursed.'

23 And she kissed him and said to him; 'May the Lord of the world love thee as the heart of thy mother and her affection rejoice in thee and bless thee.' And she ceased from blessing.

C.1 Rebecca really prayed for her son Jacob to be blessed by the Lord and that he would give him many children. Well God certainly answered Rebecca's heart-felt prayers as Jacob ended up with 4 wives and 12 sons and one daughter.

C.2 Of course, this was all part of God's plan for Israel to multiply, prosper and became a great nation. This was indeed God's commandment to Adam and Eve at the very beginning of Creation and again after the Great Flood when growth of the human population had been restarted with Noah and his three sons.

GEN.1:28 And God blessed them, and God said unto them, 'Be fruitful, and multiply, and replenish the earth, and subdue it: and have dominion over the fish of the sea, and over the fowl of the air, and over every living thing that moves upon the earth'.

THE TESTAMENTS OF THE TWELVE PATRIARCHS 'INSIGHTS'

TESTAMENT OF REUBEN

The First-Born Son of Jacob and Leah.

Chapter 1: Lecture against Fornication

THE Copy of the Testament of Reuben, even the commands which he gave his sons before he died in the hundred and twenty-fifth year of his life.

2 Two years after the death of Joseph his brother, when Reuben fell ill, his sons and his sons' sons were gathered together to visit him.

3 And he said to them: My children, behold I am dying, and go the way of my fathers.

4 And seeing there Judah, and Gad, and Asher, his brethren, he said to them: Raise me up that I may tell to my brethren and to my children what things I have hidden in my heart, for behold now at length I am passing away.

5 And he arose and kissed them, and said unto them: Hear, my brethren, and do ye my children, give ear to Reuben your father, in the commands which I give unto you.

[Author's Disclaimer: Please do not be offended at Reuben's attitude towards woman. Besides this person lived almost 3700 years ago, and the customs were very different back then.]

6 And behold I call to witness against you this day the God of heaven, that ye walk not in the sins of youth and fornication, wherein I was poured out, and defiled the bed of my father Jacob.

7 And I tell you that he smote me with a sore plague in my loins for seven months; and had not my father Jacob prayed for me to the Lord, the Lord would have destroyed me.

C.1 Here is information that we have not seen in either the Bible nor the apocryphal books of Jubilees or Jasher, that Reuben was punished for his crime against both his father and indeed against the Lord in defiling his father's concubine.

C.2 According to the Laws of Moses, which fortunately for Reuben didn't come into law for circa 250 years after his own time, Reuben could have been stoned to death for his illegal actions.

Leviticus 22.11: If a man has sexual relations with his father's wife, he has dishonoured his father. Both the man and the woman are to be put to death; their blood will be on their own heads.

8 For I was thirty years old when I wrought the evil thing before the Lord, and for seven months I was sick unto death.

Psalm 119.68,71. 'Before I was afflicted, I went astray, but now have I kept thy Word'. 'It is good for me that I have been afflicted that I might learn thy statutes'.

C.3 Reuben stated that he was 30 years old when he committed the crime against his father's concubine wife. This means that it happened long before Joseph was sold as a slave into Egypt by his brethren.

C.4 It also means that Joseph could have heard and seen the judgment that God himself pronounced over this brother Reuben of 7 months being sick in bed nigh unto death and this could have strengthened Joseph's convictions and faith once he was sold as a slave into Egypt, when he was tempted by a beautiful temptress who was married and the wife of Potiphar one of Pharaoh's right hand men. Joseph knew that he must not make the same mistake that his brother Reuben had made. The fear of God is what kept Joseph 'in check' once down in Egypt in my opinion.

9 And after this I repented with set purpose of my soul for seven years before the Lord.

10 And wine and strong drink I drank not, and flesh entered not into my mouth, and I ate no pleasant food; but I mourned over my sin, for it was great, such as had not been in Israel.

C.5 Reuben: 'My sin, for it was great, such as had not been in Israel'. Because Reuben's sin was so blatant and foolish and defiant of the laws of Abraham his great grandfather, therefore his punishment was long or for seven months of being in bed very sick and nigh unto death. It was only because of the diligent prayers of his father Jacob that he was not 'slain' by God Himself!

11 And now hear me, my children, what things I saw concerning the seven spirits of deceit, when I repented.

C.6 I don't know if the following list of 7 deadly sins from the Catholic church has any relevance to the 7 spirits of deceit, but they certainly sound similar: 'The seven deadly sins, also known as the capital vices or cardinal sins, is a grouping and classification of vices within Christian teachings, although they are not mentioned in the Bible. Behaviours or habits are classified under this category if they directly give rise to other immoralities. According to the standard list, they are Pride, Greed, Wrath, Envy, Lust, Gluttony, and Sloth, which are contrary to the 7 Heavenly Virtues': **Source**: Seven deadly sins - Wikipedia The virtues are identified as chastity, temperance, charity,

17

diligence, patience, kindness, and humility. The 7 Virtues and the 7 Deadly Sins | Faith and the Intuitive Arts (wordpress.com)

C.7 Repentance is a powerful thing. When we repent, then God starts to strengthen us and to fill us with righteousness, knowledge and wisdom as he did with Reuben, and he became a totally different person who walked in the fear of God. He also stopped being so physical and also stopped being one who leaned to his own understanding a lot of the time. It is possible that he had become a little lifted up in pride before his crime against his father, as he was so exalted as the eldest brother and was mighty in deeds and in warfare against his enemies. So, God had to take him down a peg to show him that his own strength was nothing without God.

1 John 1.9 'If we confess our sins God is faithful and just to forgive us our sins and to cleanse us from all unrighteousness'.

> 12 Seven spirits therefore are appointed against man, and they are the leaders in the works of youth.
>
> 13 And seven other spirits are given to him at his creation, that through them should be done every work of man.

C.8 We see in contrast that there are listed nine fruits of the Spirit or Virtues in the New Testament Book of Galatians chapter 5.

Galatians 5.22-23 But the fruit of the Spirit is love, joy, peace, longsuffering, gentleness, goodness, faith,

[23] Meekness, temperance: against such there is no law.

> 14 The first is the spirit of life, with which the constitution of man is created.

Genesis 2.7 And the Lord God formed man of the dust of the ground and breathed into his nostrils the breath of life; and man became a living soul.

C.9 What Reuben calls the 7 spirits assigned to mankind, these are what we call today the senses, or they sound very similar. Could this mean that our senses are more than just physical? Notice that in the New Testament, that frequently Jesus in healing some person from a serious ailment like deafness, that he would first cast out a bad spirit of deafness. Could it be that the opposite also exists: the spirit of 'hearing'?

> 15 The second is the sense of sight, with which arise desire.

C.10 It is indeed the sense of sight that causes people to notice something beautiful like a cute baby or a flower or a beautiful woman.

> 16 The third is the sense of hearing, with which cometh teaching.

C.11 We do learn a lot from our sense of hearing especially when we are listening. Like noticing how things grow in God's nature and that it is not just chaos or random.

> 17 The fourth is the sense of smell, with which tastes are given to draw air and breath.
>
> 18 The fifth is the power of speech, with which cometh knowledge.
>
> 19 The sixth is the sense of taste, with which cometh the eating of meats and drinks; and by it strength is produced, for in food is the foundation of strength.
>
> 20 The seventh is the power of procreation and sexual intercourse, with which through love of pleasure sins enter in.

C.12 All these 'senses' are for the good of mankind and not for evil. Many things are not actually evil if used with the right 'intention' and often with moderation. God gave us our senses so how could they be evil? The gifts of sex and procreation are also beautiful gifts from God to us to be used in the right kind of relationships such as marriage.

Philippians 4.5 'Let your moderation be known unto all men. The Lord is at hand.'

C.13 I think that Reuben is telling us something profound and that is that there is a good spirit linked to human beings that help them with many of their functions and especially with their thinking.

> 21 Wherefore it is the last in order of creation, and the first in that of youth, because it is filled with ignorance, and leadeth the youth as a blind man to a pit, and as a beast to a precipice.
>
> 22 Besides all these there is an eighth spirit of sleep, with which is brought about the trance of nature and of death.

C.14 This last verse sounds very deep. 'An eighth spirit of sleep with which is brought about a trance of nature and of death'?! It would appear that Reuben is talking about a topic that most of us are totally unfamiliar with. A sort of dangerous spiritual sleep which can cause death and leads people into a trance. What is Reuben talking about? To cut a long story short, it is often when we are young and inexperienced that we sometimes do erratic and dangerous deeds.

C.15 When people get to their late 20's and 30's in general, they wonder why they had done such crazy things when they had been a teenager.

C.16 Teenagers can be totally reckless and 'dare-devils' living just for the present 'moment' and for the latest 'thrill'. This eight 'spirit of sleep and death sounds like a very dangerous spirit and sounds like the Horseman of Death, lurking around tempting the youth to get into all kinds of wickedness early on in life before they have time to grow up and come to their senses.

C.17 Acting in a 'senseless way' is indeed giving into this 'spirit' of 'sleep' in my opinion.

C.18 Sadly, many people, although they become wiser in many ways as they emerge from the age of youth still living in the 'land of sleep''. What does that mean? Well, as we have heard top politicians saying in their arrogance and lack of concern and love for others: 'The Truth is whatever I say it is' The Elite of the planet are living fully in the 'land of sleep' and Death.

C.19 If we go back in time to the early days in Pre-Flood times, it was all started by Cain, the brother of Abel, in the Land of Nod, some 6000 years ago. Nod means the 'Land of Forgetfulness'. Forgetting the reality that God is the Creator and that we owe Him our dedication and obedience. Cain was living in rebellion against God and was followed by his descendants.

Proverbs 23.7 'As a man thinketh in his heart so is he.' Eat and drink, saith he to thee; but his heart is not with thee.

---

23 With these spirits are mingled the spirits of error.

24 First, the spirit of fornication is seated in the nature and in the senses.

25 The second, the spirit of insatiableness in the belly.

26 The third, the spirit of fighting, in the liver and gall.

27 The fourth is the spirit of *obsequiousness and chicanery, that through officious attention one may be fair in seeming.

C.20 What does this last verse mean? 1) obsequiousness = grovelling and snivelling 2) Chicanery: the use of deception or subterfuge to achieve one's purpose. In modern lingo: 'kissing ass' for benefit.

---

28 The fifth is the spirit of pride, that one may be boastful and arrogant.

29 The sixth is the spirit of lying, in perdition and jealousy to practise deceits, and concealments from kindred and friends. (perdition = complete and utter ruin)

30 The seventh is the spirit of injustice, with which are thefts and acts of rapacity, that a man may fulfil the desire of his heart; for injustice

---

> worketh together with the other spirits by the taking of gifts. (Rapacity = aggressive greed.)
>
> 31 And with all these the spirit of sleep is joined which is that of error and fantasy.

C.21 It is interesting that the 'spirit of spiritual sleep' and slumber accompanies all these other bad spirits that tend to tempt the youth. We see today that a lot of the youth are atheistic and unbelieving in God, which makes them a target for evil spirits.

> 32 And so perishes every young man, darkening his mind from the truth, and not understanding the law of God, nor obeying the admonitions of his fathers, as befell me also in my youth.

Ephesians 4:18 They are darkened in their understanding and alienated from the life of God because of the ignorance that is in them due to the hardness of their hearts.

1 Timothy 4:2 «Speaking lies in hypocrisy; having their conscience seared with a hot iron;»

> 33 And now, my children, love the truth, and it will preserve you: hear ye the words of Reuben your father.

C.22 It is tragic that in modern times we know relatively nothing of all these things, just mentioned by Reuben.

C.23 It is a great tragedy that in modern times most of the parents have totally abdicated their responsibilities of teaching and training their own children in every sense of the word. They give their children over to the gods of false education, evolution and unbelief in God. They unwittingly do as the ancient evil nations who sacrificed their own children to Molech and Mammon.

C.24 Most Parents in the West no longer teach their children about God and Jesus, but just tell them 'Do you own thing' and hope for best. No rhyme or order in modern living as most people are being led around by the spirit of Satan himself in their unbelief and never-ending idolatry.

C.25 Of course, there are Christians who do still teach their own children and try to keep them away from worldly influence, but it is very difficult with all the electronic gadgets constantly available even to small kids which spew out evil and nonsense and certainly not teaching children to behave in a godly way.

C.26 I just read how that 70% of American pastors 'no longer hold to a biblical view of life in 2022. It is no wonder, as they have largely been teaching their flocks about the 'abundant life' which has absolutely nothing to do with true Christianity. A MINORITY OF PASTORS IN THE USA HOLD A BIBLICAL WORLDVIEW | LIVING ETERNAL NOW

Ecclesiastes 8.5 "Whoso keeps the commandment shall feel no evil thing: and a wise man's heart discerns both time and judgment."

---

34 Pay no heed to the face of a woman,

35 Nor associate with another man's wife,

36 Nor meddle with affairs of womankind.

37 For had I not seen Bilhah bathing in a covered place, I had not fallen into this great iniquity.

C.27 It is my personal opinion that we should not blame our sins on somebody else and make excuses for our sins. That is passing the 'buck' of responsibility.

---

38 For my mind taking in the thought of the woman's nakedness, suffered me not to sleep until I had wrought the abominable thing.

C.28 The spirit of lust is a 'restless spirit' and keeps persistently trying to tempt people to do the ungodly thing and give in to their evil temptations and perversions.

Genesis 3.12 'The man said, "The woman you put here with me—she gave me some fruit from the tree, and I ate it."

---

39 For while Jacob our father had gone to Isaac his father, when we were in Eder, near to Ephrath in Bethlehem, Bilhah became drunk and was asleep uncovered in her chamber.

Ephesians 5.18 Do not get drunk on wine, which leads to debauchery. Instead, be filled with the Spirit.

C.29 A definition concerning 'debauchery', which this world if fast descending into, due to demonic influences, and modern liberal teachings. [Debauchery – 'free for all sex including perversities' with whoever is available at the time of drunkenness]

C.30 It is tragic that teenagers are encouraged in such horrors as wanton drunkenness and saying that it is a manly thing to do. No, it is not, it is ungodly behaviour. But how can one blame the teenagers when they are never taught 'right and wrong' by their unbelieving parents.

C.31 Schools don't teach children to understand the opposite sex and how to get on with them and how to treat them kindly and with consideration. Schools teach the children to be selfish with a me first attitude.

---

40 Having therefore gone in and beheld her nakedness, I wrought the

---

impiety without her perceiving it, and leaving her sleeping, departed.

C.32 King David was also tempted in seeing a naked woman and he was also judged for it as she was a married woman and he committed adultery with her because she was so beautiful to look at.

2 Samuel 11.2-5 One evening King David got up from his bed and walked around on the roof of the palace. From the roof he saw a woman bathing. The woman was very beautiful, [3] and David sent someone to find out about her. The man said, "She is Bathsheba, the daughter of Eliam and the wife of Uriah the Hittite." [4] Then David sent messengers to get her. She came to him, and he slept with her. Then she went back home. [5] The woman conceived and sent word to David, saying, "I am pregnant."

41 And forthwith an angel of God revealed to my father concerning my impiety, and he came and mourned over me, and touched her no more.

C.33 The angel of the Lord revealed to Jacob what Reuben had just done with his concubine wife Bilhah. I think it was tragic that Jacob never went into this wife Bilhah again. That turned out to be a tragedy as Bilhah died shortly after this time, as her mistress Rachel already had died at the hard birth of Benjamin.

C.34 Poor Bilhah she got a raw deal! Did Bilhah, Jacob's concubine, lose the will to live because Jacob abandoned her? There was far too much 'letter of the law' in the Old Testament - no real forgiveness and only an eye for an eye and a tooth for a tooth. Thank God for the coming of the Messiah – Jesus who radically changed the Old Testament to the New Testament. Instead of an 'eye for an eye', Jesus preached 'forgive others' be 'merciful' to others, have 'compassion' on others and certainly not 'abandon' them for breaking a rule that was not even their mistake as in the case of Bilhah with Reuben!
[See Jubilees Insights & Jasher Insights]

CHAP. II.

PAY no heed, therefore, my children, to the beauty of women, nor set your mind on their affairs; but walk in singleness of heart in the fear of the Lord, and expend labour on good works, and on study and on your flocks, until the Lord gives you a wife, whom He will, that ye suffer not as I did.

C.1 Editor: I would put in a disclaimer here for the women reading this book to not be offended by what was written by this first Patriarch, and eldest brother Reuben about relationships and sex. The Patriarchs lived some 3700 years ago and their thinking was very different than those in modern times. Being not so long since the Great Flood (600 years), men were still afraid that the women would become as the 'licentious daughters of Cain' and attract fallen angels or demons.

C.2 Good advice about not stalking women, or following them around, just because they are beautiful creatures. A young man is not supposed to have the 'hunter' instinct, as taught by Evolution, but to get his mind on some useful job that needs doing. Trust in the Lord and He will give you a good wife and companion all in His good time. I think that God's original intention was for men and women to marry young like Adam and Eve did when they were around 19 and 16 years of age. That would cut out years of loneliness and modern promiscuity would not be an issue.

C.3 Having excessive desire even for a seemingly good thing, like sex can become an obsession, which can lead to sin, iniquity and crimes. No woman should be forced to have sex against her will, under any circumstances, even if you are married to her.

C.4 I have often heard the ridiculous excuse by rapists that it was the woman's fault for being beautiful and seductive. Man is not supposed to be a wild beast which is totally out of control, but he has to learn to get his sexuality under control. The more one disciplines a certain area in one's life, the less 'lust and addictions' have control over one's soul.

C.5 There is a time and place for everything 'under the sun', as King Solomon would say. We just need to make sure that what we are doing in any given relationship is God's will, and that we are harming no one by our actions as regards to relationships with women. What age to get married? Now that is a very good question. Some people get married very young, but that custom seems to have changed in modern times where in today's Western world people generally get married at a later age -often in their thirties, which sadly I think is a mistake. Better to get married when you are still flexible in your mind and body, and not yet rigid in your thinking.

C.6 I think that it would be good on average for people to get married in their twenties, if at all possible. Of course, finding the right person isn't always so easy these days. That is what many women have told me. According to obstetricians and gynaecologists the human female body is best suited for having babies between 22-25 years old. This is when the body is the most flexible at this age for having a first baby. My wife had her first baby when she was 22. Having babies much later we are told, can result in health issues.

C.7 The scriptures make it clear that it is a good thing for people to get married. Paul stated, *'If they cannot contain - then let them marry'*. He also said, *'Marriage is honourable in all and the bed undefiled'*.

Hebrews 13.4 Marriage is honourable in all, and the bed undefiled; but whoremongers and adulterers God will judge.

2 For until my father's death I had not boldness to look in his face, or to speak to any of my brethren, because of the reproach.

Romans 8.1 There is now therefore no condemnation to them which are in Christ Jesus, who walk not after the flesh but after the spirit.

1Jn 1.9 If we confess our sins God is Faithful and Just to forgive us our sins and cleanse us from all unrighteousness.

3 Even until now my conscience causes me anguish on account of my impiety. [Impiety = unholy]

C.8 So sad to see that Reuben's conscience was still pricking him 90 years after he had committed a serious crime. The Messiah changed all that in that once one had been forgiven for a sin, the person was no longer supposed to meditate upon that sin.

Proverbs 28:13 «He that covers his sins shall not prosper: but whoso confesses and forsakes [them] shall have mercy.

4 And yet my father comforted me much, and prayed for me unto the Lord, that the anger of the Lord might pass from me, even as the Lord showed.

5 And thenceforth until now I have been on my guard and sinned not.

C.9 The Bible tells us that 'All have sinned and come short of the Glory of God' In the book of Job also written around 4000 years ago, Job stated 'If I profess myself to be innocent, my own mouth shall condemn me.' In verse 5 above, Reuben is stating that that particular sin - 'iniquity of adultery', he did not commit ever again in his lifetime.

6 Therefore, my children, I say unto you, observe all things whatsoever I command you, and ye shall not sin.

1 John 3:9 "Whosoever is born of God doth not commit sin; for his seed remains

in him: and he cannot sin, because he is born of God."

1 John 2.5 Whoso keeps His Word in him verily is the love of God perfected.

C.10 What these above Bible verses are stating is that if you keep reading and obeying God's Word, then the Word itself being Jesus, (according to John 1.1-14:) will keep you from doing the wrong things or sinning against God.

> 7 For a pit unto the soul is the sin of fornication, separating it from God, and bringing it near to idols, because it deceives the mind and understanding, and leadeth down young men into Hades before their time.

C.11 Why can fornication bring young men down to Hades or death before their time? Is there something going on that young men in particular are totally unaware of. Some serious danger by going to houses of prostitution? Sickness, or perhaps violence, a brawl or something even more sinister is lurking in the background? To know about that one needs to know what happened to the young men who gave into the temptations and lures of the 'licentious' daughters of Cain before the Great Flood, which I covered in another of my *Insights books.*

Proverbs 9.18 But he knows not that the dead are there; and that her guests are in the depths of hell.

Gal 5:16 This I say then, 'Walk in the Spirit, and ye shall not fulfil the lust of the flesh'.

Gal 5:17 For the flesh lusts against the Spirit, and the Spirit against the flesh: and these are contrary the one to the other: so that ye cannot do the things that ye would.

> 8 For many hath fornication destroyed; because, though a man be old or noble, or rich or poor, he bringeth reproach upon himself with the sons of men and derision with Beliar.

Gal 5:19 Now the works of the flesh are manifest, which are these: Adultery, fornication, uncleanness, lasciviousness,

Gal 5:20 Idolatry, witchcraft, hatred, variance, emulations, wrath, strife, seditions, heresies,

Gal 5:21 Envyings, murders, drunkenness, revellings, and such like: of the which I tell you before, as I have also told you in time past, that they which do such things shall not inherit the kingdom of God

> 9 For ye heard regarding Joseph how he guarded himself from a woman, and purged his thoughts from all fornication, and found favour in the sight of God and men.

> 10 For the Egyptian woman did many things unto him, and summoned magicians, and offered him love potions, but the purpose of his soul admitted no evil desire, sharp as a two-edged sword.

Proverbs 5.3-5 'For the lips of a strange woman drop as an honeycomb, and her mouth is smoother than oil. But her end it bitter as wormwood. Her feet go down to death; her steps take hold on hell

> 11 Therefore the God of your fathers delivered him from every evil and hidden death.
>
> 12 For if fornication overcomes not your mind, neither can Beliar (Satan) overcome you.
>
> 13 For evil are women, my children; and since they have no power or strength over man, they use wiles by outward attractions, that they may draw him to themselves.

C.12 Women are not evil, at least not most of them and certainly not those who are godly and believe in the Messiah - Jesus Christ. According to the Book of Proverbs there are 'seductive spirits' which can be very dangerous. I think they are like unto the 'Sirens' mentioned in the Book of Enoch:

ENOCH 19.1-2 And Uriel said unto me, 'Here shall stand the angels who have connected themselves with women, and their spirits assuming many different forms are defiling mankind and shall lead them astray into sacrificing to demons as gods, (here they shall stand [in the prison]) until the day of judgement, in the which they shall be judged and made an end of.' And the women also of the angels who went astray shall become sirens, and I Enoch alone saw this vision, the end of all things and no man shall see as I have seen.

> 14 And whom they cannot bewitch by outward attractions, him they overcome by craft.
>
> 15 For moreover, concerning them, the angel of the Lord told me, and taught me, that women are overcome by the spirit of fornication more than men, and in their heart, they plot against men; and by means of their adornment they deceive first their minds, and by the glance of the eye instil the poison, and then through the accomplished act they take them captive.

C.13 It would seem that Reuben had a problem in blaming women for the sin that he committed.

Book of Enoch 8.1a 'And Azazel taught men to make swords and knives, and shields, and breastplates, and made known to them the metals of the earth and the art of working with them.

C.14 This verse in the 'Book of Enoch' then goes on to describe how the fallen angel Azazel taught the women how they could beautify themselves to attract and seduce both men and angels.

Enoch 8.1b 'And bracelets, and ornaments, and the use of antimony, and the beautifying of the eyelids, and all kinds of costly stones, and all colouring tinctures'.

Book of Enoch 8.2 'And there arose much godlessness, and they committed fornication and were led astray, and became corrupt in all their ways.'

> 16 For a woman cannot force a man openly, but by a harlot's bearing she beguiles him.

C.15 Here is a description of a harlot from Proverbs 9.13-18

[13] A foolish woman is clamorous: she is simple and knows nothing.

[14] For she sits at the door of her house, on a seat in the high places of the city,

[15] To call passengers who go right on their ways:

[16] Whoso is simple, let him turn in hither: and as for him that needs understanding, she saith to him,

[17] Stolen waters are sweet, and bread eaten in secret is pleasant.

[18] But he knows not that the dead are there; and that her guests are in the depths of hell.

> 17 Flee, therefore, fornication, my children, and command your wives and your daughters, that they adorn not their heads and faces to deceive the mind: because every woman who uses these wiles hath been reserved for eternal punishment.

C.16 Just to make this point very clear, the Patriarch here was very concerned that the women in his time would not *return* to the ways of the 'licentious daughters of Cain' from before the Great Flood and attract the Fallen Angels yet again. In my opinion, 'The Patriarch Reuben should have made a distinction between normal relationships and those relationships which were done unto idols and unto fallen angels or devils such as sexual ceremonies of witchcraft.

1 Cor 11.4-5,10 Every man who prays or prophesies with his head covered dishonours his head. [5] But every woman who prays or prophesies with her head uncovered dishonours her head—it is the same as having her head shaved. [10] For this cause ought the woman to have power on *her* head because of the angels.

28

C.17 It is so sad that the church in general gets this point by Paul the apostle all wrong. There is nothing wrong with women and the beauty of their hair. The Bible itself states that the 'crown' of a woman is her hair.

1 Corinthians 11.15 'But if a woman have long hair, it is a glory to her: for her hair is given her for a covering.

1 Corinthians 11:7 For a man indeed ought not to cover his head, forasmuch as he is the image and glory of God: but the woman is the glory of the man. For a man indeed ought not to cover his head, forasmuch as he is the image and glory of God: but the woman is the glory of the man.

C.18 The apostle Paul was not stating that women should cover their heads as some sort of 'religious custom' but as a protection as they are beautiful. He was aware of what happened before the Great Flood when the angels (Fallen ones) came down to the earth and committed fornication with the daughters of Cain. Paul was hypothesizing that the women covering their heads might protect them from evil angels lusting after them as had happened in Pre-flood times and many times since then, especially in witchcraft circles.

> 18 For thus they allured the Watchers who were before the flood; for as these continually beheld them, they lusted after them, and they conceived the act in their mind; for they changed themselves into the shape of men and appeared to them when they were with their husbands.

C.19 Apparently in witchcraft 90% are women even in modern times. Women having sex with Fallen angels is still a great danger in modern times. Sex seems to be very much involved in certain satanic rituals.

> 19 And the women lusting in their minds after their forms, gave birth to giants, for the Watchers appeared to them as reaching even unto heaven.

DANIEL 4:13 «I saw in the visions of my head upon my bed, and, behold, a Watcher and an holy one came down from heaven;"

C.20 The Watchers were originally a special group of angels created by God to take care of mankind and they were especially 'in tune' with man's thinking processes and knew all about man and how his body and mind and spirit operated. Unfortunately, in the Celestial Rebellion fomented by Lucifer and later called Satan, many of the Watcher class of angels went into rebellion against God. Because of their 'link' with humans it was very easy for them to manipulate humans through their minds.

C.21 In the actual story of the Watchers, when they came down to earth and had sex with the women, it was brought out in the Apocryphal books that the Fallen angels took the women away from their husbands by force. [Genesis

6; Jubilees 5.1-4; Jasher 4.16-18.] Read my books 'Enoch Insights', 'Jasher Insights' and 'Jubilees Insights'.

> 20 Beware, therefore, of fornication; and if you wish to be pure in mind, guard your senses from every woman.

C.22 Women are evil sounds like religious 'letter of the law' attitude put in by religionists at a much later date. It sounds like the 'Essenes' sect of monks of 100 BCE pushing the point of chastity in order to justify themselves. Disobedience to God's first commandment, 'Be fruitful and multiply' was encouraged by celibate monks. Not a smart idea, as within a generation or two without having children the sect would have died out!

C.23 *'Guard your senses'* - Guard your senses from drunkenness and what it leads to such as fornication and even adultery

C.24 Note that Reuben and Jacob's concubine were both drunk. Why? It lead to adultery.

C.25 In the days before the Great Flood initially when the Fallen angels came down to earth it was not all woman that they committed fornication with, but the licentious and promiscuous daughters of Cain. Cain whom the scripture states was born of Satan. [See my book **Jasher Insights** for more about Cain, the child of Satan]

1 John 3.12 "Not as Cain, *who* was of that wicked one, and slew his brother. And wherefore slew he him? Because his own works were evil, and his brother's righteous."

C.26 *'Cain who was of that wicked one'* - the serpent. He was the child of the serpent. Adam was the Son of God, and we know that God is not wicked. That can only mean that the serpent had intercourse with Eve thus producing Cain with all the ungodly manifestations that his father (the devil) had.

> 21 And command the women likewise not to associate with men, that they also may be pure in mind.

C.27 The idea of separating the sexes in order to avoid fornication from happening is a very short-sighted and religious narrow-minded idea. It does not work in general.

C.28 If you cloister up young women in a boarding school for example and also cloister boys up in another segregated boarding-school like I was. Sexual problems do develop, when young and having lots of hormones. Some people become same- sex orientated. Another problem is, as happened in our 400 'boys only' boarding school when I was 17 years old. The girls came over from the 600 'girls only' boarding school for a 'dance' and they were 'wild as alley cats' let loose. They wanted sex! I thought we boys were wild enough, but the girls were even wilder. I will leave the rest up to your imagination, as to what happened on that 'dance night' and it wasn't having cups of tea or reading the Bible together either. Of course, I was not a 'saved 'person' when

I was 17 years old.

C.29 I mentioned the above simply to show that you can't control people by laws and religious practices. As, in regards to sex: people will find a way to 'meet each other'. I do agree that modern society does not work when it comes to relationships and marriage a lot of the time. Why? For exactly the reason that Reuben is stating. When there are 'no rules', as in this modern unbelieving Western world, then anything goes, and that itself is not a good thing. We do need godly rules of some sort - but they need to be both balanced and fair and not extreme as well as kind and loving.

C.30 Notice that in the New Testament that Jesus was very kind and loving and forgiving of a woman whom the Jews wanted to 'stone' because she has apparently committed adultery and had been caught in the very act. Did Jesus, the creator start to throw stones at the poor woman. No, he forgave her and cautioned her not to commit fornication again! What about the man involved? Why did he get away with it? How did the Pharisees know that the woman had committed adultery?

John 8:3 'Then the scribes and Pharisees brought to Him a woman caught in adultery.

C.31 Those Pharisees must have been watching her house all the time like peeping-toms.

John 8.4-12 And when they had set her in the midst, they said to Him, "Teacher, this woman was caught in adultery, in the very act. Now Moses, in the law, commanded us that such should be stoned. But what do You say?" This they said, testing Him, that they might have something of which to accuse Him. But Jesus stooped down and wrote on the ground with His finger, as though He did not hear. So, when they continued asking Him, He raised Himself up and said to them, "He who is without sin among you, let him throw a stone at her first." And again, He stooped down and wrote on the ground. Then those who heard it, being convicted by their conscience, went out one by one, beginning with the oldest even to the last. And Jesus was left alone, and the woman standing in the midst. When Jesus had raised Himself up and saw no one but the woman, He said to her, "Woman, where are those accusers of yours? Has no one condemned you?" She said, "No one, Lord." And Jesus said to her, "Neither do I condemn you; go and sin no more."

> 22 For constant meetings, even though the ungodly deed be not wrought, are to them an irremediable disease, and to us a destruction of Beliar and an eternal reproach.

C.32 This seems to be talking about whoremongering could lead to the body being destroyed by Beliar (Satan)

Ephesians 5.5 "For this ye know, that no whoremonger, nor unclean person, nor covetous man, who is an idolater, hath any inheritance in the kingdom of Christ and of God."

> 23 For in fornication there is neither understanding nor godliness, and

31

all jealousy dwelleth in the lust thereof.

24 Therefore, then I say unto you, ye will be jealous against the sons of Levi, and will seek to be exalted over them; but ye shall not be able.

25 For God will avenge them, and ye shall die by an evil death. For to Levi God gave the sovereignty and to Judah with him and to me also, and to Dan and Joseph, that we should be for rulers.

26 Therefore I command you to hearken to Levi, because he shall know the law of the Lord, and shall give ordinances for judgement and shall sacrifice for all Israel until the consummation of the times, as the anointed High Priest, of whom the Lord spake.

27 I adjure you by the God of heaven to do truth each one unto his neighbour and to entertain love each one for his brother.

Matthew 22.39 'Thou shalt love thy neighbour as thyself.

28 And draw ye near to Levi in humbleness, of heart, that ye may receive a blessing from his mouth.

29 For he shall bless Israel and Judah, because him hath the Lord chosen to be king over all the nation.

30 And bow down before his seed, for on our behalf it will die in wars visible and invisible and will be among you an eternal king.

31 And Reuben died, having given these commands to his sons. And they placed him in a coffin until they carried him up from Egypt and buried him in Hebron in the cave where his father was.

Book of Jasher 62.1 In that year, being the seventy-ninth year of the Israelites going down to Egypt, died Reuben the son of Jacob, in the land of Egypt; Reuben was a hundred and twenty-five years old when he died, and they put him into a coffin, and he was given into the hands of his children.

C.33 Why does Reuben not mention his daughters? It is very sad when men can't relate to women and see them only as a sex object.

C.34 The New Testament tells clearly that there is 'No male or female' in

32

Christ Jesus'.

Galatians 3:28 There is neither Jew nor Greek, there is neither bond nor free, there is neither male nor female: for ye are all one in Christ Jesus.

C.35 It would appear that back then, at least Reuben had a hard time understanding women, and apparently Paul the apostle was very much influenced in the teachings of Reuben or the 'Testament of Reuben'.

C.36 Is it possible that Paul was not physically attractive to women?

2 Cor 10.10 'For his letters, say they, are weighty and powerful; but his bodily presence is weak, and his speech contemptible.'

C.37 Did Paul have the wrong attitude against women as he confesses in 1 Cor 7:

1 Cor 7.1,7 Now concerning the things whereof ye wrote unto me: It is good for a man not to touch a woman. 'For I would that all men were even as I myself.'

C.38 Did Paul get soured on some relationships that he had had with women and thus held onto some of the anti-women stances of some of the Patriarchs? He certainly advocated celibacy, which when you think long and hard about, can't be a good idea, as it goes against God's first commandment 'To be fruitful and multiply' – One can certainly not do that without the woman!

C.39 Fornication as mentioned by some of the Patriarchs:

[Testament of Simeon 5:3

Beware, therefore, of fornication, for fornication is mother of all evils, Separating from God, and bringing near to Beliar.

Testament of Judah 14

1 And now, my children, I say unto you, be not drunk with wine; for wine turns the mind away from the truth, and inspires the passion of lust, and leadeth the eyes into error. For the spirit of fornication hath wine as a minister to give pleasure to the mind; for these two also take away the mind of man. For if a man drink wine to drunkenness, it disturbs the mind with filthy thoughts leading to fornication and heats the body to carnal union; and if the occasion of the lust be present, he worketh the sin, and is not ashamed.

Testament of Judah 15

1 He that commits fornication is not aware when he suffers loss and is not ashamed when put to dishonour. For even though a man be a king and commit fornication, he is stripped of his kingship by becoming the slave of fornication, as I myself also suffered. For I gave my staff, that is, the stay of my tribe; and my girdle, that is, my power; and my diadem, that is, the glory of my kingdom. And indeed, I repented of these things; wine and flesh I eat not until my old age, nor did I behold any joy. And the angel of God showed me that for ever do women bear rule over king and beggar alike. And from the

king they take away his glory, and from the valiant man his might, and from the beggar even that little which is the stay of his poverty.

Testament of Judah 18:2-6

2 Beware, therefore, my children, of fornication, and the love of money, and hearken to Judah your father. 3 For these things withdraw you from the law of God, and blind the inclination of the soul, And teach arrogance, And suffer not a man to have compassion upon his neighbour. They rob his soul of all goodness, and oppress him with toils and troubles, And drive away sleep from him, And devour his flesh. 5 And he hinders the sacrifices of, God And he remembers not the blessing of God, He hearkens not to a prophet when he speaks, And resents the words of holiness. 6 For he is a slave to two contrary passions, and cannot obey God, Because they have blinded his soul, And he walketh in the day as in the night. **SOURCE**: Flee Fornication | Hebrew Readers]

TESTAMENT OF SIMEON

The Second Son of Jacob and Leah.

CHAP. I.

THE copy of the words of Simeon, the things which he spoke to his sons before he died, in the hundred and twentieth year of his life, at which time Joseph, his brother, died.

2 For when Simeon was sick, his sons came to visit him. and he strengthened himself and sat up and kissed them, and said:

3 Hearken, my children, to Simeon your father and I will declare unto you what things I have in my heart.

4 I was born of Jacob as my father's second son; and my mother Leah called me Simeon, because the Lord had heard her prayer.

5 Moreover, I became strong exceedingly; I shrank from no achievement nor was I afraid of ought. For my heart was hard, and my liver was immovable, and my bowels without compassion. [Definition: Ought =anything]

6 Because valour also has been given from the Most High to men in soul and body.

7 For in the time of my youth I was jealous in many things of Joseph, because my father loved him beyond all.

C.1 The life of Jacob who became called Israel was a tough and heart-breaking life in many ways. Maybe that is why he became so great. As it is through breakings that God Himself fashions people for His own purposes.

C.2 It is indeed sad that Jacob spoiled Joseph because of his mother being Rachel and that Rachel died young when Joseph was only 10 years old.

C.3 Benjamin was only 7 years old when his brother Joseph then 17 was sold as a slave into Egypt. Obviously, Jacob was very grieved with the loss of his beloved wife Rachel at only 46 years of age.(According to the apocryphal book of Jubilees)

C.4 However, when Rachel's sister Leah, the other wife of Jacob also died at the young age of 51. (According to the apocryphal book of Jubilees), Jacob finally realized what a gem Leah had been, as she had been a person who never said anything amiss about another person according to the apocryphal book of Jubilees.

C.5 At the time that the 11 brethren sold Joseph as a slave, both Rachel and

Leah had already died.

C.6 According to the Book of Jubilees Jacob's only daughter Dinah died young when hearing of the news of the so-called 'death of Joseph'. Also Rachel's handmaiden died at that time also. This meant that Jacob ended up with Leah's handmaiden as his only wife remaining out of 4 wives.

C.7 Jacob had originally only wanted Rachel as his wife, but he was tricked by his corrupted uncle Laban into marrying Rachel's sister Leah first in the darkened bed-chamber.

C.8 From the twistings and sorrows and breakings of Jacob's life came the victory of Jacob becoming named Israel by God Himself.

C.9 Israel means: one who 'wrestles with God'. It also means Prince of God and man.

C.10 What is outstanding about Jacob is that he was given by God many prophecies about the future of the nation of Israel and the Messiah which he passed on to the 12 Patriarchs.

Genesis 37.3-4 Now Israel loved Joseph more than all his children because he was the son of his old age: and he made him a coat of many colours. 4 And when his brethren saw that their father loved him more than all his brethren, they hated him, and could not speak favourably unto him.

> 8 And I set my mind against him to destroy him because the prince of deceit sent forth the spirit of jealousy and blinded my mind, so that I regarded him not as a brother, nor did I spare even Jacob my father.

C.11 'Prince of Deceit' is referring to Satan the Prince of Darkness.

Proverbs 6.34-35 For jealousy is the rage of a man: therefore, he will not spare in the day of vengeance. He will not regard any ransom: neither will he rest content though thou give him many gifts.

C.12 'Rage' is a very evil spirit known for causing wars, abortions, murders and deaths of all sorts.

> 9 But his God and the God of his fathers sent forth His angel and delivered him out of my hands.

Psalm 34.7 The angel of the Lord encompasses round about them that fear him and delivers him.

> 10 For when I went to Shechem to bring ointment for the flocks, and Reuben to Dothan, where were our necessaries and all our stores, Judah my brother sold him to the Ishmaelites.
>
> 11 And when Reuben heard these things he was grieved, for he wished

> to restore him to his father.

Genesis 37.22 And Reuben said unto them, 'Shed no blood, but cast him into a pit that is in the wilderness and lay no hand upon him; that he might rid him out of their hands, to deliver him to his father again.

> 12 But on hearing this I was exceedingly wroth against Judah in that he let him go away alive, and for five months I continued wrathful against him.
>
> 13 But the Lord restrained me and withheld from me the power of my hands; for my right hand was half withered for seven days.

C.13 Here is a detail that we have not heard about before. Simeon's hand was cursed and withered for seven days. That reminds me of the story of King Jeroboam of the Ten Northern Tribes of Israel who became king when the kingdom was split at the death of Solomon. Jeroboam's hand also became cursed and withered.

1 Kings 13.4-6 'And it came to pass, when king Jeroboam heard these sayings of the man of God, which had cried against the altar in Bethel, that he put his hand forth from the altar saying lay hands on him. And his hand which he put forth dried up. So that he could not pull it in again to him. The altar also was rent, and the ashes poured out from the altar according to the sign which the man of God had given by the word of the Lord. 6 And the king answered and said unto the man of God, 'Entreat now the face of the Lord thy God and pray for me than my hand might be restored to me again'. And the man of God besought the Lord and the King's hand was restored him again and became as before.

> 14 And I knew, my children, that because of Joseph, this had befallen me, and I repented and wept; and I besought the Lord God that my hand might be restored and that I might hold aloof from all pollution and envy and from all folly.
>
> 15 For I knew that I had devised an evil thing before the Lord and Jacob my father, on account of Joseph my brother, in that I envied him.
>
> 16 And now, my children, hearken unto me and beware of the spirit of deceit and envy.
>
> 17 For envy rules over the whole mind of a man, and suffers him neither to eat nor to drink, nor to do any good thing. But it ever suggests to him to destroy him that he envies; and so long as he that is envied flourishes,

> he that envies fades away.

Proverbs 14.30 A sound heart is the life of the flesh: but envy the rottenness of the bones

> 18 Two years therefore I afflicted my soul with fasting in the fear of the Lord, and I learnt that deliverance from envy cometh by the fear of God.

Proverbs 14.26 In the fear of the Lord is strong confidence and His children shall have a place of refuge

C.14 Bad spirits need to be both rebuked and cast out or sent away in no uncertain terms.

Matthew 8.16 When the even was come, they brought unto him many that were possessed with devils: and he cast out the spirits with his word, and healed all that were sick:

> 19 For if a man flee to the Lord, the evil spirit runs away from him and his mind is lightened.

C.15 For the Devil flees when he sees the weakest saint upon his knees. 'Take up that white hot 'Sword of the Spirit' which is the Word of God and cut the Devil to the heart, lay it on him, sock it to him with the Word of God. Rebuke him in the Name of Jesus.

2 Corinthians 10:4 For the weapons of our warfare are not carnal, but mighty through God to the pulling down of strongholds.

> 20 And henceforward he sympathises with him whom he envied and forgives those who are hostile to him, and so cease from his envy.

CHAP. II: Israel, Judah, and Levi

AND my father asked concerning me, because he saw that I was sad; and I said unto him, I am pained in my liver.

C.1 Why is Simeon pained in his liver? He seems to affirm that his liver is hurting because of his sins and iniquities and in particular his bitterness and ill treatment of his brother Joseph when he sold him as a slave when Joseph was 17 years old. The Patriarchs mention the different organs in the body, as also having connections with our actions and deeds and sins. This is a very interesting concept.

2 For I mourned more than they all, because I was guilty of the selling of Joseph.

3 And when we went down into Egypt, and he bound me as a spy, I knew that I was suffering justly, and I grieved not.

4 Now Joseph was a good man and had the Spirit of God within him: being compassionate and pitiful, he bore no malice against me; but loved me even as the rest of his brethren.

5 Beware, therefore, my children, of all jealousy and envy, and walk in singleness of heart, that God may give you also grace and glory, and blessing upon your heads, even as ye saw in Joseph's case.

Proverbs 27.4 Wrath is cruel and anger is outrageous; but who is able to stand before envy?

6 All his days he reproached us not concerning this thing, but loved us as his own soul, and beyond his own sons glorified us, and gave us riches, and cattle and fruits.

C.2 Joseph was in many ways an excellent sample of forgiveness to his brethren that had done him evil and injustice - like the Christ. Joseph could have had his brethren killed when he was the right hand of Pharaoh. However, he chose not to, but to 'try them', and see if they had changed from their evil ways. Then he rewarded them all when they passed the 'test'. It is such a beautiful story of love, mercy and forgiveness.

7 Do ye also, my children, love each one his brother with a good heart, and the spirit of envy will withdraw from you.

C.3 'Let the light in, and the darkness will flee of itself'.

> 8 For this makes savage the soul and destroys the body; it causes anger and war in the mind, and stirs up unto deeds of blood, and leadeth the mind into frenzy, and causes tumult to the soul and trembling to the body.

C.4 'Frenzy' is another very evil demon.

> 9 For even in sleep malicious jealousy gnaws, and with wicked spirits disturbs the soul, and causes the body to be troubled, and wakes the mind from sleep in confusion; and as a wicked and poisonous spirit, so appears it to men.

C.5 An interesting description of a demon of jealousy which has sharp teeth that gnaw on a person.

Song of Solomon 8.6 Set me upon thine heart as a seal upon thine arm: for love is strong as death; jealousy is cruel as the grave: the coals thereof are coals of fire, which hath a most vehement flame.

James 3.16 For where envying and strife is, there is confusion and every evil work

> 10 Therefore was Joseph comely in appearance, and goodly to look upon, because no wickedness dwelt in him; for some of the trouble of the spirit the face manifests.

C.6 This is a good point, that the face of a person starts to reveal what kind of person he has been during his lifetime. Kindness and a gentle humble disposition, shows on a person's face, as does also wickedness of different sorts. As it has been said 'The 'eyes' are the 'window of the soul'.

> 11 And now, my children, make your hearts good before the Lord, and your ways straight before men, and ye shall find grace before the Lord and men.

C.7 Look at the contrast to today when seemingly 'anything goes' with no moral rules! Total madness and insanity are seeking to take over, so that chaos will rule! Well, that is the plan of the Satanists, but it is a plan that will fail and be defeated by God himself.

> 12 Beware, therefore, of fornication, for fornication is mother of all evils, separating from God, and bringing near to Beliar.

C.8 Who is the 'mother of all evils'? - **Rev. 17.4** The Great Whore: [4] And the woman was arrayed in purple and scarlet colour, and decked with gold and precious stones and pearls, having a golden cup in her hand full of abominations and filthiness of her fornication:

> 13 For I have seen it inscribed in the writing of Enoch that your sons shall be corrupted in fornication and shall do harm to the sons of Levi with the sword.

C.9 The Book of Enoch does indeed describe the 'History of Israel' from its beginning unto the New Heaven and the New Earth or New Jerusalem.

C.10 It also predicts that many false shepherds would lead Israel with a few good shepherds. Looking at Bible history, some leaders of ancient Israel did indeed try to kill the Levites throughout the period of the Kings of Israel.

C.11 Here the word Levite is referring to a person who is totally dedicated to God and to prayer and supplicating for the people.

C.12 Sometimes Israel had prophets and priests who exhorted the wicked kings of Israel to turn from their wicked ways such as Jeremiah. The kings either killed them or put them in jail.

C.13 In Jeremiah's case he was put in jail until rescued by the conquering Babylonian empire and its king Nebuchadnezzar.

C.14 Many times, God miraculously protected His Levites just as predicted in the above verse 13.

> 14 But they shall not be able to withstand Levi; for he shall wage the war of the Lord and shall conquer all your hosts.

C.15 Here the Patriarchs are prophesying about the future relative to our time and as mentioned in Revelation chapter 19 when the King of Kings and High Priest Melchizedek Himself comes to slaughter the wicked and those who have opposed the truth of the Love of God at the Battle of Armageddon. [For the complete story See Revelations 19.11-21]

Rev 19.15 'And out of His mouth goes a sharp two-edged sword that with it He should smite the nations; and He shall rule them with a rod of iron: and he treads the winepress of the fierceness of the Wrath of God.

Rev 19.16 'And on His vesture and on his thigh a name written King of Kings and Lord of Lords'

C.16 Levi here is representing the truly 'righteous warriors'. who fight for the Lord in spirit and who cannot be defeated, because the King of Kings is their leader and God, who is also a High Priest of the order of Melchizedek as related in Genesis 14.18 & in more detail in Hebrews 7

Hebrews 7.3 'Without father, without mother, without descent, having neither beginning of days, nor end of life; but made like unto the Son of God abides a (High) Priest continually.

> 15 And they shall be few in number, divided in Levi and Judah, and there shall be none of you for sovereignty, even as also our father proph-

esied in his blessings.

C.17 Israel did indeed become very few in numbers in 70 AD, when the Romans kicked out the Jews from Israel. This action was prophesied and mentioned by the 12 Patriarchs as happening as a coming judgement upon Israel because Israel would kill their own Messiah. Imagine the Patriarchs predicting that event of the death of their own Messiah some 1700 years before the birth of Christ.

CHAP. III. A prophecy of the coming of the Messiah.

BEHOLD I have told you all things, that I may be acquitted of your sin.

C.1 'Acquitted of your sin' This is like saying, I have confessed and told you the truth and how to obey God and keep His commandments, now it is up to you to do the right thing, and not make the same mistakes that I did when I was young.

2 Now, if ye remove from you your envy and all stiff-neckedness, as a rose shall my bones flourish in Israel, and as a lily my flesh in Jacob, and my odour shall be as the odour of Libanus; and as cedars shall holy ones be multiplied from me for ever, and their branches shall stretch afar off.

C.2 The Patriarch Simeon is making the point that his sons and grandsons and great grandsons, and great-great grandsons are already showing signs of being guilty of *'envy and all stiff-neckedness.'* Simeon lived to be 120 years old, so he must have many generations of descendants.

1 Samuel 15.22-23 And Samuel said 'Hath God as great delight in burned offerings and sacrifices as in obeying the voice of the Lord. For rebellion is as the sin of witchcraft and stubbornness is as iniquity and Idolatry. Because thou has rejected the Word of the Lord, He also has rejected you from being king.' (King Saul)

C.3 'as a rose shall my bones flourish in Israel' - Simeon is stating that Israel will become as the Rose of Sharon or the Rose of the Lord Himself.

C.4 'as a lily my flesh in Jacob, and my odour shall be as the odour of Libanus'. Israel is also mentioned as a Lily in the Apocryphal book of II Esdras.

II Ezdras '5.12 And I said, 'O Sovereign Lord, from every forest of the earth and from all of its trees thou hast chosen one vine, and from all the lands of the world thou has chosen for thyself one region, and from all the flowers of the world, thou has chosen for thyself one Lily. Jesus the Messiah is called the 'Lily of the valley' at least in song.

C.5 'He's the Lily of the valley and the bright and morning star. He's the fairest of 10,000 that everybody ought to know'- that is a song talking about Jesus.

Song of Solomon 2.1-2 I am the rose of Sharon, and the lily of the valleys.

As the lily among thorns, so is my love among the daughters.

C.6 The Patriarch Simeon is clearly prophesying that he can see the Messiah coming in the future who will be the Rose of Sharon and the Lily of the valley and the bright and Morning Star.

3 Then shall perish the seed of Canaan, and a remnant shall not be

> unto Amalek, and all the Cappadocians shall perish, and all Hittites shall be utterly destroyed.

Exodus 17.13 And Joshua discomfited Amalek and his people with the edge of the sword.

1 Samuel 15.18 And the Lord sent thee on a journey and said, go and utterly destroy the sinners the Amalekites and fight against then until they be consumed.

C.7 The Amalekites were indeed totally destroyed and dramatically so, as pointed out in 1 Samuel 15, which is an excellent chapter about kings obeying the prophet of God and thus the Lord Himself. It shows how king Saul lost the kingdom through disobedience to God circa 1079 BC.

Joshua 1.3 Every place that the sole of your foot shall tread upon, that have I given unto you, as I said unto Moses and all the land of the Hittites.

Jubilees 20.4 'For the seed of Canaan will be rooted out of the land.'

> 4 Then shall fail the land of Ham, and all the people shall perish.

C.8 The land of Ham was devastated because of the 10 Plagues brought upon Pharaoh and Egypt in the times of Moses and Aaron his brother the high Priest some 170 years after the death of the Patriarchs, and exactly 430 years from the time of Abraham's son Isaac being born.

C.9 The descendants of Esau are mentioned by Isaac the father of Jacob, as being 'rooted out' in the Book of Jubilees.

Jubilees 26.34 And by thy sword thou shalt live and thou wilt serve thy brother. And it shall come to pass that when thou become great, and dost shake his yoke from off thy neck, thou shalt sin a complete sin unto death, and thy seed shall be rooted out from under heaven.

> 5 Then shall all the earth rest from trouble, and all the world under heaven from war.

C.10 Here it is mentioning that there shall be *no more war. This will happen when the Messiah returns the 2nd time and puts an end to evil and to violence and war by locking up Satan and his minions in the Bottomless Pit for 1000 years at the beginning of the 1000-year Golden Age of the coming Millennium or better known as Christ's reign on earth. *** **No More War** -song: NuBeat Music - Main Albums - HOT OR COLD

Isaiah 2.2-4 And it shall come to pass in the last days, that the mountain of the LORD's house shall be established in the top of the mountains and shall be exalted above the hills; and all nations shall flow unto it.

[3] And many people shall go and say, 'Come ye, and let us go up to the mountain of the LORD, to the house of the God of Jacob; and he will teach us of his ways, and we

will walk in his paths: for out of Zion shall go forth the law, and the word of the L ORD from Jerusalem'.

[4] And he shall judge among the nations and shall rebuke many people: and they shall beat their swords into plow shares, and their spears into pruninghooks: nation shall not lift up sword against nation, neither shall they learn <u>war</u> anymore.

> 6 Then the Mighty One of Israel shall glorify Shem.
>
> 7 For the Lord God shall appear on earth, and Himself save men.

Isaiah 7.14 Therefore the Lord shall give you a sign: behold a virgin shall conceive and bear a son, and shall call his name Immanuel (Christ)

Isaiah 22.21 I will commit thy government into his hand; and he shall be a father to the inhabitants of Jerusalem.

> 8 Then shall all the spirits of deceit be given to be trodden under foot, and men shall, rule over wicked spirits.

C.11 'Spirits of deceit' shall be 'trodden under foot'. The messiah gave us the power to cast out evil spirits in His powerful name - Jesus.

Luke 10.19 "Behold, I give unto you power to tread on serpents and scorpions, and over all the power of the enemy: and nothing shall by any means hurt you.

> 9 Then shall I arise in Joy and will bless the Most High because of his marvellous works, because God hath taken a body and eaten with men and saved men.

John 1.14 And the Word was made flesh, and dwelt among us, and we beheld his glory, the glory as of the only begotten of the Father, full of grace and truth.

Matthew 15:36 "And he took the seven loaves and the fishes, and gave thanks, and brake them, and gave to his disciples, and the disciples to the multitude."

> 10 And now, my children, obey Levi and Judah, and be not lifted up against these two tribes, for from them shall arise unto you the salvation of God.

In Hebrew, Judah means 'thanksgiving' or 'praise' - הדוהי.

Psalm 100:4–5 Enter his gates with thanksgiving and his courts with praise; give thanks to him and praise his name. For the Lord is good and his love endures forever; his faithfulness continues through all generations.

C.12 Levi – In Hebrew the word Levi means "united," "joined," or, sometimes, "joined in harmony."

> 11 For the Lord shall raise up from Levi as it were a High Priest, and from Judah as it were a King, God and man, He shall save all the Gentiles and the race of Israel.

C.13 It is true that Jesus the Messiah is known as King of Kings and that he came out of the Tribe of Judah when born upon earth. However, Jesus is also known as the High Priest of the order of Melchizedek mentioned in Hebrews 7.

> 12 Therefore I give you these commands that ye also may command your children, that they may observe them throughout their generations.

C.14 It is interesting to note that both the parents of Moses who delivered Israel from Egypt were Levites.

Exodus 2.1-2,10. And there went a man of the house of Levi and took a wife a daughter of Levi. And the woman conceived and bare a son; and when she saw him that he was a goodly child, she hid him three months. And the child grew, and she brought him unto Pharaoh's daughter, and he became her son. And she called his name Moses; and she said, Because I drew him out of the water.

> 13 And when Simeon had made an end of commanding his sons, he slept with his fathers, an hundred and twenty years old.

Book of Jasher 61.4 And in the seventy-fifth year died his brother Simeon, he was a hundred and twenty years old at his death, and he was also put into a coffin and given into the hands of his children.

> 14 And they laid him in a wooden coffin, to take up his bones to Hebron. And they took them up secretly during a war of the Egyptians. For the bones of Joseph, the Egyptians guarded in the tombs of the kings.

C.15 This last verse seems to be telling us that when Simeon died, they secretly took him in a wooden coffin to Hebron. They were afraid that his body would get stuck in Egypt as they saw that the body of Joseph was guarded by the Egyptians in the tombs of their Pharaohs. Joseph and Simeon both died in the same year.

> 15 For the sorcerers told them, that on the departure of the bones of Joseph there should be throughout all the land darkness and gloom, and an exceeding great plague to the Egyptians, so that even with a lamp a man should not recognize his brother.

C.16 Here is a bit of new information in that the sorcerers of Egypt predicted that one day there would be a terrible plague and darkness and gloom upon the land of Egypt at the time that Joseph's bones were removed from Egypt. Let's check the Bible for the time of Moses and the 10 Plagues of Egypt some 170 years after the death of Joseph.

Exodus 10.21 And the Lord said unto Moses, stretch forth thine hand towards heaven, that there may be darkness over the land of Egypt, even darkness which may be felt.

Exodus13.19 And Moses took the bones of Joseph with him: for he had straight sworn the children of Israel, saying, God will surely visit you; and ye shall carry up my bones away with you

16 And the sons of Simeon bewailed their father.

17 And they were in Egypt until the day of their departure by the hand of Moses.

TESTAMENT OF LEVI

The Third Son of Jacob and Leah.

CHAP. I.

THE copy of the words of Levi, the things which he ordained unto his sons, according to all that they should do, and what things should befall them until the day of judgement.

C.1 Levi is giving his sons a pre-view of what will happen to the nation of Israel in the hope that they would stay close to the Lord and not go astray like unto all the nations around them.

2 He was sound in health when he called them to him; for it had been revealed to him that he should die.

C.2 Is this something that is unique to Abraham's time, or does it go all the way back to Adam? Not only Levi knew he was going to die on a specific day, but also according to the Book of Jubilees his grandmother Rebecca also was in perfect health when she died at 155 years old and told her son Jacob that she was about to die.

Book of Jubilees: Ch 35.7 'And yet I will tell you the truth, my son: I shall die this year, and I shall not survive this year in my life; for I have seen in a dream the day of my death, that I should not live longer beyond 155 years: and behold I have completed all the days of my life which I am to live.

C.3 The same is the case with Adam in the '**Lost Books of Adam and Eve Book II**' at 930 years old, as he knew he was about to die. The above-mentioned book is included in my book **Eden Insights**.

'**EDEN INSIGHTS**': **Chapter 87.1** When Adam our father saw that his end was near, he called his son Seth, who came to him in the Cave of Treasures and he said unto him: 'O Seth, my son bring the children and thy children's children that I may shed my blessing on them ere I die.

C.4 In doing some research, I found out that a doctor who took care of the 'old and dying', stated that about two weeks before patients died, that they were 'visited' by relatives that had already 'passed on', encouraging them not to be afraid to die. Hospice caregivers claim patients experience visions of loved ones before death - YouTube

3 And when they were gathered together, he said to them:

4 I, Levi, was born in Haran, and I came with my father to Shechem.

5 And I was young, about twenty years of age, when, with Simeon, I wrought vengeance on Hamor for our sister Dinah.

Book of Jubilees 30.2 'And there they carried off Dinah, the daughter of Jacob, into the house of Shechem, the son of Hamor, the Hivite, the prince of the land, and he lay with her and defiled her, and she was a little girl, a child of twelve years old.

C.5 Hamor was the father of Shechem after which the city was named. Such a terrible crime committed against what was but a child!

C.6 Read my book '**Jasher Insights' Book 1** for a very dramatic account of Shechem and how Simeon and Levi and afterwards their brethren fought against Shechem with supernatural strength from God and they took vengeance against Shechem the prince.

> 6 And when I was feeding the flocks in Abel-Maul, the spirit of understanding of the Lord came upon me, and I saw all men corrupting their way, and that unrighteousness had built for itself walls, and lawlessness sat upon towers.

Isaiah 61.1 The Spirit of the Lord God is upon me; because the Lord hath anointed me to preach good tidings unto the meek; he hath sent me to bind up the broken-hearted, to proclaim liberty to the captives, and the opening of the prison to them that are bound

1Timothy 6.5 "Perverse disputings of men of corrupt minds, and destitute of the truth, supposing that gain is godliness: from such withdraw thyself."

C.7 Levi was with righteous indignation at the very evil city of Shechem whose inhabitants were totally lawless, meaning 'anything goes'. Levi was wondering what he should do about the prince of Shechem who had abused his sister Dinah.

> 7 And I was grieving for the race of the sons of men, and I prayed to the Lord that I might be saved.

C.8 Here Levi is stating in exasperation after seeing the abominable wickedness of Shechem that he wanted God to save him from the wickedness or deliver him from it. We all wish that we could be delivered out of this world sometimes when we see the awful state that it has descended into but we must be patient until our Deliverer comes for each of us in His good time and truly 'save us'. In the case of Levi God had a plan for him to destroy the wickedness of Shechem and that must have been satisfying in a sense. However, in modern times we will have to wait upon God to deliver us all from the wickedness in God's perfect time.

> 8 Then there fell upon me a sleep, and I beheld a high mountain, and I was upon it.

C.9 Here Levi had a dream or vision, where he was taken up to heaven or a high mountain. Similar things happened to Enoch in the Book of Enoch as well as the prophets Isaiah and Ezekiel and John in the book of Revelation

> 9 And behold the heavens were opened, and an angel of God said to

> me, Levi, enter.

C.10 'behold the heavens were opened:

Enoch 14.5 'And the vision was shown to me thus: behold in vision clouds invited me and a mist summoned to me and the course of the stars and lightnings sped and hastened me, and the winds in the vision caused me to fly and lifted me upwards and bore me into heaven'.

> 10 And I entered from the first heaven, and I saw there a great sea hanging.

C.11 *'a great sea hanging'* -This is quite the statement' The first thing that comes to mind about this is Revelation 4.6. There are other scriptures as well.

Rev.4.6 And before the throne there was a **'sea of glass'** like unto crystal.

C.12 I will attempt to hypostasize what could the above verse 10 mean '*a great hanging sea*'. The book of Revelation tells us about a gigantic Crystal City, which from the dimensions given sounds like a giant pyramid. I have seen artists attempts at drawing the Heavenly City as a giant pyramid which is surrounded by the blue 'sea of glass'. It is like putting a giant pyramid inside a sphere, fitting perfectly. Since the Heavenly City is described in Revelation 21-22 as having its height and length and breadth all equal at 1500 miles, this would also mean that if one put such a large pyramid inside a sphere of the 'Crystal Blue Sea', that the apex of the pyramid and the 4 corner points of the base of the Heavenly City would all touch the sphere. If a person was inside the City on any given level, one would see this flowing Sea of Crystal Blue just below the City and all around it.

C.13 Read my recent book 'Eden Insights' chapter 1, which just happens to be talking about the 'Crystal Sea'. What is remarkable is that 'Eden Insights' is based on the Pre-Flood books of the 'Lost Books of Adam and Eve', and therefore is an even older source of information than the 'Testaments of the 12 Patriarchs'.

C.14 The Testaments of the 12 Patriarchs were originally written around 3700 years ago, but the Lost books of Adam and Eve were written circa 5200 years ago, making them probably the oldest books on the planet, along with the Book of Enoch which was also written in Pre-flood times.

C.15 I suspect that it was Enoch who not only wrote the original Book of Enoch but that he also 'put together' the 'Lost Books of Adam and Eve' that is in their original form. It is stated that Enoch was the first person to learn to read and write.* quote

> 11 And further I saw a second heaven far brighter and more brilliant, for there was a boundless light also therein,

Revelation 22.5 And there shall be no night there: and they need no candle, neither light of the sun: for the Lord God giveth them light: and they shall reign for ever and ever.

> 12 And I said to the angel, Why is this so? And the angel said to me, Marvel not at this, for thou shalt see another heaven more brilliant and incomparable.
>
> 13 And when thou hast ascended thither, Thou shalt stand near the Lord, and shalt be His minister, and shalt, declare His mysteries to men, and shalt proclaim concerning Him that shall redeem Israel.

C.16 This sounds like the famous 7th Heaven of the actual Throne Room of God and Jesus and the Holy Spirit in the Highest level of the Heavenly City.

C.17 *'shalt be His minister'* and *'declare His mysteries to men'* - Levi was taken up to the 7th Heaven, and was there appointed to be the High Priest, and also his Levite descendants after him, to represent Israel before the Lord, until the Lord Himself returns to rule the earth at His 2nd coming.

> 14 And by thee and Judah shall the Lord appear among men, saving every race of men.

C.18 *'Lord appear among men, *saving every race of men'.* This is a contrast to what was taught in Israel for a very long time until New Testament times. Until the time of Christ, it was taught by the Pharisees 'To the Jew first', and that only Jews could be 'saved by the laws of Moses' to even be part of the 'Chosen Race.'

C.19 However, we can see that the 'founding fathers' of Israel the 12 Patriarchs said something totally different than what was preached in the times just before Christ. The Pharisees had twisted the laws of Moses to suit their own nefarious purposes of politics and power.

C.20 The Bible in the Old Testament, and the 'Testament of the 12 Patriarchs' both stated that Israel was supposed to be an example of a nation that believed in God and their Messiah to all the nations round about them. Israel became so rebellious before God in the 300 years between the Testaments, that most of them got slaughtered or driven out of Israel by the Romans in 70 AD for murdering the only begotten Son of God the Messiah – Jesus in what is known as the Diaspora.

C.21 This is also why Jesus the Christ came exactly when He did, in order to do away with the corrupted old laws which had been designed to help the people to stay in line with God's will, but not to enslave them as the Pharisees did.

John 1.7 For the Law came by Moses, but Grace and Truth came by Jesus Christ.

C.22 'The Pharisees 'sit in Moses Seat' – that was a good lecture that Jesus gave about the condition of the hierarchy of Israel' in circa 33 AD. The

53

Pharisees were not only Priests but a powerful political party. Their opposition party was the Sadducees.

Matthew 23.1-5 Then spake Jesus to the multitude, and to his disciples, Saying the Scribes sit in Moses's seat: 'All therefore whatsoever they bid you observe, *that* observe and do'; but do not ye after their works: for they say, and do not. ⁴For they bind heavy burdens and grievous to be borne and lay *them* on men's shoulders; but they *themselves* will not move them with one of their fingers. But all their works they do for to be seen of men. [**Read the rest of Matthew 23 to see Jesus blasting the Pharisees for their diabolical crimes against both God and His people.**]

C.23 Judah was the Tribe of the Kings in Israel and Judah survived longer than the 10 Northern Tribes of Reuben, Simeon, Issachar, Zebulun, Dan, Naphtali, Gad, Asher, Joseph & Benjamin which went into captivity in circa 730 BC into Assyria.

C.24 Levi was a Tribe but was not given its own territory. The Levites were originally dispersed throughout all the Tribes of Israel as the priests. In the times of the kings of Judah (after 730 BC), most of the Levites had moved to Jerusalem or into the cities of Judah.

---

15 And from the Lord's portion shall be thy life, and He shall be thy field and vineyard, and fruits, gold, and silver.

C.25 Here it is showing that 'tithing' and giving of offerings is blessed by God Himself. Jacob the father of the 12 Patriarchs along with Abraham brought in the idea of tithing 10% of one's income and giving it to help the poor and the work of God at the Temple to the Levite priests.

---

16 Hear, therefore, regarding the heavens which have been shown to thee.

C.26 What is defined as heaven? Is it physical or spiritual? It would appear that the word dimension is more appropriate than the word heaven or heavens in certain cases. In modern English 'Heaven' means by definition a place of joy and ecstasy. However, here we see not only a good heaven mentioned but the 'lowest heaven' which sounds more like Hell. In modern terms it would be more useful to say that there are many dimensions. The earth is in a physical dimension, and surrounding it are higher dimensions. Below it or within it are lower dimensions. The higher one goes in the spirit or to higher dimensions, the more light there is and the more joy and happiness there is. The physical dimension and the lower dimensions are not so happy and are distinctly physical in nature, where one feels the 'weights and burdens' and 'unrighteous deeds' of mankind hanging over you.

---

17 The lowest is for this cause gloomy unto thee, in that it beholds all the unrighteous deeds of men.

C.27 In the lower dimensions is the place where the dead go who are not saved and where the wicked also go.

C.28 I have been in haunted castles and buildings with bad spirits in them. I went into one of the Main Media buildings of one of the top newspapers, and believe it or not, it had a 'dark and fore-boding spirit' and it felt very uncomfortable being there. It had a blanket of spiritual darkness hanging over it. Buildings tend to accumulate the spirits of bad deeds that have been done of negativity, lying or evil things.

Book of Enoch 22 .2 Then Raphael answered, one of the Holy angels who was with me, and said unto me, 'these hollow places have been created for this very purpose, that the spirits of the souls of dead should assemble therein, yea that all the souls of the children of men should assemble here.

C.29 See my book 'Enoch Insights' and read the whole 22nd chapter about the souls in hell, limbo, as well as the souls of the righteous as to where they all go when they die.

[See 'Journey to Gragau', which is an amazing book about the spirit world.]

18 And it has fire, snow, and ice made ready for the day of judgement, in the righteous judgement of God; for in it are all the spirits of the retributions for vengeance on men.

C.30 *'fire, snow, and ice' made ready for the day of judgement, in the righteous judgement of God'* This verse is quite remarkable, as I have read this same statement of 'Judgment' many times in the scriptures and apocryphal books. *'for in it are all the spirits of the retributions for vengeance on men'.* Here are a few examples:

Job 38.22-23 Hast thou entered into the treasures of the snow? Or hast thou seen the treasures of the hail. Which I have reserved against the time of trouble, against the day of battle and war?

Psalm 147 16-17 He giveth snow like wool: he scatters the hoarfrost like ashes. He casts forth his ice like morsels: who can stand before his cold?

Psalm 148.8 Fire and hail; snow and vapour; stormy wind fulfilling his word.

Psalm 149.7 To execute vengeance upon the heathen and punishments upon the people.

Book of Enoch 100.8 When the hoarfrost and the snow with their chilliness and snowstorms with all their plagues fall upon you, in those days ye shall not be able to stand before them.

C.31 There are so many verses mentioning snow, ice and frost coming as a judgement on the wicked, both in the Book of Psalms, the Book of Job in the Bible, also in the Book of Enoch, and now in the 'Testament of the 12 Patriarchs'. What are these verses all saying? Are they indicating, or even pointing to a judgment of God, in the near future? Could a great judgment come from God in the form of a sudden ICE-AGE?

> 19 And in the second are the hosts of the armies which are ordained for the day of judgement, to work vengeance on the spirits of deceit and of Beliar.

C.32 *'hosts of the armies which are ordained for the day of judgement'.* There are quite a few verses like this one, both in the apocryphal books and the Bible:

Joel 2.11 And the Lord shall utter his voice before his army: for his camp is very great: for he is strong to execute his word: for the day of the Lord is great and terrible; and who can abide it?

Rev 19.11,14 And I saw heaven opened and behold a white horse; and he that sat upon him was called Faithful and True, and in righteousness he doth judge and make war. And the armies which were in heaven followed him upon white horses, clothed in fine linen, white and clean.

> 20 And above them are the holy ones. *Need to explain all the levels so-far mentioned for clarity.

Revelations 5.11 And I beheld and heard the voice of many angels round about the throne and the 4 Beasts and Elders: and the number of them was 10,000 times 10,000 and 1000's of 1000's

> 21 And in the highest of all dwelleth the Great Glory, far above all holiness.

Book of Enoch 24.2 And the 7th mountain was in the midst of these, and it excelled them in height resembling the seat of a throne.

> 22 In the heaven next to it are the archangels, who minister and make propitiation to the Lord for all the sins of ignorance of the righteous. What Are the 9 Orders of Angels? | 9 Choirs of Angels - Beliefnet

C.33 *'Angels who minister and make propitiation to the Lord for all the 'sins of ignorance' of the righteous'.* What is this talking about? It would appear that we, the righteous, sometimes inadvertently commit sins that we are unaware of and therefore there are spirits or angels to intercede to God on our behalf, so that we are not immediately judged for those sins that we are unaware of, in our ignorance.

> 23 Offering to the Lord a sweet-smelling savour, a reasonable and a bloodless offering.

C.34 Notice that in the 'heavenly dimensions', sacrifices are no longer used as in the 'days of Abraham' using a 'blood sacrifice'.

> 24 And in the heaven below this are the angels who bear answers to the angels of the presence of the Lord.

Isaiah 63.9 'And the angel of his presence saved them: In his love and in his pity he redeemed them'.

C.35 *'In the heaven below are angels who bear answers to the angels of the Presence'.* There is a system of command of angels in heaven. Who are the angels of the Presence? There are apparently '7 Angels of the Presence', who stand around the Throne of God awaiting His orders. Many angels come to the angels of the Presence with information to pass on directly to God Himself. They, the angels of the Presence, are the chiefs of all the angels. Here are listed all of them in the Book of Enoch:

Book of Enoch Chapter 9.1 Then Michael, Uriel, Raphael, and Gabriel looked down from heaven...

Luke 1.19 'I am Gabriel who stands in the Presence of God'.

Book of Enoch Chapter 10.1 Then said the Most High the Holy and Great one spoke and sent Uriel unto Noah..

Book of Enoch Chapter 20.1-2 Raguel, Saraquel, & Remiel.

Book of Jubilees 1.27 And He said to the angel of the presence 'write for |Moses from the beginning of Creation til My sanctuary has been built among them for eternity

II Ezdras 4.1 Then the angel which was sent to me whose name was Uriel..

> 25 And in the heaven next to this are **thrones** and **dominions**, in which always they offer praise to God. Angelic Orders of Seraphim, Thrones, Dominions, Virtues And Principalities, - Writings - Our Ultimate Reality

Revelations 4.2 And immediately I was in the spirit: and behold, a Throne was set in Heaven, and one sat on the throne. And He that sat thereon was to look upon like a jasper and a sardine stone; and there was a rainbow round about the throne insight like unto emerald.

Isaiah 6.1-4 In the year that king Uzziah died I saw also the Lord sitting upon a throne, high and lifted up, and his train filled the temple. Above it stood the Seraphim: each one had six wings; with twain he covered his face, and with twain he covered his feet, and with twain he did fly. And cried one to another and said 'Holy, Holy, Holy is the Lord of Hosts: the whole earth is full of His glory.

> 26 When, therefore, the Lord looks upon us, all of us are shaken; yea, the heavens, and the earth, and the abysses are shaken at the presence of His majesty.

Book of Jubilees 5.29 And on the new moon in the fourth month the fountains of the great deep were closed and the floodgates of heaven were restrained; and on the new moon of the seventh month all the mouths of the abysses of the earth were opened, and the water began to descend into the deep below.

2 ESDRAS 16.3 The Lord will threaten, and who will not be utterly shattered at his presence. The earth and the foundations quake, the sea is churned up from the depths and its waves and the fish shall be troubled at the presence of the Lord and before the glory of His power.

> 27 But the sons of men, having no perception of these things, sin and provoke the Highest.

Romans 1.20-21 For the invisible things of him from the beginning of the world are clearly seen, being understood by the things that are made, even His eternal power and Godhead, so that they are without excuse. Because that when they knew God, they glorified him not as God, neither were thankful; but became vain in their imaginations, and their foolish heart was darkened.

C.36 The Spirit world, Heaven, Hell and other dimensions: The Heavenly City described in the Book of Revelation Chapters 21-22 shows the city as having the height, length and width as 1500 miles. The city is 1500 miles high, and I have heard it described as having 15 major levels or one level every 100 miles. There are many different levels in heaven. Paul said in the New Testament that he knew about the 3rd Heaven in (II Corinthians 12.2-4). Jesus also mentioned that there was a place called Paradise which was right next to Hell and was inside the earth (Luke 16.19-31) Jesus mentioned as he died on the cross that he was going down to Paradise or a place in the earth in (Luke 23.43).

C.37 Paradise is a beautiful place inside the earth, and some would call it a waiting place. Many souls go there waiting to go up to the Heavenly City when they are invited to do so. I have just mentioned our final heavenly home and the wayfaring station where souls wait. This is also described very well in the **Book of Enoch chapter 22**. It would appear that God has many places where souls can rest until it is time for them to go up to the Heavenly City to whatever level they are assigned, according to their works in the physical life. Salvation is for free (Jn 3.16) and is only by the Grace of God (Titus 3.5) but your good works determine your position in the afterlife.

C.38 Apparently apart from semi-physical (part spiritual and part physical) places as I have just mentioned, there are also many different dimensions going up and down in the spirit world. The spirit world is a vast place full of amazing things.

C.39 A comparison between the size of our physical universe and spiritual space has been described by those who have been to the spirit world and come back and told us about it in the following manner: 'If you were to imagine your physical universe as an ice-cube, and the spiritual universe as all the oceans of the world, then the ice-cube floating on the oceans would be a good comparison as to the difference in size between the physical universe and the spiritual universe.(See the following books: **Journey to Tricon** – about Heaven and **Journey to Gragau** about Hell by A.Trenholm which are available at Amazon) These books are absolutely fascinating, and are by a writer who claims to have visited both heaven and hell on two different occasions.

CHAP. II.

NOW, therefore, know that the Lord shall execute judgement upon the sons of men.

2 Because when the rocks are being rent, and the sun quenched, and the waters dried up, and the fire cowering, and all creation troubled, and the invisible spirits melting away, and Hades taketh spoils through the visitations of the Highest, men will be unbelieving and persist in their iniquity.

Revelations 9.20-21 And the rest of the men who were not killed by these plagues yet repented not of the works of their hands, that they should not worship devils and idols of gold and silver and brass and stone and of wood: which can neither see not hear nor walk. Neither repented they of their murders, nor of their sorceries nor of their fornication nor of their thefts.

3 On this account with punishment shall they be judged.

Revelation 6.15 And the kings of the earth, and the great men, and the rich men and the chief captains and the mighty men, and every bondman and every free man hid themselves in the dens and the rocks of the mountains And said to the mountains and rocks, 'Fall on us and hide us from the face of him that sits on the throne and from the Wrath of the Lamb, for the day of his Wrath is come and who shall be able to stand?

INQUISITION

The Book of Enoch 60.6 And when the day, and the power, and the punishment, and judgement come, which the Lord of Spirits hath prepared for those who worship not the righteous law, and for those who deny the righteous judgment and those who take His name in vain. That day is prepared, for the elect a covenant, but for sinners an inquisition. When the punishment of the Lord of Spirits shall rest upon them, it shall rest in order that the punishment of the Lord of Spirits may not come in vain, and it shall slay the children with their mothers and fathers. Afterwards the judgment shall take place according to His mercy and His patience.

4 Therefore the Highest hath heard thy prayer, to separate thee from iniquity, and that you should become to Him a son, and a servant, and a minister of His presence.

5 The light of knowledge shalt thou light up in Jacob, and as the sun shalt thou be to all the seed of Israel.

6 And there shall be given to thee a blessing, and to all thy seed until the

Lord shall visit all the Gentiles in His tender mercies for ever.

7 And therefore there have been given to thee counsel and understanding, that thou might instruct thy sons concerning this.

8 Because they that bless Him shall be blessed, and they that curse Him shall perish.

9 And thereupon the angel opened to me the gates of heaven, and I saw the holy temple, and upon a throne of glory the Highest.

Book of Enoch 14.10 And I looked and saw therein a lofty throne. Its appearance was as crystal, and the wheels thereof as the shiny sun, and there was the vision of the cherubim. And from underneath the throne came streams of flaming fire, so that I could not look thereon, and the Great Glory sat thereon and His raiment shone more brightly than the sun and was whiter than any snow.

Revelation 4.6 And before the throne was there a sea of glass like unto crystal: and round about the throne were four beasts full of eyes before and behind.

10 And He said to me: Levi, I have given thee the blessing of the priesthood until I come and sojourn in the midst of Israel.

Hebrews 7:5 "And verily they that are of the sons of Levi, who receive the office of the priesthood, have a commandment to take tithes of the people according to the law, that is, of their brethren, though they come out of the loins of Abraham:"

11 Then the angel brought me down to the earth, and gave me a shield and a sword, and said to me: Execute vengeance on Shechem because of Dinah, thy sister, and I will be with thee because the Lord hath sent me.

C.1 Why was Levi given and shield and sword by God almighty? It was time for vengeance.

Ephesians 6.16-17 Above all, taking the shield of faith, wherewith ye shall be able to quench all the fiery darts of the wicked. And take the helmet of salvation, and the sword of the Spirit, which is the word of God:

12 And I destroyed at that time the sons of Hamor, as it is written in the heavenly tables.

13 And I said to him: I pray thee, O Lord, tell me Thy name, that I may call upon Thee in a day of tribulation.

14 And he said: I am the angel who intercedes for the nation of Israel that they may not be smitten utterly, for every evil spirit attacks it.

C.2 The angel who defends the true Israel is called Uriel and is one of the 7 angels of the 'Presence of God'. He is also known as Ariel.

15 And after these things I awaked, and blessed the Most High, and the angel who intercedes for the nation of Israel and for all the righteous.

CHAP. III.

> AND when I was going to my father, I found a brazen shield; wherefore also the name of the mountain is Aspis, which is near Gebal, to the south of Abila.

C.1 Where are these locations: Gebal and Abila? - Gebal: An ancient Phoenician city, situated on a bluff of the foothills of Lebanon, overlooking the Mediterranean. It was one of the principal seaports of Phoenicia and had a small but good harbour for small ships. It was regarded as a holy city by the ancients. It is mentioned by Joshua in the book of Joshua 13:5, as the land of the Gebalites, and also mentioned in 1 Kings 5:18 as aiding in the construction of Solomon's temple. The «elders» and the «wise men» of Gebal are among the workmen employed on Tyrian ships (Ezekiel 27:9 (Source: Bible Map: Gebal (bibleatlas.org)

Abila is situated to the NW of Damascus. AbilaMapRevB-914x1024.jpg (914×1024) (bibleplaces.com)

C.2 What was the 'brazen shield' that Levi found? It sounds like one of the pieces of the 'armour of God' described in Ephesians chapter 6. [See later in this chapter.]

> 2 And I kept these words in my heart. And after this I counselled my father, and Reuben my brother, to bid the sons of Hamor not to be circumcised; for I was zealous because of the abomination which they had wrought on my sister.

C.3 Levi, being the High Priest of God considered 'tricking the men of Shechem using 'circumcision' as a ruse' as suggested by his brothers, was not a godly idea as circumcision was supposed to be a remembrance of the Hebrews dedication to God. A gift not supposed to be given away to others who were not dedicated.

C.4 The Bible describes the men of Shechem being slaughtered in 'tortures'. (Genesis Ch.34), as do other apocryphal books such as Jasher and Jubilees. The Patriarchs decided to trick the men of Shechem. If they were willing to get circumcised, then prince Shechem could keep their sister Dinah whom Shechem had raped. It was a ruse, and when the men of Shechem were 'sore after 3 days' after 'being circumcised', then Levi and Simeon set upon them when they were weakened and slaughtered them all by the sword.

> 3 And I slew Shechem first, and Simeon slew Hamor. And after this my brothers came and smote that city with the edge of the sword.

Psalm 149.6-9 Let the high praise of God be in their mouth and a two-edged sword in their right hand. To execute vengeance upon the heathen, and punishments upon the people. To bind their kings with chains, and their nobles with fetters of iron; to execute upon them the judgement written: This honour have all the saints. Praise ye the Lord.

> 4 And my father heard these things and was wroth, and he was grieved in that they had received the circumcision, and after that had been put to death, and in his blessings he looked amiss upon us.

Genesis 35-36 'And Jacob said to Simeon and Levi, Ye have troubled me to make my name stink among the inhabitants of the land, among the Canaanites and the Perizzites: and I being few in number, they shall gather themselves together against me and slay me; and I shall be destroyed and my house. 36 And they said, Should he (Shechem, the prince of Shechem) deal with our sister as with a harlot?

> 5 For we sinned because we had done this thing against his will, and he was sick on that day.
>
> 6 But I saw that the sentence of God was for evil upon Shechem; for they sought to do to Sarah and Rebecca as they had done to Dinah our sister, but the Lord prevented them.

C.5 No wonder the Patriarchs were very angry at the town of Shechem as they had not only raped their sister Dinah who was only twelve years old, but they had attempted the same with Rebecca the wife of Isaac and Sarah the wife of Abraham in much earlier times

> 7 And they persecuted Abraham our father when he was a stranger, and they vexed his flocks when they were big with young; and Eblaen, who was born in his house, they most shamefully handled.
>
> 8 And thus they did to all strangers, taking away their wives by force, and they banished them (their husbands).

C.6 This extreme cruelty against strangers was the exact reason God destroyed Sodom and Gomorrah. It was also one of the reasons for the Great Flood that destroyed most of mankind.

> 9 But the wrath of the Lord came upon them to the uttermost.
>
> 10 And I said to my father Jacob: 'By thee will the Lord despoil* the Canaanites and will give their land to thee and to thy seed after thee'. [*despoil = destroy]

C.7 Levi comforts his father that he and his family will not be destroyed by the peoples around them, as God is on their side, and that He had promised to

Abraham that His descendants would get rid of the Canaanites from the lands around them. This was largely fulfilled in the days of Moses and Joshua.

> 11 For from this day forward shall Shechem be called a city of imbeciles; for as a man mocks a fool, so did we mock them.
>
> 12 Because also they had wrought folly in Israel by defiling my sister. And we departed and came to Bethel.

C.8 History of Bethel: What is the History and Importance of Bethel in the Bible? What is the History and Importance of Bethel in the Bible? | Spiritual Insights for Everyday Life (leewoof.org)

> 13 And there again I saw a vision as the former, after we had spent there seventy days.
>
> 14 And I saw seven men in white raiment saying unto me: Arise, put on the robe of the priesthood, and the crown of righteousness, and the breastplate of understanding, and the garment of truth, and the late* of faith, and the turban of the head, and the ephod of prophecy.

C.9 These 7 men are the 7 'Angels of the Presence' mentioned in the Book of Enoch and also present in the Book of Jubilees talking with Moses. They are Michael, Uriel, Raphael, Gabriel, as well as others such as Phanuel who is mentioned in the Book of Enoch Ch 40 as a good angel. Also Raguel, Saraquael and Remiel are mentioned in the Book of Enoch chapter 20 as good angels. Structure of angelology. It is very important not to get the names of angels wrong in case it is talking about a Fallen angel like Ramiel, who is also mentioned in the Book of Enoch

C.10 Very important information here: 'Arise, put on the robe of the priesthood, and the crown of righteousness,

2 Tim 4.8 "Henceforth there is laid up for me a crown of righteousness, which the Lord, the righteous judge, shall give me at that day: and not to me only, but unto all them also that love his appearing."

C.11 'breastplate of understanding', high-priest-wearing-breastplate.jpg (228×207) (biblestudy.org) Breastplate of Righteousness - The Armor of G-d - What Scripture Says About... - Psalm11918.org

C.12 'Garment of truth', and the '*late of faith', and the 'turban of the head'

Ephesians 6.10-17 Finally, my brethren, be strong in the Lord, and in the power of his might.

[11] Put on the whole armour of God, that ye may be able to stand against the wiles of the devil.

¹² For we wrestle not against flesh and blood, but against principalities, against powers, against the rulers of the darkness of this world, against spiritual wickedness in high places.

¹³ Wherefore take unto you the **whole armour of God**, that ye may be able to withstand in the evil day, and having done all, to stand.

¹⁴ Stand therefore, having your **loins girt** about with **truth**, and having on the **breastplate of righteousness.**

¹⁵ And your **feet shod** with the **preparation** of the **gospel of peace;**

¹⁶ Above all, taking the **shield of faith**, wherewith ye shall be able to **quench** all the **fiery darts** of the **wicked (the Devil).**

¹⁷ And take the **helmet of salvation**, and the **sword of the Spirit**, which is the **Word of God:**

C.13 Ephod of prophecy'. Ancient Israelite Divination: Urim ve-Tummim, Ephod, and Prophecy - TheTorah.com

15 And they severally carried these things and put them on me and said unto me: From henceforth become a priest of the Lord, thou and thy seed for ever.

16 And the first anointed me with holy oil and gave to me the staff of judgement.

C.14 What is a '***staff of judgement***'? Is that what Moses carried in his hand and which Aaron often used in the10 Plagues Judgments against Pharaoh when God delivered Israel out of Egypt? That staff was also known as 'Aaron's Rod' that budded.

17 The second washed me with **pure water** and fed me with '**bread and wine'** even the most holy things and clad me with a holy and glorious robe.

C.15 '*Washed me with 'pure water' and fed me with 'bread and wine'.* **Why was this necessary?** It is very interesting that Christ performed a ceremony just like this with his 12 disciples. Christ both washed the 'disciples' feet' and also had the Last Supper with His disciples on the evening before He died. He also had 'communion' using bread and wine in the ceremony which has been observed by Christians for the past 2000 years since the death of Christ. When Peter protested to Christ that He should never wash Peter's feet. Jesus then said if I wash not your feet then you will have no part in me. Peter replied then wash my whole body. To which Christ responded 'He who has had his feet washed is every wit cleansed. Christ was showing this same sample of humility. [Paraphrasing of John 13.8 -10]

> 18 The third clothed me with a linen vestment like an ephod. *

C.16 *An Ephod consisted of a rectangular small breastplate made of cloth and it was embedded with 12 gems representing the12 Tribes of Israel. That garment was used only by the High Priest. - Ephod of prophecy'. Ancient Israelite Divination: Urim ve-Tummim, Ephod, and Prophecy - TheTorah.com

> 19 The fourth put round me a **girdle** like unto purple

C.17.The Lord Jesus as High Priest is mentioned as wearing a 'Golden Girdle' in the Book of Revelation.

Revelation chapter 1.13 And in the midst of the seven candlesticks one like unto the Son of man, clothed with a garment down to the foot, and girt about the paps with a golden girdle.

> 20 The fifth gave me a branch of rich olive.

C.18 An Olive branch today means 'Peace'. In the End of days they will have an even more important meaning as 2 fiery prophets of God.

Genesis 8:11 And the dove came to him in the evening; and, lo, in her mouth was an olive leaf plucked off: so Noah knew that the waters were abated from off the earth.

Revelation 11:4 "These are the two olive trees and the two candlesticks that stand before the Lord of the earth"

> 21 The sixth placed a 'crown' on my head.

C.19 A 'crown' symbolizes 'time of reigning and ruling'. Levi was righteous in the eyes of God and received a 'crown' of righteousness from heaven in humility.

Revelation 6.2 And I saw and behold a white horse: and he that sat on him had a bow; and a crown was given unto him: and he went forth conquering, and to conquer.

Revelation 1.12-13 His eyes were as a flame of fire, and on his head were many crowns; and he had a name written, that no man knew, but he himself. And he was clothed with a vesture dipped in blood: and his name is called The Word of God.

> 22 The seventh placed on my head a 'diadem of priesthood', and filled my hands with incense, that I might serve as priest to the Lord God.

C.20 For a diadem of 12 stars see the Book of Revelation chapter 12 that the Woman or the church wears. The story of Revelation 12 is actually physically written in the stars and results in The 12 Star signs. Why is this connection important? Because the 12 Patriarchs were all born under different star signs just like the diadem crown of Revelations 12. The 12 apostles were also all different star signs. The 12 patriarchs and the 12 apostles and the Bride with a diadem of 12 stars. Why would God bring out this point from the beginning to the ending of the story unless it is very important. I think it is to represent all the different people that God has created. God did not create three 'Leos' among the Patriarchs or the 12 Apostles. God likes to create perfect balance. And that way everyone knows that they are represented, as God loves each person.

Revelation 12.12 And there appeared a great wonder in heaven; a woman clothed with the sun, and the moon under her feet, and upon her head a <u>crown of twelve stars</u>

[**Definition**: A <u>diadem</u> is a type of crown, specifically an ornamental headband worn by monarchs and others as a badge of royalty.]

---

23 And they said to me: Levi, thy seed shall be divided into three offices, for a sign of the glory of the Lord who is to come.

Numbers 3.17 "These were the sons of Levi, by their names; Gershon, Kehat, and Merari."

C.21 The Levites were divided into three clans, the descendants of Levi's three sons.

C.22 *'for a sign of the glory of the Lord who is to come'. This could only be talking about Jesus. The Levites as a tribe are working for the High Priest Jesus - Melchizedek. -See Hebrews 7*

---

24 And the first portion shall be great; yea, greater than it shall none be.

25 The second shall be in the priesthood.

26 And the third shall be called by a new name, because a king shall arise in Judah, and shall establish a new priesthood, after the 'fashion of the Gentiles'.

C.23 There is an interesting passage is Isaiah, right toward the end, where the Lord explains that he will choose "priests" and "Levites" from among the Gentiles.

This is remarkable because in order to be a Levite, one must be born of the tribe of Levi. Moreover, to be a priest (Kohan), one must be not only a Levite but a descendent of Aaron. Here the Lord says that he shall choose men who are not Levites, Aaronites, nor even Jews! (**Source**: Gentile Priests and Levites - Taylor Marshall)

Is 66:19-21 And some of them (Gentiles) also I will take for priests and for Levites, says the LORD.

C.24 Christ the Messiah was the one who gave the 'priesthood' to the Gentiles in giving the Holy Ghost to 'all of his disciples', many of whom were not Jewish.

Acts 5.32 And we are His witnesses of these things; and so also is the Holy Ghost whom God hath given to them that obey Him.

C.25 God gave Peter the leader of the Early church a 'vision of unclean animals'. God said call not 'unclean' that which God has made clean. This meant that from that point on the disciples were to witness to the Gentiles as well as the Jews.

Acts 10.9-16 (condensation): 11 'And I saw heaven opened, and a certain vessel descending unto him, as it had been a great sheet knit at the four corners and let down to the earth.

[12] Wherein were all manner of four-footed beasts of the earth, and wild beasts and creeping things, and fowls of the air

[13] And there came a voice to him' Rise, Peter, kill, and eat.

[14] but Peter said, Not so, Lord; for I have never eaten any thing that is common or unclean

[15] And the voice spake unto him again the 2nd time 'what God have cleansed call thou not unclean'.

Acts 10.28 And he said unto them, Ye know how that it is unlawful for a man that is a Jew to keep company or come unto one of another nation; but God hath showed me that I should not call any man common or unclean.

---

27 And His presence is beloved, as a prophet of the Most High, of the seed of Abraham our father.

28 Therefore, every desirable thing in Israel shall be for thee and for thy seed, and ye shall eat everything fair to look upon, and the table of the Lord shall thy seed apportion.

29 And some of them shall be high priests, and judges, and scribes; for by their mouth shall the holy place be guarded.

30 And when I awoke, I understood that this dream was like the first dream. And I hid this also in my heart and told it not to any man upon the earth.

31 And after two days I and Judah went up with our father Jacob to Isaac our father's father.

Book of Jubilees Ch.31.4,6 And Jacob went up on the new moon of the seventh month to Bethel. And Jacob went to his father Isaac and to his mother Rebecca to the house of his father Abraham, and he took his two sons with him Levi and Judah, and he came to his father Isaac an to his mother Rebecca

32 And my father's father blessed me according to all the words of the visions which I had seen. And he would not come with us to Bethel.

Book of Jubilees Ch.31.8,13-16 (Rebecca, the wife of Isaac and mother of Jacob): And she saw his (Jacob's) two sons, and she recognised them, and said unto him: 'Are these thy sons, my son', and she embraced them and kissed them, and blessed them, saying: In you shall the seed of Abraham become illustrious, and ye shall prove a blessing in the earth. 13 (Isaac speaking) 'And the spirit of prophecy came down into his mouth and he took Levi by the right hand and Judah by his left 14 And he turned to Levi first, and began to bless him first, and said unto him: May God of all, the very Lord of all the ages, bless thee and thy children throughout all the ages 15 And may the Love give to thee and to thy seed greatness and great glory, and cause thee and thy seed, from among all flesh, to approach Him to serve in His sanctuary as the angels of the Presence and as the Holy ones. Even as they, shall the seed of thy sons be for glory and greatness and holiness, and may He make them great unto all ages 16 And they shall be judges and princes and chiefs of all the sons of Jacob. [See my book **Jubilees Insights** to see the rest of Isaacs blessing on Jacob's sons]

33 And when we came to Bethel, my father saw a vision concerning me, that I should be their priest unto God.

Book of Jubilees 32.1 And he abode that night at Bethel, and Levi dreamed that they has ordained and made him the priest of the Most High God, him and his sons forever: and he awoke from his sleep and blessed the Lord.

C.26 It is wonderful how God spoke so clearly to Jacob and Isaac and Abraham and then to Levi in visions and dreams and in prophecies. From the Great flood times until Christ and the New Testament it would appear that only certain people were anointed with the Holy Spirit such as prophets and High Priests. That all changed in the New Testament where it is stated that 'We are witness of these things and so also is the Holy Ghost whom God gives to those that obey Him'.

Acts 5.32 'And we are his witnesses of these things; and so is also the Holy Ghost, whom God has given to them that obey him.'

34 And he rose up early in the morning, and paid tithes of all to the Lord through me. And so we came to Hebron to dwell there.

Book of Jubilees 32.2 And Jacob rose up early in the morning on the fourteenth of this month and he gave a tithe of all that came with him, both of men and cattle, both of gold and every vessel and garment, yea he gave tithes of all. [Read **Jubilees**

C.27 Jacob started to pay tithes through his son Levi, who became the High Priest by the command of God Himself. This would suggest a tangible event that happened to Levi himself back circa in 1700 BC. Jacob had promised God that if when he was young and unmarried that if he brought him safely back to his father and mother Isaac and Rebecca's house, which happened some 21 years later, then Jacob would give 10% of his income to God.

> 35 And Isaac called me continually to put me in remembrance of the law of the Lord, even as the angel of the Lord showed unto me.

C.28 Here is evidence that Levi was trained by his grandfather Isaac in the ways of the Priesthood. This book is full of evidence that the original Testaments of the 12 Patriarchs were indeed written by them and not some pseudo-epigraphical writer in 100 BC as suggested by some. How could a writer in 100 BC know about the different sufferings of the Christ that would come and why he would he write about the Messiah when these Testaments of the 12 Patriarchs was a condemnation against Israel at the time of the Messiah and in times leading up to the Messiah. That would be counter-productive for the Pharisees to produce a book or books which speak specifically in very derogatory terms about them and God's subsequent judgment against them as indeed prophesied by Jesus himself in Matthew 23

Matthew 23:38 'Behold, your house is left to you desolate'

Matthew 27:25 'Then answered all the people, 'His blood be on us and our children'

C.29 Here the Jews self-cursed themselves when they gave consent to Pontius Pilate the governor to crucify Jesus.

C.30 Forty years later Israel was totally eliminated by God Himself because they killed their own Messiah in cold blood.

> 36 And he taught me the law of the priesthood of sacrifices, whole burnt-offerings, first-fruits, freewill-offerings, peace-offerings.

C.31 I'm sure that the law of the priesthood also included fasting sometimes: Fasting—The Astonishing Physical And Spiritual Benefits » SkyWatchTV

> 37 And each day he was instructing me, and was busied on my behalf before the Lord, and said to me: Beware of the spirit of fornication; for this shall continue and shall by thy seed pollute the holy place.
>
> 38 Take, therefore, to thyself a wife without blemish or pollution, while yet thou are young, and not of the race of strange nations.
>
> 39 And before entering into the holy place, bathe; and when thou offer

the sacrifice, wash; and again, when thou finish the sacrifice, wash.

40 Of twelve trees having leaves offer to the Lord, as Abraham taught me also.

41 And of every clean beast and bird offer a sacrifice to the Lord.

42 And of all thy first fruits and of wine offer the first, as a sacrifice to the Lord God; and every sacrifice thou shalt salt with salt.

43 Now, therefore, observe whatsoever I command you, children; for whatsoever things I have heard from my fathers I have declared unto you.

C.32 Levi is stating that the laws and ordinances and commandments of God that he himself has followed during his life, were passed down to him from his father Jacob, and his ancestors Isaac and Abraham as well as Noah and Enoch.

44 And behold I am clear from your ungodliness and transgression, which ye shall commit in the end of the ages against the Saviour of the world, Christ, acting godlessly, deceiving Israel, and stirring up against its great evils from the Lord.

C.33 It was in the gospel of John, where Jesus told the Pharisees and Levites, that they were of their father the Devil.

John 8.44 "Ye are of *your* father the devil, and the lusts of your father ye will do. He was a murderer from the beginning, and abode not in the truth, because there is no truth in him. When he speaks a lie, he speaks of his own: for he is a liar, and the father of it." [Satan invented lying]

C.34 What happened in Jewish history? Levi, one of the 12 Patriarchs, was a good man and a High Priest of God and so were many of his descendants, but in the centuries before Christ the priesthood had become totally corrupted and ruled by power and wealth as many rich religions are so today. How does a people turn from being godly to being satanic? Well, compare Cain and Abel. [See much more about this topic in my books **Eden Insights**, **Jasher Insights Book 1** and **Jubilees Insights**]

45 And ye shall deal lawlessly together with Israel, so He shall not bear with Jerusalem because of your wickedness; but the veil of the temple shall be rent, so as not to cover your shame.

C.35 Here is an amazing prophecy in verse 45 about the coming Messiah:

'veil of the temple being rent' so as not to cover your shame.

Matthew 27:51-53 [51]And, behold, the veil of the temple was rent in twain from the top to the bottom; and the earth did quake, and the rocks rent; [52]And the graves were opened; and many bodies of the saints which slept arose, "And came out of the graves after his resurrection, and went into the holy city, and appeared unto many."

C.36 Matthew 27. 51-53The above verse 45 is also in the New Testament being mirrored by Mark 15.38 and Luke 23.45 concerning **the 'veil of the temple being rent'**

C.37 Why does verse 45 also say **'so as not to cover your shame.'** The following link explains it very well in that the veil was rent by God Himself to show the hypocrisy of the religious system in 'killing its own Messiah' Jesus Christ. The veil was rent to show that the Messiah had just died and that the old religion of 'works' was now dead and departed because of the Jews rejection of their own Messiah.

C.38 Why was the temple's veil rent when Christ the Messiah died?: Why was the Temple's veil rent when Christ died? | For What Saith the Scriptures?

***The difference between the 2nd Temple and the 1st Temple. The 2nd temple no longer had the Ark of the Covenant and the Shekinar Glory of God was missing and many other objects: See my article: the 3rd Temple in the appendix of this book.

> 46 And ye shall be scattered as captives among the Gentiles and shall be for a reproach and for a curse there.
>
> For more on the story of the Ark of the Covenant- see my article on the 3rd Temple.
>
> 47 For the house which the Lord shall choose shall be called Jerusalem, as is contained in the book of Enoch the righteous.

C.39 **'Enoch the righteous'** - Here Levi is referring back to the Book of Enoch - so obviously it was indeed a very real and important book. Today the book of Enoch is referred to as a pseudepigraphic book – in other words written by someone other than Enoch after the fact. However, that assumption is simply false, as there is plenty of evidence that the Book of Enoch was in fact written by Enoch himself in Pre-Flood times, as Noah mentions the Book of Enoch. It is stated that the Book of Enoch was written in 300 BC. When in fact that was when the book was put together from a much older manuscript. See my book '**Enoch Insights'** for much more information on this topiC.

C.40 The Book of Enoch is mentioned by 6 of the 12 Patriarchs: Reuben, Simeon, Levi, Naphtali, Dan, and Benjamin and the New Testament early church quoted from the Book of Enoch as in the Book of Jude.

> 48 Therefore when I took a wife, I was twenty-eight years old, and her

name was Melcha.

49 And she conceived and bare a son, and I called his name Gersam, for we were sojourners in our land.

50 And I saw concerning him, that he would not be in the first rank.

51 And Kohath was born in the thirty-fifth year of my life, towards sunrise.

52 And I saw in a vision that he was standing on high in the midst of all the congregation.

53 Therefore I called his name Kohath which is, beginning of majesty and instruction.

C.41 It confirmed in the Book of Jubilees - that Levi's sons were indeed called Gershon, Kohath and Merari

Jubilees 44.13 Levi and his sons; and these are the names of the sons: Gershon, Kohath and Merari

54 And she bare me a third son, in the fortieth year of my life; and since his mother bare him with difficulty, I called him Merari, that is, 'my bitterness,' because he also was like(ly) to die.

55 And Jochebed was born. in Egypt, in my sixty-fourth year, for I was renowned (famous) then in the midst of my brethren.

56 And Gersam took a wife, and she bare to him Lomni and Semei. And the sons of Kohath, Ambram, Issachar, Hebron, and Ozeel. And the sons of Merari, Mooli, and Mouses.

57 And in the ninety-fourth year Ambram took Jochebed my daughter to him to wife, for they were born in one day, he and my daughter.

58 Eight years old was I when I went into the land of Canaan, and eighteen years when I slew Shechem, and at nineteen years I became priest, and at twenty-eight years I took a wife, and at forty-eight I went into Egypt.

59 And behold, my children, ye are a third generation. In my hundred and eighteenth year Joseph died.

C.42 Joseph died at 110 years old when Levi was 118 years old. This means that Levi, who was the 3rd son of Jacob and Leah, and Joseph who was born to Jacob and Rachel as his 11th child were 8 years apart. This means that Jacob's 4 wives had an average of one baby/year between all of them during that time period. Benjamin the 12th and last child of Jacob and Rachel was born 10 years after Joseph. So, there was 18 years between Levi the 3rd child & the 12th or last child born to Jacob.

CHAP. IV.

> AND now, my children, I command you: Fear the Lord your God with your whole heart and walk in simplicity according to all His law.

C.1 'Fear the Lord your God' with your 'whole heart':

Deuteronomy 10.12-13 'And now, Israel, what doth the Lord thy God require of thee, but to fear the Lord thy God and to walk in His ways and to love Him and to serve the Lord thy God with all of thy heart and with all of thy soul. To keep the commandments of the Lord and His statutes, which I command thee this day for thy good.

C.2 *'walk in simplicity' according to all His law*. There is only one verse in the entire Bible which talks about 'simplicity' in a positive context, and it is in the New Testament:

2 Cor 11.3 But I fear lest by any means, as the serpent beguiled Eve through his subtility, so your minds should be corrupted from the 'simplicity' that is in Christ

C.3 There is a mention of 'simplicity' in the Old Testament, but it is a warning of what not to do:

Proverbs 1.22 How long ye simple ones will ye love simplicity and ye scorners, delight in their scorning, and fools hate knowledge.

> 2 And do ye also teach your children letters, that they may have understanding all their life, reading unceasingly the law of God.

Proverbs 2.1-2 My son, if thou wilt receive my words, and hide my commandments with thee. So that thou incline thine ear unto wisdom and apply thine heart to understanding.

C.4 The word 'letter' is found in various places in the Old Testament 2 Samuel 11.14 when king David sent a letter to his top general Joab. In around 1037 BC.

> 3 For every one that knows the law of the Lord shall be honoured and shall not be a stranger whithersoever he goes.

Psalm 37.31 The law of his God is in his heart and none of his steps shall slide.

Proverbs 3.4 So shalt thou find favour and good understanding in the sight of God and man.

> 4 Yea, many friends shall he gain more than his parents, and many men shall desire to serve him, and to hear the law from his mouth.

> 5 Work righteousness, therefore, my children, upon the earth, that ye may have it as a treasure in heaven.

Matthew 6.21 For where your treasure is, there will your heart be also.

Proverbs 3.13-14 Happy is the man that finds wisdom, and the man that gets understanding. For the merchandize of it is better than the merchandise of silver and the gain thereof than fine gold.

> 6 And sow good things in your souls, that ye may find them in your life.

Hosea 10.12 Sow to yourselves in righteousness, reap in mercy; break up your fallow ground: for it is time to seek the Lord, until he come and rain righteousness upon you.

> 7 But if ye sow evil things, ye shall reap every trouble and affliction.

Hosea 10.13 Ye have ploughed in wickedness, ye have reaped iniquity; ye have eaten the fruit of lies: because thou did trust in thy way, in the multitude of thy mighty men.

> 8 Get wisdom in the fear of God with diligence; for though there be a leading into captivity, and cities and lands be destroyed, and gold and silver and every possession perish, the wisdom of the wise nought can take away, save the blindness of ungodliness, and the callousness that comes of sin.

C.5 'Get wisdom' Getting godly wisdom and understanding seems to be the most important goal in this life.

Proverbs 4.5,7 Get wisdom, get understanding: forget it not; neither decline from the words of my mouth. Wisdom is the principle thing, therefore in all thy getting, get understanding.

> 9 For if one keep oneself from these evil things, then even among his enemies shall wisdom be a glory to him, and in a strange country a fatherland, and in the midst of foes shall prove a friend.
>
> 10 Whosoever teaches noble things and does them, shall be enthroned with kings, as was also Joseph my brother.

Hosea 14.9 Who is wise, and he shall understand these things? Prudent, and shall know them? For the ways of the Lord are right and the just shall walk in them: but the transgressors shall fall therein.

> 11 Therefore, my children, I have learnt that at the end of the ages ye will transgress against the Lord, stretching out hands to wickedness

against Him; and to all the Gentiles shall ye become a scorn.

C.6 Israel certainly transgressed against God throughout its history starting with the times of Moses where the whole older generation died in the wilderness for their rebellion against God. Israel was finally kicked out by God Himself through the hand of the Romans in 70 AD at the Diaspora. Above it states that later on at "**end of the ages' ye will transgress against the Lord".**

C.7 We know that when the Messiah came that the Jews killed him. What about the future? The Jews rejected the true Messiah, Jesus. When the false Messiah -the Antichrist comes along they will follow him according to the Bible. The Jews will be deceived into believing that the coming One World Leader or the Anti-Christ is the Messiah, whom they will worship as God, when he is in fact the son of the Devil. This will start with the setting up of the 3rd Temple in Jerusalem and a 7-year Pact between the Anti-Christ and the Jews, Muslims and Christians.

2 Thessalonians 3-4 Let no man deceive you by any means: for that day shall not come, except there come a falling away first, and that man of sin be revealed, the son of perdition; Who opposes and exalts himself above all that is called God, or that is worshipped; so that he as God sits in the temple of God, shewing himself that he is God.

C.8 I studied the apocryphal book of 2nd Esdras chapter 14. Where it shows different ages.

The **1st Age** was from Creation until the Great Flood.

The **2nd Age** was from the Great Flood until the birth of Christ.

The **3rd age** from the birth of Christ until the Wrath of God

Enoch 9.2 And they said to the Lord of Ages, Lord of lords, God of gods, King of kings and God of Ages, the throne of thy glory stands unto all generations of the ages and thy name Holy and glorious unto all the ages.

C.9 The **3rd Age** as mentioned in verse 11, would seem to indicate that it is talking about the modern times in which we are living today in other words not long until the end of the world and the Wrath of God.

C.10 The **4th Age** is talking about the Golden age of the Millennium when the Messiah reigns with His saints for 1000 years on the earth mentioned in the book of Isaiah and Revelations chapter 20.

C.11 The **5th Age** will be the eternal Age of the New Heaven and the New Earth as mentioned in Revelations 21-22.

12 For our father Israel is pure from the transgressions of the chief priests [who shall lay their hands upon the Saviour of the world].

C.12 Now it is clearly prophesying about the 1st coming of the Messiah and how that he would be killed by the High Priests or better known to us as the

Pharisees.

> 13 For as the heaven is purer in the Lord's sight than the earth, so also be ye, the lights of Israel, purer than all the Gentiles.

Isaiah 42.6-7 'I the Lord have called thee in righteousness, and will hold thine hand and will keep thee, and give for thee a covenant of the people, for a light to the Gentiles. To open the eyes of the blind, bring out the prisoners from prison, and them that sit in darkness out of the prison house'.

> 14 But if ye be darkened through transgressions, what, therefore, will all the Gentiles do living in blindness?

Matthew 6.22-23 The light of the body is the eye: if therefore thine eye be single the whole body shall be full of light. But if the light that is in thee be darkness how great is that darkness.

> 15 Yea, ye shall bring a curse upon our race, because the light of the law which was given for to lighten every man this ye desire to destroy by teaching commandments contrary to the ordinances of God.

1 Kings 16.33,25 And King Ahab made a grove and did more to provoke the Lord God of Israel to anger than all the kings that were before him 25 But there was none like unto Ahab who did sell himself to do wickedness in the sight of the Lord, whom Jezebel his wife stirred up.

> 16 The offerings of the Lord ye shall rob, and from His portion shall ye steal choice portions, eating them contemptuously with harlots.
>
> 17 And out of covetousness ye shall teach the commandments of the Lord, wedded women shall ye pollute, and the virgins of Jerusalem shall ye defile; and with harlots and adulteresses shall ye be joined, and the daughters of the Gentiles shall ye take to wife, purifying them with an unlawful purification; and your union shall be like unto Sodom and Gomorrah,

Hosea 4.1-2 Hear the Word of the Lord, ye children of Israel: for the Lord hath a controversy with the inhabitants of the land, because there is **no truth**, nor mercy, nor **knowledge of God** in the land. By swearing and lying and killing, and stealing, and committing adultery, they break out and blood touches blood.

> 18 And ye shall be puffed up because of your priesthood, lifting your-selves up against men, and not only so, but also against the commands

79

> of God.

1 Kings 13.33-34 'After this Jeroboam returned not from his evil way but made again of the lowest of the people priests of the high places: whosoever he would he consecrated him, and he became one the priests of the high places. And this thing became sin unto the house of Jeroboam even to cut it off, and to destroy it from off the earth.

> 19 For ye shall contemn the holy things with jests and laughter.

C.13 *'contemn the holy things with jests and laughter'.* The last king of Babylon also did exactly this and died for his trouble the very same night with the 'writing on the wall' warning by the Hand of God Himself.

Daniel 5.3-4 Then they brought the golden vessels that were taken out of the temple of the house of God which was at Jerusalem and the king and his princes, his wives and his concubines drank in them. They drank wine and praised the gods of gold, and of silver, of brass, or iron, and of wood, and of stone.

C.14 The third king of Babylon was called Belshazzar and he paid with his life for using the 'golden vessels' from the temple in Jerusalem in a 'drunken ungodly banquet' in honour of his princes, wives and concubines.

Daniel 5.30 In that night was Belshazzar the king of the Chaldeans slain.

> 20 Therefore the temple, which the Lord shall choose, shall be laid waste through your uncleanness, and ye shall be captives throughout all nations.

Jeremiah 52.4-5 And Nebuchadnezzar, king of Babylon, came, he and his army against Jerusalem, and pitched against it and built forts against it round about. So, the city was besieged unto the 11th year of King Zedekiah.

Jeremiah 52. 9-11 And they took Zedekiah to Babylon, slew his sons in front of him, and put out his eyes.

> 21 And ye shall be an abomination unto them, and ye shall receive reproach and everlasting shame from the righteous judgement of God.

Deuteronomy 4.26 'I call heaven and earth to witness against you this day that you shall soon utterly perish. Ye shall not prolong your days but shall be utterly destroyed'.

> 22 And all who hate you shall rejoice at your destruction.

Hosea 4.6 My people are destroyed for lack of knowledge: because thou hast rejected knowledge, I will also reject thee, that thou shalt be no priest to me: seeing thou hast forgotten the law of thy God, I will also forget thy children.

> 23 And if you were not to receive mercy through Abraham, Isaac, and Jacob, our fathers, not one of our seed should be left upon the earth.

Deuteronomy 4.27 And the Lord shall scatter you among the nations and Ye shall be left few in number among the heathen where the Lord will lead you.

> 24 And now I have learnt that for seventy weeks ye shall go astray, and profane the priesthood, and pollute the sacrifices.

C.15 'for seventy weeks ye shall go astray' Where is Levi getting this reference to 70 weeks in his time of circa 1700 BC? Is there a reference to 70 weeks of Israel going astray in the Book of Enoch or Noah?

Book of Enoch 93.2 And Enoch began to recount from the books and said: I was born the 7th in the 1st week.

Book of Enoch 93.5 After that in the 7th Week shall an apostate generation arise and many shall be its deeds and all of its deeds shall be apostate. And at its close shall be elected the elect righteous one, the eternal plant of righteousness to receive 7-fold instruction concerning all His creation

C.16 In Enoch's reference to a 'week' he is stating that a week is 700 years or 100 years =1 day. However, in the Bible in the book of Daniel we see 70 weeks mentioned in the book of Daniel 9. In this case one week was 7 years.

Daniel 9.24 Seventy weeks are determined upon thy people and upon thy holy city to finish the transgression, and to make an end of sins, and to make reconciliation for iniquity and to bring in everlasting righteousness and to seal up the vision and prophecy, and to anoint the most Holy.

C.17 There is also the mention in the Book of Enoch of 70 shepherds that lead the people of Israel astray.

C.18 When did Israel go astray for a period of time of 70 weeks? Was one week just 7 years as in the book of Daniel or interpreted as 700 years as in the book of Enoch? It would appear from looking at both the Book of Enoch and the book of Daniel that Israel was the most reprobate in her history in the centuries leading up to the birth of the Messiah

> 25 And ye shall make void the law and set at nought the words of the prophets by evil perverseness.
>
> 26 And ye shall persecute righteous men and hate the godly; the words of the faithful shall ye abhor.
>
> 27 And a man who renews the law in the power of the Most High, ye

81

> shall call a deceiver; and at last ye shall rush upon him to slay him, not knowing his dignity, taking innocent blood through wickedness upon your heads.

Acts 7 51-59 Ye stiff-necked and uncircumcised in heart and ears, Ye always do resist the Holy Ghost; as your fathers did so do ye. Which of the prophets have not your fathers persecuted? And they have slain them which shewed before of the 'Coming of the Just One'; of whom ye have been the betrayers and murderers. Who have received the law by the 'disposition of angels' and have not kept it. And when they heard these things, they were cut to the heart, and they gnashed upon him with their teeth. But he, being full of the Holy Ghost looked up steadfastly into heaven and saw the Glory of God and seeing Jesus standing on the right hand of God. Then they cried with a loud voice and stopped their ears and ran upon him with one accord. And cast him out the city and stoned him.

C.19 'Disposition of angels' = Fallen angels. In other words, 'Stephen the Martyr' was telling the Pharisees and rulers at Jerusalem that many of their 'laws' were not give not them by God, but by devils.

> 28 And your holy places shall be laid waste even to the ground because of him.
>
> 29 And ye shall have no place that is clean; but ye shall be among the Gentiles a curse and a dispersion until He shall again visit you, and in pity shall receive you through faith and water.

C.20 The Messiah himself had almost nothing good to say about the Pharisee priests in the last week before he himself was crucified by these children of Satan -false priests.

Matthew 23.31,34-35. Wherefore ye be witnesses unto yourselves that ye are the children of those who killed the prophets. Ye serpents, ye generation of vipers, how can ye escape the damnation of hell? Wherefore, I send unto you prophets and wise men and scribes: some of them ye shall kill and crucify; and some ye shall scourge in your synagogues and persecute from city to city. That upon you may come all the righteous blood shed upon the earth from the blood of righteous Abel unto the blood if Zacharias son of Barachias, whom ye slew between the temple and the altar.

C.21 The following link gives a lot of information as to which of the prophets did the Jews murder or have killed?: http://en.wikipedia.org/wiki/Lives_of_the_ Prophets What Prophets Did The Jews Kill? - General Discussions - Mormon Dialogue & Discussion Board

CHAP. V.

AND whereas ye have heard concerning the seventy weeks, hear also concerning the priesthood. For in each jubilee there shall be a priesthood.

C.1 There is a definite repeated mention of this 70 weeks by the angels of God's Presence to Levi. What exactly are these 70 weeks? Another example is found in the Bible concerning Jacob when he worked for his corrupt uncle Laban, who told him that if he wanted to marry Laban's daughter Rachel then he would have to work for him for 7 years. The actual wording in the scriptures was 'fulfil her week'

Genesis 29.27 'Fulfil her week and we will give thee this also for the service which thou shalt serve with me yet 7 other years.'

2 And in the **first jubilee**, the first who is anointed to the priesthood shall be great and shall speak to God as to a father.

C.2 *First 'jubilee'*. Moses was the one who wrote the Book of Jubilees, and I think that the verse 2 above is talking about Moses who was a Levite.

Deuteronomy 34.10-12 And there arose not a prophet since in Israel like unto Moses, whom the Lord knew face to face. In all the signs and the wonders, which the Lord sent him to do in the land of Egypt to Pharoah, and to all his servants and to all his land. And in all that mighty hand, and in all the great terror which Moses shewed in the sight of all Israel.

C.3 Jubilee, or more complete, the Year of Jubilee (לבויה תנש) or simply לבי ("Jabilee", as for instance in Leviticus 25) marked every fiftieth (or forty-ninth, depending how one counted) year. (Leviticus 25:13-54, 27:17-24, Numbers 36:4) The prophet Ezekiel speaks of a year of liberty, which is probably the same thing (Ezekiel 46:17).

C.4 Note that when Jesus read from the book of Isaiah in the synagogue of Nazareth, he proclaimed the release of captives as stipulated to be done in the year of Jubilee (Leviticus 25:10). Also note that much to our loss, neither the Sabbath year nor the year of Jubilee are observed in our modern world. **SOURCE**: Jubilee | The amazing name Jubilee: meaning and etymology (abarim-publications.com)

C.5 More about Jubilees: The **Book of Jubilees** is predominantly a book describing the Calendar-Cycle of a solar-schematic calendar based on Enoch's "Astronomical Book". It retells the story of Genesis and the Exodus, up to Moses receiving the law, fitting the story into **49-year Jubilee cycles**, with all major events occurring in a "Jubilee" year. This is then followed by various prophesies about the future of Israel, which, as it is written in hindsight, are mostly accurate. It is also heavily influenced by Enoch's different books, most notably the "Astronomical" and "Dreams" books. It is therefore a theological summary of Enoch's books, or at least a summary of the same ideas.

C.6 Prophecy about Moses and Aaron who were 'prophet' and 'priest' of God and were also both Levites being brothers.

> 3 And his priesthood shall be perfect with the Lord, and in the day of his gladness shall he arise for the 'salvation' of the world.

C.7 Verse 3 is most definitely talking about the Messiah. The only person ever born who could save men's souls is Jesus - the Messiah

Acts 4.12 Neither is there Salvation in any other for there is no other name under heaven given among men whereby we must be saved.

C.8 Jesus himself stated that if ye believe not my writings neither will you believe in Moses in whom ye say that ye trust, for he wrote of me.

John 5.47 But if ye believe not his writings, how shall ye believe my words?

C.9 Could verse 3 be talking about Moses or only about the Messiah? We assume that because the word 'salvation' is used that this must infer the Christ. However, if we think of the word salvation in verse three more like the word deliverance then it could also be talking about Moses delivering the children of Israel from Egypt in the Exodus.

C.10 *'day of his gladness'* This expression in verse three could be referring to Moses being in the wilderness by himself and then 'out of his sorrow' of exile from Egypt, he was given a wife – Ziporah. It was after he was married and had a few children that God called Moses on the mountain to go and deliver Israel from Egypt.

> 4 In the second jubilee, he that is anointed shall be conceived in the sorrow of beloved ones; and his priesthood shall be honoured and shall be glorified by all.

C.11 Who is this verse talking about as the birth of Moses could be described as *'conceived in the sorrow of beloved ones'* as in the famous story of Jocabed putting her little baby on the waters of the Nile and seeing her baby sailing away, as an alternative to her baby being slaughtered by the soldiers of Pharaoh. Moses was certainly a baby 'born in sorrow'. Many Israelite babies were slaughtered by Pharaoh to try and stop the growth of the 'budding' nation of Israel where Egypt had acted as the womb of the 'baby' state of Israel. It is clear here to see Satan's direct attack against the budding nation of Israel.

Ephesians 6.12 For we wrestle not against flesh and blood, but against principalities against powers, against the rulers of the darkness of this world, against spiritual wickedness in high places.

C.12 However, there also seems to be a link to the 'birth of Christ' in this verse, who born under the Roman empire also was initially born in great Joy with the choirs of the angels and the rejoicing of the 3 Kings and the Shepherds & shepherd boys at the birth of the saviour. A little while later, Joseph the father of Jesus, was told to take his little son away to the land of Egypt, as Herod sought to kill baby Jesus, as the 3 Kings had told Herod that Christ had just been born in Bethlehem. Unfortunately, many children were slaughtered at that time which had been prophesied in the book of Jeremiah and fulfilled in the book of Matthew.

Jeremiah 31.15 Thus saith the LORD; A voice was heard in Ramah, lamentation, *and* bitter weeping; Rachel weeping for her children refused to be comforted for her children, because they *were* not.

Matthew 2.18 In Rama was there a voice heard, lamentation, and weeping, and great mourning, Rachel weeping *for* her children, and would not be comforted, because they are not.

C.13 *'priesthood shall be honoured and shall be glorified by all.* This part of the verse could be either about Moses or Christ.

C.14 I find verses 2-4 to be quite remarkable, and they are verses of prophecy, given by Levi some 250 years before the time of Moses delivering Levi's descendants 'the Children of Israel' from Egypt. Levi also mentions the Christ in these few verses. This was an amazing gift of prophecy.

---

5 And the third priest shall be taken hold of by sorrow.

6 And the fourth shall be in pain, because unrighteousness shall gather itself against him exceedingly, and all Israel shall hate each one his neighbour.

7 The fifth shall be taken hold of by darkness. Likewise, also the sixth and the seventh.

8 And in the seventh shall, be such pollution as I cannot express before men, for they shall know it who do these things.

C.15 It is difficult to understand verses 4-8 except to state that from the 2nd to the 7th Jubilee is a period of time representing 7 x 49 or 7x7x7 = 343 years. I am theorizing here but could this 343 years, be the 'dark years' mentioned above, leading up to the crucifixion of Christ the Messiah who was slain by his own people in 30 AD?

C.16 This dark period is mentioned by the Patriarchs in this book. It is also said by Bible experts, that there was a '400 year gap' between the Old and New Testament times, because of the evil deeds of Israel and her rebellion against God during those times.

C.17 There were no minor or major prophets from the time of Malachi is around 390 BCE until Christ the Saviour.

C.18 The description of those 6 Jubilees is one of sorrow and unrighteousness, pain, hatred for one another, darkness, pollution. 6 Jubilees = 6 x 49 = 294 years. This could indeed be the 300 years leading up to the time of Christ. It was a time of spiritual darkness in Israel, where the wicked Pharisees and Sadducees took over during the Maccabee period of time, or the 2nd century BCE.

C.19 Some people would disagree and mention the apocryphal books of the Maccabee brothers. One question I would have about the Maccabee brothers is, if they were working for God, why didn't God protect them the way that he did the Patriarchs, as they all soon perished.

C.20 The '**Maccabee brothers**' to me seems more like Israel trying to rescue itself with a little help from God thrown in. They were certainly defiant, but was it God's will? They certainly did not have the full blessing of God, as what they did came to nought eventually, and actually caused Israel to incur more wrath and destruction from their enemies because of their defiance of the 'world empires'.

C.21 This is probably why the Protestant Bible removed the books of the Maccabees in 1885 because some experts of the Bible were not sure of the content of the **Books of Maccabees,** as to them actually being inspired writings or not, in order for them to remain part of the canon of inspired scriptures? You yourself must decide about that one, by reading those apocryphal books of **Maccabees 1-4.**

C.22 This description is a good description of our modern world which lacks the light of the true gospel of the Truth. This world is a perfect example of what Levi describes from Jubilee 2-6: A world full of greed, hatred, violence, perversion, lawlessness (in real terms the elite are the lawless ones) and spiritual darkness and yes pollution in all forms physically and spiritually. Israel was warned by God through Levi and then Moses and King David and all the prophets from Isaiah to Malachi what would happen when people largely forsake God Himself and His Word. The result would be hell on earth as we see this day.

C.23 Things are getter worse every year and especially during 2020-2022 as the Elite want to bring on their great Re-Set of humanity. What does this mean?

1) Eugenics: Get rid of the 'useless eaters' to the tune of 7 Billion + world inhabitants by all methods available- War, Famine, Plagues, artificial means, A.I methods

2) Reorganize those who remain into slaves and robots.

3) Use A.I. and transhumanism as the goal for future citizens in order to alter humans and their DNA to something which God did not create..

C.24 The problem with the 'wicked elite' who think that they can run the planet without God is that their own days are 'numbered' and into hell they are destined to go or even worse perhaps even into the jaws of the 'Lake of

Fire' along with the coming Anti-Christ and Satan. All the wicked including the 'rulers' will all have to receive the 'Mark of the Beast' (A.I technology), which the False Prophet (probably an A.I machine, who works for the Anti-Christ will set-up, and cause everyone to have to worship Satan and his Image according to Revelations 13.

Revelations 13.15 And he causes **all,** both small and great, rich and poor, free and bond, to receive a **mark** in their right hand or foreheads

C.25 Perhaps these 6 Jubilees just mentioned, are talking about the most apostate time in Israel and the ungodly kings that ruled some of the time along with corrupt priesthood.

> 9 Therefore shall they be taken captive and become a prey, and their land and their substance shall be destroyed.

C.26 In 722 BC the 2nd World Empire or the Assyrian Empire took the 10 Northern Tribes of Israel captive. In 589 Babylon the 3rd World Empire took Judah captive to Babyon and destroyed Solomons temple in Jerusalem. The temple was rebuilt over a 100 years later in the time of the 4th World Empire the Medio-Persian world empire. The 2nd Temple was beautified by King Herod. The "2nd Temple was totally destroyed in 70 AD by the Romans or the 6th World Empire, under general Titus.

C.27 Levi talks about '7 Jubilees' the one after the other or the 1st until the 7th. Then he talks about weeks also up until 7 weeks. A jubilee is defined as 49 years which equals 7 x 7

> 10 And in the fifth week they shall return to their desolate country and shall renew the house of the Lord.
>
> 11 And in the seventh week shall become priests, who are idolaters, adulterers, lovers of money, proud, lawless, lascivious, abusers of children and beasts.
>
> 12 And after their punishment shall have come from the Lord, the priesthood shall fail.
>
> 13 Then shall the Lord raise up a new priest.

C.28 Christ - the 'New High Priest

Hebrews 7.1-3 'For this Melchizedek, king of Salem, priest of the Most High God, who met Abraham returning from the slaughter of the kings, and blessed him;

[2] To whom also Abraham gave a tenth part of all; first being by interpretation King of righteousness, and after that also King of Salem, which is, King of peace;

³ Without father, without mother, without descent, having neither beginning of days, nor end of life; but made like unto the Son of God; abides a priest continually.

> 14 And to him all the words of the Lord shall be revealed; and he shall execute a righteous judgement upon the earth for a multitude of days.
>
> 15 And his star shall arise in heaven as of a king.

Numbers 24.17 'There shall come a **Star** out of Jacob, and a **Sceptre** shall arise out of Israel and shall smite the corners of Moab and destroy all the children of Sheth.

Genesis 49.10 The **sceptre** shall not depart from Judah, nor a lawgiver from between his feet until Shiloh come; and unto him shall the gathering of the people be.

C.29 The 3 Kings: The famous 'Story of Christmas' when the '3 Kings' came from the East to worship the baby Messiah -Jesus.

Matthew 2.2 'Saying, 'Where is he that is born King of the Jews? for we have seen his **star** in the east, and are come to worship him.'

Revelation 22.16 - Jesus: 'I am the root and the offspring of David, *and* the bright and morning **star**.'

2 Peter 1.19 We have also a more sure word of prophecy; whereunto ye do well that ye take heed, as unto a light that shineth in a dark place, until the day dawn, and the day **star** arise in your hearts:

> 16 Lighting up the light of knowledge as the sun the day, and he shall be magnified in the world.
>
> 17 He shall shine forth as the sun on the earth, and shall remove all darkness from under heaven, and there shall be peace in all the earth.

Isaiah 42.6,7,16 I the Lord have called you in righteousness and will hold thine hand and help thee. To open the blind eyes, to bring out the prisoners from the prison, and them that sit in darkness out of the prison house I will make darkness light before them, and crooked things straight. These things will I do unto them and not forsake them

Matthew 13.43 Then shall the righteous shine forth as the sun in the kingdom of their Father. Who hath ears to hear, let him hear.

Isaiah 9.7 Of the increase in His government and peace there shall be no end, upon the throne of David and upon his kingdom to order it and establish it with judgment and justice henceforth even for ever. The zeal of the Lord of Hosts will perform this.

> 18 The heavens shall exult in his days, and the earth shall be glad, and

the clouds shall rejoice.

19 And the knowledge of the Lord shall be poured forth upon the earth, as the water of the seas.

Isaiah 11.9 They shall not hurt nor destroy in all my holy mountain: for the earth shall be full of the knowledge of the Lord , as the waters cover the sea

20 And the angels of the glory of the presence of the Lord shall be glad in him.

C.30 'angels of the glory of the presence of the Lord'. Definition: Angels of the Presence of God: or **Angel of his presence** refers to an entity variously considered angelic or else identified with God himself.

Isaiah 63.9 'In all their affliction he was afflicted, and the '**angel of his presence**' saved them: in his love and in his pity he redeemed them; and he bare them, and carried them all the days of old'.

In the book of Enoch, four angels that stand before the Lord of Spirits are given Michael, Raphael, Gabriel and Phanuel. The 2nd book of Enoch mentions Uriel. Uriel is also known in various traditions under the names of Phanuel or Sariel, as the Angel of the Presence or else as one of the Angels of the Presence.

21 The heavens shall be opened, and from the temple of glory shall come upon him sanctification, with the Father's voice as from Abraham to IsaaC.

22 And the glory of the Most High shall be uttered over him, and the spirit of understanding and sanctification shall rest upon him in the water.

C.31 This is clearly talking about Jesus the Messiah being sanctified by God the Father

23 For he shall give the majesty of the Lord to His sons in truth for ever more;

24 And there shall none succeed him for all generations for ever.

C.32 This could only happen at the 2nd Coming of Christ when He comes to take over the world and to lock up Satan in the bottomless Pit along with all evil spirits and he takes command of the world for the 1000 years of the Millennium, known as the Golden Age.

25 And in his priesthood the Gentiles shall be multiplied in knowledge upon the earth and enlightened through the grace of the Lord. In his

> priesthood shall sin come to an end, and the lawless shall cease to do evil.
>
> 26 And he shall open the gates of paradise, and shall remove the threatening sword against Adam, and he shall give to the saints to eat from the tree of life, and the spirit of holiness shall be on them.

C.33 'sin come to an end' - Only by destroying all the evil and getting rid of both Satan and Evil spirits permanently, could 'all sin come to an end'. It would also mean that God has 'saved all the righteous of all generations of the earth' and destroyed the really wicked and rebellious 'Merchants of the Earth' and all of Satan's followers, such as those who received the Mark of Satan or the 'Mark of the Beast' in the soon to come future when the Anti-Christ is revealed to the whole world. Satan and all his co-workers are all finally coming to an end at the very end of the Millennium at the Great White Throne Judgement of God!

Revelation 20. 7-9,11,15 'And when the thousand years are expired Satan shall be loosed

[8] And shall go out to deceive the nations which are in the four quarters of the earth, Gog and Magog, to gather them together to battle: the number of whom *is* as the sand of the sea.

[9] And they went up on the breadth of the earth, and compassed the camp of the saints about, and the beloved city: and <u>fire came down from God out of heaven and</u> <u>**devoured** them.</u>

[11] And I saw a great white throne and Him that sat upon it from whose face and the earth and the heaven fled away and there was found no place for them.

[15] And whosoever was not found written in the Book of Life was cast into the Lake of Fire.

C.34 'open the gates of paradise' Finally after 6000 years God will make Paradise on earth again during the Millennium as well as a paradise in Heaven or the spirit world. The thing to understand here is that in God's original Creation he separated the spiritual world from the physical world. One day the spiritual and physical worlds will blend into the eternal realities instead of the temporal values of the physical plane

C.35 'remove the threatening sword from Adam' At present, all descendants of Adam are under the threatening sword of Death. At the end of the Millennium or the golden Age will come the eternal age.

Revelations 21.4 And God shall wipe away all tears from their eyes: and there shall be no more death, neither sorrow nor crying, neither shall be any more pain; for the former things are passed away.

C.36 The Saints and the 'tree of life' In the eternal age the 'saved' will drink of the waters of eternal life, which were originally forbidden to Adam and Eve due to their Fall in eating the fruit from the Tree of Knowledge. For that reason, Adam and Eve were kicked out of the Garden of Eden. An angel with a sword which could turn every which way guarded the Garden of Eden from would-be intruders. That angel will be reassigned to other duties in the future and make it possible for mankind to re-enter the Garden of Eden or Paradise provided the person is saved.

Revelations 22.2 In the midst of the street of it, and on either side of the river (of Life), was there the tree of Life, which bare 12 manner of fruits, and yielded her fruit every month: and her leaves were for the healing of the nations

C.37 'The spirit of holiness shall be upon them' The only truly holy persons are God the Father, God the Son, and God the Holy Spirit

Romans 3.23 'For all have sinned can come short of the glory of God

Revelations: 3.7 'And to the angel of the church of Philadelphia write: 'These things saith He that is **Holy** and He that is true, He that hath the Key of David, he that opens and no man shuts and shuts and no man opens.

Romans 1.4 'And declared *to be* the Son of God with power, according to the '**spirit of holiness'**, by the resurrection from the dead.'

> 27 And Beliar shall be bound by him, and he shall give power to His children to tread upon the evil spirits.

C.38 *'And Beliar shall be bound by him'* Meaning of the word Beliar = "lord of the forest," & is also a name of Satan: source: Strong's Greek: 955. Βελίαλ (Beliar) -- "lord of the forest," Beliar, a name of Satan (biblehub.com)

Revelation 20.1-3

[1] 'And I saw an angel come down from heaven, having the key of the bottomless pit and a great chain in his hand.

[2] 'And he laid hold on the dragon, that old serpent, which is the Devil, and Satan, and bound him a thousand years.

[3] 'And cast him into the bottomless pit, and shut him up, and set a seal upon him, that he should deceive the nations no more, till the thousand years should be fulfilled: and after that he must be loosed a little season'.

C.39 *'give power to His children to tread upon the evil spirits'.* Jesus gave power to his disciples to tread on serpents and scorpions and over all the power of the Evil One that is Satan

Luke 10.19 'Behold, I give unto you power to tread on serpents and scorpions, and over all the power of the enemy: and nothing shall by any means hurt you.'

28 And the Lord shall rejoice in His children and be well pleased in His beloved ones for ever.

29 Then shall Abraham and Isaac and Jacob exult, and I will be glad, and all the saints shall clothe themselves with joy.

Psalm 149.5 Let the saints be joyful in glory let them sing aloud upon their beds

30 And now, my children, ye have heard all; choose, therefore, for yourselves either the light or the darkness, either the law of the Lord or the works of Beliar.

Joshua 24.15 And if it seem evil unto you to serve the LORD, choose you this day whom ye will serve; whether the gods which your fathers served that were on the other side of the flood, or the gods of the Amorites, in whose land ye dwell: but as for me and my house, we will serve the LORD. And the people answered and said, God forbid that we should forsake the LORD, to serve other gods.

31 And his sons answered him., saying, Before the Lord we will walk according to His law.

32 And their father said unto them, The Lord is witness, and His angels are witnesses, and ye are witnesses, and I am witness, concerning the word of your mouth.

Acts 5.32 We are witnesses of these things; and so also is the Holy Ghost whom God hath given to them that obey Him

John 8.17 'It is written in your law that the testimony of two men is true.'

33 And his sons said unto him: We are witnesses.

34 And thus Levi ceased commanding his sons; and he stretched out his feet on the bed, and was gathered to his fathers, after he had lived a hundred and thirty-seven years.

C.40 Amazing how the ancients 'Fathers' could literally have died in God's chosen time. They all called their families together in the case of all 12 sons of Jacob upon different occasions and declared they were about to pass away! They gave instructions and warnings to their sons and then simply fell asleep and died.

35 And they laid him in a coffin, and afterwards they buried him in

Hebron, with Abraham, Isaac, and Jacob.

Jasher 63.1 And in the ninety-third year died Levi, the son of Jacob, in Egypt, and Levi was an hundred and thirty-seven years old when he died, and they put him in a coffin, and he was given into the hands of his children.

THE TESTAMENT OF JUDAH

The Fourth Son of Jacob and Leah.

CHAP. I.

THE copy of the words of Judah, what things he spake to his sons before he died.

2 They gathered themselves together, therefore, and came to him, and he said to them: Hearken, my children, to Judah your father.

3 I was the fourth son born to my father Jacob; and Leah my mother named me Judah, saying, I give thanks to the Lord, because He hath given me a fourth son also.

4 I was swift in my youth, and obedient to my father in everything.

5 And I honoured my mother and my mother's sister.

C.1 Levi's mother was Leah, but Leah's sister Rachel, was also Jacob's wife

6 And it came to pass, when I became a man, that my father blessed me, saying, 'Thou shalt be a king, prospering in all things'.

Book of Jasher chapter 58.8,9 And Jacob said unto Judah, I know my son that thou are a mighty man of thy brethren; reign over them, and thy sons shall reign over them forever. Only teach thy children the bow and all the weapons of war, in order that they might fight the battles of their brother who will rule over his enemies. [See my book JASHER INSIGHTS Book 2]

C.2 Jacob prophesied that his son Judah would become the King of Israel along with his descendants. It was prophesied that the Messiah would come out of the Tribe of Judah.

7 And the Lord showed me favour in all my works both in the field and in the house.

8 I know that I raced a hind, and caught it, and prepared the meat for my father, and he did eat.

9 And the roes I used to master in the chase and overtake all that was in the plains.

C.3 Why was Judah so fast at running and also so strong? It would appear that God made the sons of Jacob unusually strong and excellent at warfare, because they had many enemies in the land of the Canaanites who had Nephilim blood, meaning that there were giants and chimeras among the population.

1 Chronicles 12:8 And of the Gadites there separated themselves unto David into the hold to the wilderness men of might, and men of war fit for the battle, that could handle shield and buckler, whose faces were like the faces of lions, and were as swift as the roes upon the mountains.

C.4 It sounds from the Bible, that in the far past there used to be some men who were chimeras of a sort. 'Faces like lions', more human than animal and swift as a lion at running.

C.5 Look at the following strange descriptions of human chimeras from the apocryphal book of Jasher:

Book of Jasher 36.32 And those animals, from their middle downward, were in the shape of the children of men, and from their middle upwards some had the likeness of bears, and some the likeness of keephas, with tails behind them from between their shoulders reaching down to the earth, like the tails of the the ducheephath, and these animals came and mounted and rode upon the asses, and lead them away, and they went away unto this day.

Book of Jasher 61.15 And Zepho (grandson of Esau and a mighty warrior king) went and he saw and behold there was a large cave at the bottom of the mountain, and there was a great stone there at the entrance of the cave, and Zepho split the stone and he came into the cave, and looked and behold a large animal was devouring the ox; From the middle upwards it resembled a man, and from the middle downwards it resembled an animal and it slew it with his two swords.

---

10 A wild mare I overtook and caught it and tamed it.

11 I slew a lion and plucked a kid out of its mouth.

Judges 14.5-6 Samson declares his victory over a Lion that he killed with his bare hands: "As Samson and his parents were going down to Timnah, a young lion suddenly attacked Samson near the vineyards of Timnah. At that moment the Spirit of the Lord came powerfully upon him, and he ripped the lion's jaws apart with his bare hands.

---

12 I took a bear by its paw and hurled it down the cliff, and it was crushed.

Samuel 17:34-35 And David said unto Saul, 'Thy servant kept his father's sheep, and there came a lion, and a bear, and took a lamb out of the flock: and I went out after him, and smote him, and delivered it out of his mouth: and when he arose against me, I caught him by his beard, and smote him, and slew him.'

---

13 I outran the wild boar, and seizing it as I ran, I tore it in sunder.

Psalm 80.18 The boar out of the wood doth waste it, and the wild beast of the field doth devour it.

> 14 A leopard in Hebron leaped upon my dog, and I caught it by the tail, and hurled it on the rocks, and it was broken in twain
>
> 15 I found a wild ox feeding in the fields, and seizing it by the horns, and whirling it round and stunning it, I cast it from me and slew it.
>
> 16 And when the two kings of the Canaanites came sheathed, in armour against our flocks, and much people with them, single handed I rushed upon the king of Hazor, and smote him on the grieves and dragged him down, and so I slew him.
>
> 17 And the other, the king of Tappuah, as he sat upon his horse, I slew, and so I scattered all his people.

C.6 It is very helpful that the Book of Jasher also talks about the exact same battles and peoples and kings mentioned by Judah and gives even more details. This is why, in my opinion, knowing the Bible first of all is the most important. 2ndly, know some of the more important ancient Jewish books such as Enoch, Jasher, Jubilees and other apocryphal books which used to be in the canon of holy scriptures.

Book of Jasher 37:27,28,29. 'And Jashub, king of Tapnach, also came forth first with his army before Judah, and Judah saw Jashub and his army coming toward him, and Judah's wrath was kindled and his anger burned within him, and he approached to battle in which Judah ventured his life. And Jashub and all his army were advancing toward Judah and he was riding upon a very strong and powerful horse, and Jashub was a very valiant man, and covered with iron and brass from head to foot; and whilst he was upon the horse he shot arrows with both hands from before and behind, as was his manner in all his battles, and he never missed the place to which he aimed his arrows.

> 18 Achor, the king, a man of giant stature, I found, hurling javelins before and behind as he sat on horseback, and I took up a stone of sixty pounds weight, and hurled it and smote his horse, and killed it.

Book of Jasher 37.32 'And Judah took up a large stone from the ground, and its weight was sixty **shekels**, and Judah ran towards Jashub, and with the stone struck him on his shield, that Jashub was stunned with the blow and fell off his horse to the ground

> 19 And I fought with this other for two hours; and I clave his shield in

twain, and I chopped off his feet, and killed him.

Book of Jasher 37.39,40 'When Judah saw that his shield was split, he hastily drew his sword and smote Jashub at his ankles and cut off his feet, that Jashub fell upon the ground and the spear fell from his hand. And Judah hastily picked up Jashub's spear and with it he cut off his head, and cast it next to his feet

20 And as I was stripping off his breastplate, behold nine men his companions began to fight with me,

Book of Jasher 37.44 And Judah also took off the iron and brass that was about Jashub and behold nine men of the captains of Jashub came along to fight against Judah [**See my book JASHER INSIGHTS Book 1 &2 for many adventure story like these ones**]

21 And I wound my garment on my hand; and I slung stones at them, and killed four of them, and the rest fled.

Book of Jasher 37.45-46 And Judah hastened and took up a stone from the ground and with it he smote one of them on the head, and his skull was fractured, and the body also fell from the horse to the ground. And the eight captains that remained, seeing the strength of Judah were greatly afraid and fled, and Judah and his ten men pursued after them, and overtook them and slew them.

22 And Jacob my father slew Beelesath, king of all the kings, a giant in strength, twelve cubits high. ᴄ∦ 𝟠ᶦ

C.7 This was some monster of a giant of 12 cubits. A cubit of around 2 feet, so 12 cubits is around 24 feet high that was even bigger than Og the giant who was 9 cubits or around 16 feet high which was slain by the children of Israel in the time of Moses and Joshua. Jacob lived some 250 years before the times of Moses and Joshua, so it appears that the giants were getting smaller as time went by, until by the time of King David some 500 years after Moses time and yet still 3000 years ago to us today, we find that the giant that king David fought against as a young lad was only some 5 cubits tall or just under 10 feet tall. Why did the giants end up getting smaller and smaller? Now that's a good question that we need an answer for. Another question is, are there still giants around on the planet today? If so, where are they hiding? Is it just possible that the outer surface of the planet is no longer hospitable for the giants to live on with much lower oxygen levels? Are the conditions on the planet unsuitable for bigger creatures like dinosaurs and giants at the present time. The truth be known, giants have been spotted on this planet throughout the ages of mankind by different peoples from all over the world, but it is now a rare sight.

23 And fear fell upon them, and they ceased warring against us.

24 Therefore my father was free from anxiety in the wars when I was with my brethren.

25 For he saw in a vision concerning me that an angel of might followed me everywhere, that I should not be overcome.

C.8 This is very interesting, as it shows that Judah had a powerful angel with him at all times that made him invincible to defeat. Hardly surprising when Judah and his brethren were often outnumbered 1000 to 1 in many of their battles.

26 And in the south there came upon us a greater war than that in Shechem; and I joined in battle array with my brethren, and pursued a thousand men, and slew of them two hundred men and four kings.

C.9 Here Judah states himself that he pursued after 1000 men. This reminds me about King David where it was said that Saul had killed his 1000's but David his 10,000's. King David lived circa 600 years after Levi.

1 Samuel 18.6-9 And it came to pass as they came, when David was returned from the slaughter of the Philistine, that the women came out of all cities of Israel, singing and dancing, to meet king Saul, with tabrets, with joy, and with instruments of musiC. And the women answered *one another* as they played, and said, Saul hath slain his thousands, and David his ten thousands.

27 And I went up upon the wall, and I slew four mighty men.

C.10 There were chimeras at the time of Judah and afterwards. Look at the following description from the Bible in the book of Samuel of some of King David's fighting men:

2 Samuel 23.20 And Benaiah the son of Jehoiada, the son of a valiant man, of Kabzeel, who had done many acts, he slew two **lionlike** men of Moab: he went down also and slew a lion in the midst of a pit in time of snow:

28 And so we captured Hazor and took all the spoil.

29 And the next day we departed to Aretan, a city strong and walled and inaccessible, threatening us with death.

30 But I and Gad approached on the east side of the city, and Reuben and Levi on the west.

31 And they that were upon the wall, thinking that we were alone, were drawn down against us.

32 And so my brothers secretly climbed up the wall on both sides by stakes, and entered the city, while the men knew it not.

33 And we took it with the edge of the sword.

34 And as for those who had taken refuge in the tower, we set fire to the tower and took both it and, them.

35 And as we were departing the men of Tappuah seized our spoil and seeing this we fought with them.

36 And we slew them all and recovered our spoil.

37 And when I was at the waters of Kozeba, the men of Jobel came against us to battle.

38 And we fought with them and routed them; and their allies from Shiloh we slew, and we did not leave them power to come in against us.

39 And the men of Makir came upon us the fifth day, to seize our spoil; and we attacked them and overcame them in fierce battle: for there was a host of mighty men amongst them, and we slew them before they had gone up the ascent.

40 And when we came to their city their women rolled upon us stones from the brow of the hill on which the city stood.

41 And I and Simeon hid ourselves behind the town, and seized upon the heights, and destroyed this city also.

42 And the next day it was told us that the king of the city of Gaash with a mighty host was coming against us.

Book of Jasher 39.16 And the sons of Jacob came to Gaash and they found the gates of the city locked, and about 500 men standing on the top of the outer-most wall, and a people numerous as the sand upon the sea shore were in ambush for the sons of Jacob from without the city at the rear thereof.

43 I, therefore, and Dan feigned ourselves to be Amorites, and as allies went into their city.

44 And in the depth of night our brethren came and we opened to them the gates; and we destroyed all the men and their substance, and we took for a prey all that was theirs, and their three walls we cast down.

Book of Jasher 39.21 And the sons of Jacob returned against the men of Gaash who were with them from without the city, and they smote them terribly, as striking against gourds, and they could not stand against the sons of Jacob, for fright and terror had seized them at the shriek of Judah.

45 And we drew near to Thamna, where was all the substance of the hostile kings.

46 Then being insulted by them, I was therefore wroth, and rushed against them to the summit; and they kept slinging against me stones and darts.

47 And had not Dan my brother aided me, they would have slain me.

48 We came upon them, therefore, with wrath, and they all fled; and passing by another way, they fought my father, and he made peace with them.

49 And we did to them no hurt, and they became tributary to us, and we restored to them their spoil.

50 And I built Thamna, and my father built Pabael.

51 I was twenty years old when this war befell. And the Canaanites feared me and my brethren.

52 And I had much cattle, and I had for chief herdsman Iram the Adullamite.

53 And when I went to him I saw Parsaba, king of Adullam; and he spake unto us, and he made us a feast; and when I was heated he gave me his daughter Bathshua to wife.

54 She bare me Er, and Onan and Shelah; and two of them the Lord smote: for Shelah lived, and his children are ye.

Genesis 46.12 And the sons of Judah; Er, and Onan, and Shelah, and Pharez, and Zerah: but Er and Onan died in the land of Canaan

C.11 If Shelah lived from Judah's 1st marriage to the Canaanite woman, then why did Judah and Tamar's son Pharez become the 1st king of the House of Judah and thus the 1st king of Israel according to the Bible?

CHAP. II.

AND eighteen years my father abode in peace with his brother Esau, and his sons with us, after that we came from Mesopotamia, from Laban.

2 And when eighteen years were fulfilled, in the fortieth year of my life, Esau, the brother of my father, came upon us with a mighty and strong people.

3 And Jacob smote Esau with an arrow, and he was taken up wounded on Mount Seir, and as he went he died at Anoniram.

Book of Jubilees 38.1-2 And after that Judah spake to Jacob his father, and saith unto him: 'bend thy bow, father, and send forth thy arrows and cast down the adversary and slay the enemy; and mayest thou have the power, for we shall not slay thy brother, for he is such as thou, and he is like thee let us give him this honour.' Then Jacob bent his bow and sent forth the arrow and struck Esau, his brother on his right breast and slew him.

4 And we pursued after the sons of Esau.

Book of Jubilees 38.9-11 And the sons of Jacob pursued after them to the mountains of Seir. And Jacob buried his brother on the hill which is in Aduram and he returned to his house. And the sons of Jacob pressed hard upon the sons of Esau in the mountains of Seir and bowed their necks so that they became servants of the sons of Jacob.

5 Now they had a city with walls of iron and gates of brass; and we could not enter into it, and we encamped around, and besieged it.

Psalms 107:16 For he hath broken the gates of brass and cut the bars of iron in sunder.

6 And when they opened not to us in twenty days, I set up a ladder in the sight of all and with my shield upon my head I went up, sustaining the assault of stones, upwards of three talents weight; and I slew four of their mighty men.

7 And Reuben and Gad slew six others.

8 Then they asked from us terms of peace; and having taken counsel

> with our father, we received them as tributaries.

Book of Jubilees 38.12-13 And they sent to their father to inquire whether they should make peace with them or slay them And Jacob sent word that they should make peace with them and place a yoke of servitude upon them, so that they paid tribute to Jacob and his sons always.

> 9 And they gave us five hundred cors of wheat, five hundred baths of oil, five hundred measures of wine, until the famine, when we went down into Egypt.

C.1 These measurements = 500 x 8 Bushels of wheat, 3500 gallons of oil, 700 gallons of wine, was a substantial tribute from Esau's relatives to Jacob's family.

[**Definition of measurements**: The 'cor' meant measurement. We learn from Ezekiel 45:14 that the 'cor' contained 10 'baths' and was the same as the 'homer', see also 1 Kings 4:22; 1 Kings 5:11; 2 Chronicles 2:10; 2 Chronicles 27:5.] The 'measure' or 'cor' was equivalent to 8 bushels or 1 quarter. The 'bath' contained 6 or 7 gallons (= hins).] **SOURCE**: Ezra 7:22 Commentaries: even up to 100 talents of silver, 100 kors of wheat, 100 baths of wine, 100 baths of oil, and salt as needed. (biblehub.com)]

> 10 And after these things my son Er took to wife Tamar, from Mesopotamia, a daughter of Aram.

C.2 Er, Son of Judah, took a wife from another country, himself being half Canaanite through his mother and half from Abraham's seed through his father Judah. His wife was from Mesopotamia from the countries around where Babylon would stand a 1000 years later. I think it very likely that his wife was the daughter of one of the servants of Jacob.

> 11 Now Er was wicked, and he was in need concerning Tamar, because she was not of the land of Canaan.

C.3 *'In need concerning Tamar'* - Some men get what they want too easily with women, and then despise that very same woman and send her away. There was a story in the Bible about the sons of King David where one half-brother killed his half-brother because he abused his sister. He first loved her but then hated her and cast her out.

2 Samuel 13. 1,14-15: And it came to pass after this, that Absalom the son of David had a fair sister, whose name *was* Tamar; and Amnon the son of David loved her. 14 Howbeit he would not hearken unto her voice: but, being stronger than she, forced her, and lay with her.15 Then Amnon hated her exceedingly; so that the hatred wherewith he hated her *was* greater than the love wherewith he had loved her. And Amnon said unto her, Arise, be gone.

C.4 That girl's name was also Tamar.

C.5 Why would Er marry a woman, only to be discontent with her after a few days? It says that he was wicked concerning Tamar, but the verse does not elaborate on exactly what that meant. I think we find out later that the reason Er had a problem with Tamar was because his mother being a Canaanite did not like the fact that Tamar was from Mesopotamia and tried to pull her son away from his wife Tamar.

> 12 And on the third night an angel of the Lord smote him.

C.6 Why would an angel of God's suddenly slay Er, the son of Judah?

> 13 And he had not known her according to the evil craftiness of his mother, for he did not wish to have children by her.

C.7 The trouble began because of his mother was a wicked Canaanite who practised witchcraft. Why did Judah marry such a woman? Well, he will explain later in this chapter.

> 14 In the days of the wedding feast I gave Onan to her in marriage; and he also in wickedness knew her not, though he spent with her a year.

C.8 It sounds like in the period of time of the wedding, because Er died, then Judah gave Er's brother Onan as a husband for Tamar. However, Onan did not perform the office of a husband, and therefore did not have sexual intercourse with her.

> 15 And when I threatened him he went in unto her, but he spilled the seed on the ground, according to the command of his mother, and he also died through wickedness.

C.9 Judah probably got a bad report from his daughter in law concerning Onan that he was not 'taking care' of her in the proper marital way, so Judah got angry with his son and threatened him. His son then had sex with Tamar, but so as to avoid her getting pregnant, he cast his seed on the ground. Extra detail here not found in the Bible is that it was his mother who had commanded Onan not to have children with his wife.

> 16 And I wished to give Shelah also to her, but his mother did not permit it; for she wrought evil against Tamar, because she was not of the daughters of Canaan, as she also herself was.

C.10 Now we can see who has been causing all the trouble – the wife of Judah for some reason did not like Tamar, probably because Tamar was different and did not have a wicked spirit like herself who practised witchcraft.

> 17 And I knew that the race of the Canaanites was wicked, but the

> impulse of youth blinded my mind.

C.11 Judah knew that the Canaanites tended to be of a wicked 'bent', but he married her when he was young and impulsive and had been drinking too much.

> 18 And when I saw her pouring out wine, owing to the intoxication of wine I was deceived, and took her although my father had not counselled it.

C.12 Judah states here, that 'he was deceived'. What was he deceived about? He also had not consulted with his father or gotten his approval to marry his wife which was the custom back in those times.

> 19 And while I was away, she went and took for Shelah a wife from Canaan.

C.13 Unbelievably evil to go and marry your son off to another Canaanite woman whilst Judah was not at home!

C.14 Judah's third son with the Canaanite woman or his first wife. This point here in verse 19 is very important, because what it is saying is that Judah's 3rd son Shelah could not have been the ancestor of all the kings of Judah. It would also appear that he died like his mother having been cursed by his father Judah.

> 20 And when I knew what she had done, I cursed her in the anguish of my soul.
>
> 21 And she also died through her wickedness together with her sons.

C.15 Judah got so angry that he cursed his wife and she died as did her two sons? Or was it all three of her sons? This information is very important to know, so that we get the right picture, as to who was the true mother of the Kings of Judah? It would seem that this information has been 'hidden', as in the Bible it not immediately clear as to who was Judah's 2nd wife was, and who had been the mother of the first descendants of the Tribe of the kings – Judah.

> 22 And after these things, while Tamar was a widow, she heard after two years that I was going up, to shear my sheep, and adorned herself in bridal array, and sat in the city Enaim by the gate.

C.16 Why did Tamar adorn herself in bridal array? Was she fishing for a husband? Note that now Tamar was a widow and Judah was a widower.

> 23 For it was a law of the Amorites, that she who was about to marry

> should sit in fornication seven days by the gate.

C.17 What a crazy, ungodly and disgusting law of the Amorites, and yet in modern times people have a 'remnant' of that practice in some cases such as the 'Hen Night' or 'Stag Party'. Because of this tradition, some potential new marriages have been ruined, because of those type of modern parties, when yet another woman got pregnant, so the intended marriage did not go ahead.

> 24 Therefore being drunk with wine, I did not recognize her; and her beauty deceived me, through the fashion of her adorning.

C.18 Why is Judah so on the defensive, as if he thinks that he committed the ultimate crime when he simply had not? How many rich people and kings and politicians go into prostitutes in modern times? Why does he blame the incident on too much alcohol and saying that 'her beauty deceived me'. Well, there are lots of verses in the Bible and especially in the Proverbs warning about this exact situation. It would seem that Judah tended to drink too much, which did cause him problems. 'Drunkenness' is something that happens when people are young, but they do normally grow out of this potentially dangerous addiction.

> 25 And I turned aside to her and said: Let me go in unto thee.

C.19 Human Sexuality: Judah sees that the woman is both beautiful and desirable. Judah has just lost his wife and he wants to make love with the woman, not knowing that she is in fact his 'daughter in law' Tamar in disguise. The sex drive in a healthy man when he is young, usually makes him seek after women on a regular basis.

> 26 And she said: What wilt thou give me? And I gave her my staff, and my girdle, and the diadem of my kingdom in pledge.

C.20 Judah is a king of all his 11 brethren and apparently already had a staff which represents kingship or leadership not to mention the 'diadem of his kingdom' That seems frivolous to give to a woman who is seemingly a 'stranger' these things of value, which were worth more than just money.

C.21 It is almost as if God Himself took a hand in Tamar's life to elevate her to the status of the wife of Judah and to be the mother in the lineage of the future kings of Judah

> 27 And I went in unto her, and she conceived.

C.22 I think it important to point out that Tamar was a widow and Judah a widower at this time and there was no reason why they could not get married, if they so wished.

> 28 And not knowing what I had done, I wished to slay her; but she priv-

ily sent my pledges, and put me to shame.

C.23 Judah was told according to the Bible, that his 'daughter in law' had conceived by 'whoredoms' or prostitution. So, 'according to the 'letter of the law' he orders her to be taken out and burned. Where did he get that awful law from? The laws of Moses had not yet been carved in stone by God on Mount Sinai, so why the harsh treatment of the so-called 'prostitute'?

29 And when I called her, I heard also the secret words which I spoke when lying with her in my drunkenness; and I could not slay her, because it was from the Lord.

C.24 Tamar who had herself been in a difficult predicament acted very wisely in my opinion. What else could she do? Her husband had died or better said been slain by the angel of the Lord. She wanted to do the right thing and that was to marry a godly person, who would not be cursed, as her two husbands Er and Onan had been. She chose Judah knowing that he was a good man at heart and a godly one, though obviously not without his faults and sins.

30 For I said, Lest haply she did it in subtlety, having received the pledge from another woman.

31 But I came not again near her while I lived, because I had done this abomination in all Israel.

C.25 This last verse does not make any sense, and is obviously not true to human nature. Judah states in the above verse that he came not near Tamar again, as long as he lived. If that was true, then who are all the descendants that he is talking to? He stated that all the 3 children of his first wife, the Canaanite woman died along with her! So, who did Judah marry and whose son became the king of the Tribe of Judah?

32 Moreover, they who were in the city said there was no harlot in the gate, because she came from another place and sat for a while in the gate.

33 And I thought that no one knew that I had gone in to her.

C.26 It turns out that by reading the Bible in many places that it was Pharez, one of the twin sons of Tamar, the daughter in law of Judah, from which all the kings of Judah descended. And Tamar his daughter-in-law bore him Pharez and Zerah.

[See Genesis 28; 1 Chronicles Chapter 2; New Testament Luke Chapter 3.23-38]

C.27 In the New Testament in the book of Matthew Chapter 1 it specifically states:

¹ The book of the generation of Jesus Christ, the son of David, the son of Abraham.

² Abraham begat Isaac; and Isaac begat Jacob; and Jacob begat Judas and his brethren;

³ And Judah begat **Phares** and Zara of **Tamar;** and **Phares** begat **Esrom**; and **Esrom** begat **Aram**;

⁴ And **Aram** begat **Aminadab**; and **Aminadab** begat **Naasson**; and **Naasson** begat **Salmon**;

⁵ And **Salmon begat Boaz** of Rachab; and **Boaz begat Obed of Ruth**; and **Obed begat Jesse**;

⁶ And **Jesse begat David the king**; and **David the king begat Solomon** of her that had been the **wife of Urias**;

C.28 King David was the forefather of the Messiah. Often in the scriptures only the firstborn son was mentioned and not all their brothers and sisters.

C.29 If I know one thing about the kings of Judah is that they kept their wives and children very close to them, and so I believe that it is likely that Judah ended up marrying Tamar who had been his daughter-in-law. Legally speaking, or according to the laws in Old Testament times, it would have been required for Judah to marry Tamar, in order for the Judah line of kings that were to soon come to be continued. If Judah had not married Tamar then the lineage of Judah would not have continued and God's plan would have been defeated. In the New Testament Joseph married Mary in order to make her an honourable woman, according to Jewish law, since she had gotten pregnant.

1 Corinthians 7.14 "For the unbelieving husband is sanctified by the wife, and the unbelieving wife is sanctified by the husband: else were your children unclean; but now are they holy."

C.30 There are many examples in the Bible where God allowed something unusual to happen, in order to fulfil his perfect will. Not only the story of Judah and Tamar who became the ancestors of all the kings of Judah, but later in Judah's kingly lineage, we had Ruth the Moabitess grafted into the royal family, and she married Boaz, even though she was not Hebrew. King David committed adultery with another man's wife Bathsheba, whose husband was Uriah the Hittite, and she ended being the mother of Solomon. So, who knows what God's will is in a given situation? It is probably not according to strict religious rules! *Look up the laws of Moses - Leviticus about marriage to foreigners.* **1 John 3:12**, KJV: Not as Cain, who was of that wicked one, and slew his brother. And wherefore slew he him? Because his own works were evil, and his brother's righteous.

C.31 What did the Messiah say about a woman caught committing adultery? Not to excuse the crime, but Jesus made it clear that it was not right to use the 'letter of the law' to condemn a woman.

C.32 Why was it always the woman who was blamed, and not the man, when it came to adultery, and "playing the harlot? One standard for men and another for women? That does not sound right! What did God Himself think? Well, Jesus Himself made it very clear in the gospel of John chapter 8. [See the amazing story of Jesus' forgiveness in John chapter 8 for the story]

John 8.10-11 Jesus said unto her, Woman, where are those thine accusers? Hath no man condemned thee? She said, No man, Lord. And Jesus said unto her, 'Neither do I condemn thee: go, and sin no more'

34 And after this we came into Egypt to Joseph, because of the famine.

Genesis 41.57 And all the countries came into Egypt to buy corn from Joseph, for the famine was so sore in all the lands.

35 And I was forty and six years old, and seventy and three years lived I in Egypt.

C.33 Judah was in his forties when he married Tamar and their son Pharez lineage became the lineage of the Kings of Judah.

C.34 Judah lived a total of 73 years in the land of Egypt. He went to Egypt when he was 46 years old, and he died when he was 119 years old

CHAP. III.

AND now I command you, my children, hearken to Judah your father, and keep my sayings to perform all the ordinances of the Lord, and to obey the commands of God.

2 And walk not after your lusts, nor in the imaginations of your thoughts in haughtiness of heart; and glory not in the deeds and strength of your youth, for this also is evil in the eyes of the Lord.

C.1 *'lusts, nor in the imaginations of your thoughts in haughtiness of heart'*. I think that it is very important to quantify what 'lusts' or desires are actually 'wrong' in the 'eyes of God' Himself. Contrary to what most churches teach today, there is nothing wrong with normal sex, as it was God who created it, as shown clearly in the story of Adam and Eve. The so-called 'Fall of man' was not mankind having normal healthy sex for both pleasure, oneness, harmony and to obey God's first commandment 'Be fruitful and multiply'. Now one can't obey that command without having sex.

C.2 The fall of man was because of direct disobedience to God the Creator and not because of 'normal sex' between and a man and a woman. I think that is was a woman having sex with Satan, as in the case of Satan fathering Cain, which was more the issue as to why Adam and Eve got kicked out of the Garden of Eden.

C.3 Adam must have also known about it as he got kicked out of the Garden of Eden. This appears to have started with Eve in the Garden of Eden and continued with the Fallen angels and the daughters of Cain some 500 years after Creation.

C.4 Religions have used 'abstinence from sex' as a control mechanism. The 'controllers' have often been found guilty of the worst crimes such as child-abuse or paedophilia. Monks and nuns secretly have gotten together and had sex in the Catholic church of old, and resultant babies were killed or aborted, and buried in the church graveyard. What Horror of Horrors! Religions have failed to quantify sexual relationships, and just lump the good and bad together with a 'control' and 'punish' sort of attitude. This has led to a lot of homosexuality in boarding schools, monasteries, and with the priests within the Catholic church.

1John 3.2 Not as Cain who was of that wicked one and slew his brother and why slew he him? Because Abel's deeds were righteous and his own wicked.

C.5 In many cases, sexual relationships are innocent and natural. However, other relationships are demonic, and that is where you have to draw the line, as to what is good and what is bad. What was the motive? Was it out of real love for someone, or was is in worship of Satan and his idol worshipping 'excessive desire' and lust? It is the excess that can be dangerous and lead to addition or even obsession.

C.6 See the story of '**Joseph the Patriarch'** at the end of this book, as he had an obsessive woman chasing after him, who clearly was demonic, and she was already married to Potiphar who was a top official, close to Pharaoh himself.

C.7 Look at the contrast when considering the evil spirit world and demonic 'lust'. Look at this from the Book of Enoch Chapter 67 to get some sort of a deeper perspective as to what dangerous devilish 'lust' is:

Book of Enoch 67. 6 And through its valleys proceed streams of fire, where the angels are punished who had led astray those who dwell on the earth. But those waters shall be in those days serve for the kings and the mighty and the exalted, and those who dwell upon the earth for the healing of the body but for the punishment of the spirit; now their <u>spirit is full of lust,</u> that they may <u>be punished in the body</u> for they have <u>denied the Lord of Spirits</u> and see their punishment daily, and yet <u>believe not</u> in His Name.

C.8 Let's face it, the religionists throughout all time have tried to 'control' sex and make money off doing so. Man's laws without God, which have nothing to do with the way God sees things. Jesus told us how God thinks when He was here on earth in person. How did Jesus behave? Certainly not like the self-righteous Pharisees. He was not condemning of people's sins. Jesus was not like Satan and his crowd or the 'Accuser' of the Saints.

Revelation 12:10 "And I heard a loud voice saying in heaven, Now is come salvation, and strength, and the kingdom of our God, and the power of his Christ: for the accuser of our brethren is cast down, which accused them before our God, day and night."

C.9 Religionists have been misled by Satan himself as in the case of the Catholic 'Inquisitions' that murdered millions of innocent peoples from the 1250 until 1820 Just absolutely monstrous.

C.10 The New Testament tells us clearly to be moderate in all things:

Philippians 4.5 Let your moderation be known unto all men.

C.11 If normal sex is not a sin, then why do the religions play down sex? It is because it is a very good 'control mechanism'. I have heard priests in the Catholic church telling the women to 'withhold' sex from their husbands 'until they come to church', which is totally against the scriptures on marriage.

'1 Corinthians 7:5 Defraud ye not one the other, except *it be* with consent for a time, that ye may give yourselves to fasting and prayer; and come together again, that Satan tempt you not for your incontinency.

C.12 What does the above verse mean exactly concerning sex within marriage? Here is a very good explanation: What does 1 Corinthians 7:5 mean? | BibleRef.com

3 Since I also gloried that in wars no comely woman's face ever enticed

113

me, and reproved Reuben my brother concerning Bilhah, the wife of my father, the spirits of jealousy and of fornication arrayed themselves against me, until I lay with Bathshua the Canaanite, and Tamar, who was espoused to my sons.

C.13 I would suggest: 'Don't accuse, or you in turn will be condemned'. For every 'pointing finger' that you have accusing and condemning others, there are three fingers pointing back at you and Satan and his demons will take advantage of that fact, as apparently this is exactly what happened to Judah. He condemned his brother Reuben for a crime, but then was himself soon attacked by Satan through the spirits of jealousy, temptation and subsequent fornication, as he clearly mentions in the last verse.

C.14 It would seem that Judah had some trials concerning women, mostly because he felt condemned for some of his escapades with them, when maybe it was not really a big deal at all. It has been made into a big deal by the 'religionists' who came later in time and decided that Judah's behaviour did not fit into the 10 Commandments put forth by God to Moses some 250 years later in time.

C.15 I can think of at least 3 sexy women in the Bible who took advantage of their beauty and their sexuality in order to marry into the royal family of the House of Judah. First of all Tamar, who was not Hebrew but from Mesopotamia. I suspect that she was the daughter of one of the workers of Jacob's tribe. Abraham also married the daughter of one of his Canaanite workers, after Sarah his wife had died, and she bore him 6 sons. Another sexy woman in the Bible was Ruth the Moabitess, who ended up marrying Boaz, who was the great grandfather of King David. Then King David got his eyes on a naked woman called Bathsheba, who just happened to by taking a bath on the other side of his garden wall. How convenient! Of course, David could not resist his urges towards such a beautiful woman and had her brought to him and he committed adultery with her, even though he knew that she was the wife of Uriah the Hittite. Her name was Bathsheba or 'Sheba in the bath'. Was she herself a Hebrew or a Hittite like her warrior husband Uriah? It would seem, that God's ways are not man's religious 'letter of the law' ways. God is merciful and compassionate unlike Satan and the religionists who use religion to control the masses and steal from them throughout history starting with Cain. Hebrews were supposed to marry Hebrews, but it did not always happen, as sometimes there simply weren't enough Hebrews to marry, especially during the times of Abraham, Isaac, Jacob, and Judah. Once Israel grew into a budding nation whilst in the 'womb' of Egypt, then eventually there would have been enough selection of Hebrews to marry. In other words, by the time of Moses and the Exodus, some 250 years after Judah got married.

C.16 It would appear that throughout the Bible history of the Kings of Judah, that sometimes God did something radical or certainly allowed it to happen in order to bring a certain result such as Judah getting a good and godly wife,

114

Boaz the old bachelor finally getting married and becoming the great grand-father of King David and Bathsheba unexpectedly becoming the mother of King Solomon. These events just mentioned were divinely planned by God Himself. Here is a good verse from the New Testament that explains this situation very well:

Romans 11:17 And if some of the branches be broken off, and thou, being a wild olive tree, wert grafted in among them, and with them partakes of the root and fatness of the olive tree.

C.17 Examining verse 2: 'And walk not after your lusts, nor in the imagina-tions of your thoughts in haughtiness of heart; and glory not in the deeds and strength of your youth, for this also is evil in the eyes of the Lord.'

Proverbs 18.12 Before destruction the heart of man is haughty, and before honour is humility.

Psalm 147:10 (God) He delights not in the strength of the horse: he taketh not pleasure in the legs of a man.

Proverbs 14.26 In the fear of the LORD is strong confidence: and his children shall have a place of refuge.

> 4 For I said to my father-in-law: I will take counsel with my father, and so will I take thy daughter.

C.18 Judah stated that he counselled with his father as to whether he should marry Bathshua the Canaanite woman, but his father consented not; and yet he went ahead and married her anyway, because her father offered him an 'endless supply of gold'. As mentioned in the very next verse as *'a boundless store of gold'*

> 5 And he was unwilling, but he showed me a boundless store of gold in his daughter's behalf; for he was a king.

C.19 Who was unwilling? He is talking about his father Jacob not agreeing with Judah marrying a Canaanite woman, then the verse goes on to talk about the Canaanite woman's father offering Judah boundless gold if he married his daughter.

> 6 And he adorned her with gold and pearls and caused her to pour out wine for us at the feast with the beauty of women.
>
> 7 And the wine turned aside my eyes, and pleasure blinded my heart.
>
> 8 And I became enamoured of and I lay with her, and transgressed the commandment of the Lord and the commandment of my fathers, and I took her to wife.

C.20 This description of his Canaanite wife Bathshua sounds more like a description of the 'Great Whore' of Babylon the Great from Revelation chapter 17-18, which is talking more about spiritual whoredoms rather than physical. Of course, Judah's wife Bathshua was into spiritual whoredoms, as she was into sorcery and witchcraft, which caused all the trouble in both Judah's marriage to her, and in the death of her three sons.

Revelation 17.4-6 And the woman was arrayed in purple and scarlet colour, and decked with gold and precious stones and pearls, having a golden cup in her hand full of abominations and filthiness of her fornication: **5** And upon her forehead *was* a name written, MYSTERY, BABYLON THE GREAT, THE MOTHER OF HARLOTS AND ABOMINATIONS OF THE EARTH. **6** And I saw the woman drunken with the blood of the saints, and with the blood of the martyrs of Jesus: and when I saw her, I wondered with great admiration.

> 9 And the Lord rewarded me according to the imagination of my heart, inasmuch as I had no joy in her children.

C.21 Judah stated, 'I had no joy in her children'. What a snare to Judah's soul his marrying a Canaanite woman called Bathshua, against his father's wisdom. She was a curse and so were her 3 children.

> 10 And now, my children, I say unto you, be not drunk with wine; for wine turns the mind away from, the truth, and inspires the passion of lust, and leadeth the eyes into error.
>
> 11 For the spirit of fornication hath wine as a minister to give pleasure to the mind; for these two also take away the mind of man.
>
> 12 For if a man drink wine to drunkenness, it disturbs the mind with filthy thoughts leading to fornication and heats the body to carnal union; and if the occasion of the lust be present, he worketh the sin, and is not ashamed.
>
> 13 Such is the inebriated man, my children; for he who is drunken reverences no man.

Proverbs 23.29-33 Who hath woe? who hath sorrow? who hath contentions? who hath babbling? who hath wounds without cause? who hath redness of eyes?

[30] They that tarry long at the wine; they that go to seek mixed wine.

[31] Look not thou upon the wine when it is red, when it giveth his colour in the cup, when it moves itself aright.

³² At the last it bites like a serpent, and stings like an adder.

³³ Thine eyes shall behold strange women, and thine heart shall utter perverse things.

> 14 For, lo, it made me also to err, so that I was not ashamed of the multitude in the city, in that before the eyes of all I turned aside unto Tamar, and I wrought a great sin, and I uncovered the covering of my sons' shame.

C.22 Why does Judah suddenly start talking about Tamar for just the end of the last verse, before he returns to talking about his first or Canaanite wife again? There was no crime legally speaking in Judah and Tamar's days - in Judah being with Tamar, as both of them had lost their mates. Judah's wife had died. Tamar's husband had died. So where is the sin? Tamar pretended to be a harlot in order to get Judah to marry her was a much more likely story if you knew what it was like to be a widow in those days.

C.23 It would seem that the 'religionists' have gone over this story and applied the letter of the laws of Moses to the story and made Judah state things that he never actually said.

C.24 'Religionists' are defined by Jesus in the New Testament. Jesus stated that the religionist went by the 'letter of the law' and had no mercy for others. He also stated that they were of their father the Devil.

Matthew 23.24 Ye blind guides, which strain at a gnat, and swallow a camel. '***By a proud pretence steal widows houses.***'

John 8.44 Ye are of your father the devil, and the lusts of your father ye will do. He was a murderer from the beginning, and abode not in the truth, because there is no truth in him. When he speaks a lie, he speaks of his own: for he is a liar, and the father of it.

C.25 Now in the next verse Judah is talking about his first wife, the Canaanite woman again.

> 15 After I had drunk wine I reverenced not the commandment of God, and I took a woman of Canaan to wife.

C.26 Judah seems to be confessing that he had a problem with alcohol and that it got him 'out of sorts' in his judgment of what was right and wrong.

> 16 For much discretion needs the man who drinks wine, my children; and herein is discretion in drinking wine, a man may drink so long as he preserves modesty.
>
> 17 But if he go beyond this limit the spirit of deceit attacks his mind, and it makes the drunkard to talk filthily, and to transgress and not to

> be ashamed, but even to glory in his shame, and to account himself honourable.

C.27 This is true, 'knowing your limit', as we say in modern times, is wisdom itself. Many people in modern times 'limit' how much they drink - due to them having to drive a car. Learning discipline in different areas of our lives is very helpful so that God's Spirit will have better control over how we behave under almost any circumstances. Life is designed by God Himself to 'test' people's faith like he did Abraham, Isaac and Jacob and his 12 Patriarch sons.

> 18 He that commits fornication is not aware when he suffers loss and is not ashamed when put to dishonour.
>
> 19 For even though a man be a king and commit fornication, he is stripped of his kingship by becoming the slave of fornication, as I myself also suffered.
>
> 20 For I gave my staff, that is, the stay of my tribe; and my girdle, that is, my power; and my diadem, that is, the glory of my kingdom.

C.28 Of course it was very unwise for Judah to give the 'staff of his tribe' and 'diadem of the glory of his kingdom' to a seemingly unknown woman just for being with her on one occasion. That was very risky business, and it seems to be that Judah was impulsive and rash when he was young as many young men still are to this day.

C.29 Judah is trying to bring out the point to his young descendants that fleshly desires should never cause one to 'let down one's guard' just for a little fleshly pleasure. That is certainly very good advice for a soldier on the battlefield of this life. Unfortunately, that was Esau, the twin brother of Jacob's mistake, in valuing a mess of pottage over his birth right, so he lost it!

Genesis 25:30-33 And Esau said to Jacob, 'Feed me, I pray thee, with that same red pottage; for |I am faint': Therefore was his name called Edom.

³¹ And Jacob said, Sell me this day thy birth right.

³² And Esau said, Behold, I *am* at the point to die: and what profit shall this birth right do to me?

³³ And Jacob said, 'Swear to me this day'; and he swore unto him: and he sold his birth right unto Jacob.

2 Tim 2.3 Thou therefore endure hardness as a good soldier of Jesus Christ

Galatians 5:17: "For the flesh lusts against the Spirit, and the Spirit against the flesh: and these are contrary the one to the other: so that ye cannot do the things that ye would."

21 And indeed I repented of these things; wine and flesh I eat not until my old age, nor did I behold any joy.

C.30 Of course Judah did eat flesh in his old age. If we don't eat we die. However, I think that what he was saying was that once he became a mature person, that 'food and drink' did not 'control him' neither any lust for that matter.

22 And the angel of God showed me that for ever do women bear rule over king and beggar alike.

23 And from the king they take away his glory, and from the valiant man his might, and from the beggar even that little which is the stay of his poverty.

24 Observe, therefore, my children, the right limit in wine; for there are in it four evil spirits--of lust, of hot desire, of profligacy, of filthy lucre.

25 If ye drink wine in gladness, be ye modest in the fear of God.

26 For if in your gladness the fear of God departs, then drunkenness arises and shamelessness steals in.

C.31 Of course it is never wise to allow oneself to get drunk as you could lose control of many things.

27 But if ye would live soberly do not touch wine at all, lest ye sin in words of outrage, and in fighting and slanders, and transgressions of the commandments of God, and ye perish before your time.

Ephesians 5:18 - And be not drunk with wine, wherein is excess; but be filled with the Spirit;

Proverbs 20.1 Wine is a mocker, strong drink is raging: and whosoever is deceived thereby is not wise.

Galatians 5:19-21 Now the works of the flesh are manifest, which are these; Adultery, fornication, uncleanness, lasciviousness,

28 Moreover, wine reveals the mysteries of God and men, even as I also revealed the commandments of God and the mysteries of Jacob my father to the Canaanite woman Bathshua, which God bade me not to reveal.

29 And wine is a cause both of war and confusion.

Romans 13.13 Let us walk honestly, as in the day; not in rioting and drunkenness, not in chambering and wantonness, not in strife and envying.

Luke 21.34 And take heed to yourselves, lest at any time your hearts be overcharged with surfeiting, and drunkenness, and cares of this life, and so that day come upon you unawares.

Proverbs 23.20 Be not among winebibbers; among riotous eaters of flesh:

Isaiah 5.11 Woe unto them that rise up early in the morning, that they may follow strong drink; that continue until night, till wine inflame them!

30 And now, I command you, my children, not to love money, nor to gaze upon the beauty of women; because for the sake of money and beauty I was led astray to Bathshua the Canaanite.

1 Timothy 6:10 "For the love of money is the root of all evil: which while some coveted after, they have erred from the faith, and pierced themselves through with many sorrows."

31 For I know that because of these two things shall my race fall into wickedness.

Proverbs 6.25 Lust not after her beauty in thine heart; neither let her take thee with her eyelids.

32 For even wise men among my sons shall they mar and shall cause the kingdom of Judah to be diminished, which the Lord gave me because of my obedience to my father.

Isaiah 28.7 But they also have erred through wine, and through strong drink are out of the way; the priest and the prophet have erred through strong drink, they are swallowed up of wine, they are out of the way through strong drink; they err in vision, they stumble in judgment.

33 For I never caused grief to Jacob, my father; for all things whatsoever he commanded I did.

34 And Isaac, the father of my father, blessed me to be king in Israel, and Jacob further blessed me in like manner.

35 And I know that from me shall the kingdom be established.

> 36 And I know what evils ye will do in the last days.

Ephesians 5:16 For I know that after my death ye will utterly corrupt yourselves and turn aside from the way which I have commanded you; and evil will befall you in the latter days; because ye will do evil in the sight of the LORD, to provoke him to anger through the work of your hands.

> 37 Beware, therefore, my children, of fornication, and the love of money, and hearken to Judah your father.

1 Corinthians 6.18 Flee fornication. Every sin that a man doeth is without the body; but he that commits fornication sins against his own body.

1 Timothy 6:10 For the love of money is the root of all evil: which while some coveted after, they have erred from the faith, and pierced themselves through with many sorrows.

> 38 For these things withdraw from the law of God, and blind the inclination of the soul, and teach arrogance, and suffer not a man to have compassion upon his neighbour.
>
> 39 They rob his soul of all goodness, and oppress him with toils and troubles, and drive away sleep from him, and devour his flesh.
>
> 40 And he hinders the sacrifices of God; and he remembers not the blessing of God, he hearkens not to a prophet when he speaks, and resents the words of godliness.
>
> 41 For he is a slave to two contrary passions, and cannot obey God, because they have blinded his soul, and he walketh in the day as in the night.
>
> 42 My children, the love of money leadeth to idolatry; because, when led astray through money, men name as gods those who are not gods, and it causes him who hath it to fall into madness.

C.32 This wickedness of Idolatry and the worship of money and sorcery as well as licentiousness are what led to the Great Flood as well prophesied by Enoch some 500 years before the Great Flood when he talked with Noah after he had been translated:

Book of Enoch 65.5 And a command has gone forth from the presence of the Lord concerning those who swell on the earth that their ruin is accomplished, because they have learned the secrets of the angels, and all the violence of the Satans, and all their powers, the most secret ones, and all the power of those who practice sorcery, and the power of witchcraft and the power of those who make molten images for the whole earth.

43 For the sake of money I lost my children, and had not my repentance, and my humiliation, and the prayers of my father been accepted, I should have died childless.

44 But the God of my fathers had mercy on me, because I did it in ignorance.

45 And the prince of deceit blinded me, and I sinned as a man and as flesh, being corrupted through sins; and I learnt my own weakness while thinking myself invincible.

46 Know, therefore, my children, that two spirits wait upon man-the spirit of truth and the spirit of deceit.

47 And in the midst is the spirit of understanding of the mind, to which it belongs to turn whithersoever it will.

And the works of truth and the works of deceit are written upon the hearts of men, and each one of them the Lord knows.

49 And there is no time at which the works of men can be hid; for on the heart itself have they been written down before the Lord.

50 And the spirit of truth testifies all things and accuses all; and the sinner is burnt up by his own heart and cannot raise his face to the judge.

1 Cor 6.19-20 What? know ye not that your body is the temple of the Holy Ghost which is in you, which ye have of God, and ye are not your own?

CHAP. IV.

AND now, my children, I command you, love Levi, that ye may abide, and exalt not yourselves against him, lest ye be utterly destroyed.

2 For to me the Lord gave the kingdom, and to him the priesthood, and He set the kingdom beneath the priesthood.

3 To me He gave the things upon the earth; to him the things in the heavens.

4 As the heaven is higher than the earth, so is the priesthood of God higher than the earthly kingdom, unless it falls away through sin from the Lord and is dominated by the earthly kingdom.

C.1 Here Judah is stating that the spiritual is much more important than the physical rather than only mentioning that the Priesthood is more important than the Kingship of Israel. To be guided by God Himself and not by the ways of man in his rebellion and unbelief in God.

5 For the angel of the Lord said unto me: The Lord chose him rather than thee, to draw near to Him, and to eat of His table and to offer Him the firstfruits of the choice things of the sons of Israel; but thou shalt be king of Jacob.

6 And thou shalt be amongst them as the sea.

7 For as, on the sea, just and unjust are tossed about, some taken into captivity while some are enriched, so also shall every race of men be in thee: some shall be impoverished, being taken captive, and others grow rich by plundering the possessions of others.

C.2 What is the meaning of the word 'sea' in verse 6? From the Book of Revelation 17 we can deduce that the 'sea' represents the people.

Revelation 17.15 And the waters which thou saw, where the Whore (Babylon the Great Whore of Materialism) sit, are peoples and nations and tongues

8 For the kings shall be as sea-monsters. German U-boat 'attacked by sea monster' found on seabed off Scotland - Tales from out there (weebly.com)

Revelation 13.1 And I stood upon the sand of the sea, and saw a beast rise up out of the sea having seven heads and ten horns and upon his horns 10 crowns and upon his heads the name of blasphemy

C.3 In Judah's time the 1st of the 7- headed monster was manifested in the head of Egypt. The book of Revelation mentions 7 heads. What were they? 1) Egypt which was followed by the empire of 2) Assyria. That in turn was followed by 3) Babylon. Babylon fell to the 4) Medio-Persians. Their empire fell to 5) Alexander the Great and the Grecian empire. The Grecian empire fell to the 6) Romans. The ten horns on the last head are 10 kings that arise of the 7) 7th head of the coming Anti-Christ government and the last of man's insane world empires. Each empire became more extensive than the one before it, and the 7th will cover the whole world. The 6th Empire being Rome was shown as the worst head and most ferocious as described also in the Book of Daniel chapter 7.

Daniel 7.7 After this I saw in the night visions and behold a fourth beast, dreadful and terrible and strong exceedingly; and it had great iron teeth: it devoured and break in pieces and stamped the residue with the feet of it: and it was diverse from the beasts that were before it and it had 10 horns.

---

9 They shall swallow men like fishes: the sons and daughters of freemen shall they enslave; houses, lands, flocks, money shall they plunder.

10 And with the flesh of many shall they wrongfully feed the ravens and the cranes; and they shall advance in evil in covetousness uplifted, and there shall be false prophets like tempest, and they shall persecute all righteous men.

11 And the Lord shall bring upon them divisions one against another.

12 And there shall be continual wars in Israel; and among men of another race shall my kingdom be brought to an end, until the salvation of Israel shall come.

C.4 *'Continual wars in Israel' ..'kingdom brought to an end ''Until the Salvation of Israel shall come'.* It is true that Israel faced continual wars and mostly because most of her kings and leaders did not obey God and their enemies were allowed to invade time and time again during the empires of Egypt all the way to the Romans. It was the Romans who destroyed Israel in 70 AD and was a fulfilment of prophecy because Israel had crucified their own Messiah.

C.5 Salvation did come through the Messiah, but it was a spiritual Salvation and not a physical deliverance from the Roman occupation as many thought that it would be. The Pharisees expected some sort of new 'Maccabean' style revolt against Rome and that is why they rejected Jesus and his message of

Love and forgiveness - even for one's enemies.

13 Until the appearing of the God of righteousness, that Jacob, and all the Gentiles may rest in peace.

14 And He shall guard the might of my kingdom for ever; for the Lord made aware to me with an oath that He would not destroy the kingdom from my seed for ever.

C.6 Judah's kingdom will indeed be fully restored under the Messiah who shall shortly return to planet earth.

15 Now I have much grief, my children, because of your lewdness and witchcrafts, and idolatries which ye shall practise against the kingdom, following them that have familiar spirits, diviners, and demons of error.

16 Ye shall make your daughters singing girls and harlots, and ye shall mingle in the abominations of the Gentiles.

17 For which things' sake the Lord shall bring upon you famine and pestilence, death and the sword, beleaguering by enemies, and revilings of friends, the slaughter of children, the rape of wives, the plundering of possessions, the burning of the temple of God, the laying waste of the land, the enslavement of yourselves among the Gentiles.

Revelation 18.23 For thy merchants were the great men of the earth; for by thy sorceries were all nations deceived. And in her were found the blood of prophets and of saints, and of all who were slain upon the earth

18 And they shall make some of you eunuchs for their wives.

19 Until the Lord visit you, when with perfect heart ye repent and walk in all His commandments, and He bring you up from captivity among the Gentiles.

20 And after these things shall a star arise to you from Jacob in peace,

Numbers 24.17 'There shall come a Star out of Jacob and a Sceptre shall arise out of Israel'.

Matthew 2.1-2 Now when Jesus was born in Bethlehem of Judea in the days of Herod the king, behold there came (three) wise men from the East to Jerusalem. 2 Saying, where is he that is born King of the Jews? For we have seen his star in the

East.

Isaiah 60.3 And the Gentiles shall come to thy light, and kings to the brightness of thy rising

> 21 And a man shall arise from my seed, like the sun of righteousness,

Malachi 4.2a Unto you that fear my name shall the Sun of Righteousness arise with healing in His wings

C.7 The Sun of Righteousness is talking about Jesus the Messiah.

Book of Enoch: 58.2 Blessed are ye, ye righteous, for glorious shall be your lot. And the righteous shall be in the light of the Sun. and the elect in the light of eternal life. The days of their life shall be unending and the days of the holy without number. And they shall seek the light and find righteousness with the Lord of Spirits. There shall be peace to the righteous in the name of the Eternal Lord.

> 22 Walking with the sons of men in meekness and righteousness;

Matthew 21.5 'Behold thy King cometh unto thee, meek and sitting upon an ass and a colt the foal of an ass.

> 23 And no sin shall be found in him.

John 1.28 'Behold the Lamb of God which taketh away the sins of the world.'

Galatians 1.4 Who gave Himself for our sins that he might deliver us from this present evil world, according to the will of God and our Father.

2 Timothy 2.14 Who gave Himself for us that He might redeem us from all iniquity and purify unto himself a peculiar people, zealous of good works.

> 24 And the heavens shall be opened unto him, to pour out the spirit, even the blessing of the Holy Father; and He shall pour out the spirit of grace upon you.

Book of Enoch 49.1 For wisdom is poured out like water, and glory fails not before Him for evermore. For he is mighty in all the secrets of righteousness, and unrighteousness shall disappear as a shadow, and have no continuance; because the Elect One stands before the Lord of Spirits and his glory is forever and ever, and his might unto all generations.

> 25 And ye shall be unto Him sons in truth, and ye shall walk in His commandments first and last.
>
> 26 Then shall the sceptre of my kingdom shine forth; and from your

> root shall arise a stem; and from it shall grow a rod of righteousness to the Gentiles, to judge and to save all that call upon the Lord.

Isaiah 9.6-7 For unto us a child is born unto us a son is given: and the government shall be upon his shoulders: his name shall be called Wonderful, Counsellor, The might God, The Everlasting Father, The Prince of Peace. 7 The increase of his government and peace there shall be no end, upon the throne of David, and upon his kingdom, to order it, and establish it with judgment and with justice from henceforth even for ever. The zeal of the Lord of Hosts will perform this.

C.8 It is remarkable how God plans things so perfectly and that his plans always work out. Judah was told by his grandfather Isaac and by his father Jacob that through him (Judah) would come the Messiah and that is exactly what happened. The lineage of Judah is miraculous, considering his first three sons all died as did his first wife. He had twin sons through Tamar who had been his daughter in law. He claims in this story not to have ever touched Tamar again after the twins were born, and yet we find by studying the Bible that Tamar was indeed the ancestor of the kings of Judah. In order for that to happen, by law, Judah must have ended up marrying Tamar in order for her son Pharez to be the forefather of all of kings of Judah.

C.9 The religionists would not have liked that fact and have tried to cover up the origins of the lineage of the Kings of Judah, but it is there for all to see in the scriptures. God was the one who took a strong hand in the situation concerning Judah and Tamar in my opinion.

Matthew 1.1-6,16. The book of the generation of Jesus Christ, the son of David, the son of Abraham. Abraham begat Isaac and Isaac begat Jacob and Jacob begat Judah and his brethren. And Judah begat Phares and Zara of Tamar. And Phares begat Esrom. Esrom begat Aram And Aram begat Aminadab. Aminadab begat Naasan Naasan begat Salmon. Salmon begat Boaz. Boaz begat Jesse of Ruth. Jesse began King David. David begat king Solomon of Bathsheba.... Joseph the husband of Mary of whom was born Jesus who is called the Christ.

> 27 And after these things shall Abraham and Isaac and Jacob arise unto life; and I and my brethren shall be chiefs of the tribes of Israel:
>
> 28 Levi first, I the second, Joseph third, Benjamin fourth, Simeon fifth, Issachar sixth, and so all in order.
>
> 29 And the Lord blessed Levi, and the Angel of the Presence, me; the powers of glory Simeon; the heaven, Reuben; the earth, Issachar; the sea, Zebulun; the mountains, Joseph; the tabernacle, Benjamin; the luminaries, Dan; Eden, Naphtali; the sun, Gad; the moon, Asher.

C.10 This above verse is very unclear as to its meaning and is somewhat confusing. It sounds like God has summoned his Powers and Principalities and Virtues to all come and bless the Patriarchs. So, each one of them gave their blessing. If you read my book 'Enoch Insights', you will see that God appointed angels and powers over all creation. I think what the original text was trying to say was that the Lord blessed Levi and the Angel of God's Presence blessed Judah. The Powers of Glory blessed Simeon. The Powers of the Heaven's Reuben. The Powers or spirits of the earth blessed Issachar. The Powers of the seas blessed Zebulun. The Powers or spirits of the mountains blessed Joseph. The Holiness of the tabernacle blessed Benjamin. The luminaries (angels) blessed Dan. The Guardian of Eden - a Cherubim with a flaming sword blessed Naphtali. The angel of the sun blessed Gad and the angel of the moon blessed Asher.

> 30 And ye shall be the people of the Lord and have one tongue; and there shall be there no spirit of deceit of Beliar (The Devil), for he shall be cast into the fire for ever.

Revelations 20.10 And the Devil that deceived them was cast into the lake of fire and brimstone where also the Beast and the False prophet are and shall be tormented day and night for ever and ever.

> 31 And they who have died in grief shall arise in joy, and they who were poor for the Lord's sake shall be made rich, and they who are put to death for the Lord's sake shall awake to life.
>
> 32 And the harts of Jacob shall run in joyfulness, and the eagles of Israel shall fly in gladness; and all the people shall glorify the Lord for ever.
>
> 33 Observe, therefore, my children, all the law of the Lord, for there is hope for all them who hold fast unto His ways.

Book of Enoch 53.6-7 And after this the Righteous and Elect One shall cause the 'house of his congregation' to appear; henceforth these shall be no more hindered in the name of the Lord of Spirits. But the hills shall be as a fountain of water, and the righteous shall have rest from oppression of sinners.

Revelation 21.1 And I John saw the Holy City - New Jerusalem coming down from God out of Heaven prepared as a Bride adorned for her husband.

> 34 And he said to them: Behold, I die before your eyes this day, a hundred and nineteen years old.

Book of Jasher 62.23 And it came to pass at that time that Judah the son of Jacob died in Egypt, in the eighty-sixth year of Jacob's going down to Egypt, and Judah was an hundred and twenty-nine years old at his death, and they buried and embalmed him and put him into a coffin, and he was given into the hands of his children.

> 35 Let no one bury me in costly apparel, nor tear open my bowels, for this shall they who are kings do; and carry me up to Hebron with you.

C.11 Today, when a person dies often his organs are taken out and used for medicine and often without the consent of the relatives. An ungodly practice indeed. Do the transplanted organs affect the receiver of these organs emotionally? Look at the following from a medical journal: *'Aside from scientific studies, there have been several real-life cases that support the cell memory theory. Claire Sylvia, a heart transplant recipient who received the organ from an 18-year-old male that died in a motorcycle accident, reported having a craving for beer and chicken nuggets after the surgery. The heart transplant recipient also began to have reoccurring dreams about a man named 'Tim L.' Upon searching the obituaries, Sylvia found out her donor's name was Tim and that he loved all of the food that she craved, according to her book A Change of Heart.* Can An Organ Transplant Change A Recipient's Personality? Cell Memory Theory Affirms 'Yes' (medicaldaily.com)

> 36 And Judah, when he had said these things, fell asleep; and his sons did according to all whatsoever he commanded them, and they buried him in Hebron, with his fathers.

THE TESTAMENT OF ISSACHAR

The Fifth Son of Jacob and Leah.

CHAP. I.

> THE copy of the words of Issachar.
>
> 2 For he called his sons and said to them: Hearken, my children, to Issachar your father; give ear to the words of him who is beloved of the Lord.

C.1 There are only a handful of people in the Bible who owned the title *'beloved'* One was King David whom God called 'A man after His own heart' and then there was Daniel the prophet whom the Archangel called ' Daniel beloved of God' and John the Beloved or John who wrote the Book of Revelation. This means that Issachar was definitely a very unusual person and also highly dedicated to God himself.

> 3 I was born the fifth son to Jacob, by way of hire for the mandrakes.

C.2 I agree that initially, the Mandrake story, is very difficult to fathom or understand. Here is what I think that it meant in the following comments below:

> 4 For Reuben my brother brought in mandrakes from the field, and Rachel met him and took them.

Genesis 30.14 And Reuben went in the days of wheat harvest, and found mandrakes in the field, and brought them unto his mother Leah. Then Rachel said to Leah, Give me, I pray thee, of thy son's mandrakes.

C.3 Rachel kept the mandrakes in the hope that they would represent two sons that would be born to her if she made a sacrifice of them, Because she did sacrifice the two mandrakes to represent two sons it was counted unto her for righteousness according to this story and the angel of Lord announced that Rachel would bear 2 sons, which she did – Joseph and Benjamin.

C.4 It would seem that initially Rachel took away the mandrakes as she did not want Leah using the mandrakes to make a 'love' potion that could lure Jacob over to Leah's side and be much more attracted to her.

C.5 Here is a definition of Mandrakes: Genesis 30.14; Song of Solomon 7.13 the marginal reading "love apples": They are still used in folklore medicine in Palestine. The plant was well known as an aphrodisiac by the ancients (Song of Solomon 7.13) Source: Mandrakes Definition and Meaning - Bible Dictionary (biblestudytools.com)

> 5 And Reuben wept, and at his voice Leah my mother came forth.
>
> 6 Now these mandrakes were sweet-smelling apples which were

produced in the land of Haran below a ravine of water.

7 And Rachel said: I will not give them to thee, but they shall be to me instead of children.

8 For the Lord hath despised me, and I have not borne children to Jacob.

9 Now there were two apples; and Leah said to Rachel: Let it suffice thee that thou hast taken my husband: wilt thou take these also?

10 And Rachel said to her: Thou shalt have Jacob this night for the mandrakes of thy son,

Genesis 30.15 And she said unto her, 'Is it a small matter that thou hast taken my husband? and would thou take away my son's mandrakes also? And Rachel said, Therefore, he shall lie with thee to night for thy son's mandrakes.'

11 And Leah said to her: Jacob is mine, for I am the wife of his youth.

12 But Rachel said: Boast not, and vaunt not thyself; for he espoused me before thee, and for my sake he served our father fourteen years.

13 And had not craft increased on the earth and the wickedness of men prospered, thou wouldst not now see the face of Jacob.

14 For thou art not his wife, but in craft wert taken to him in my stead.

C.6 Rachel is stating that her father used witchcraft in order to fool and deceive Jacob into mistaking Leah for her sister Rachel in the Bridal bed chamber, and that he lay with her whilst under the influence of alcohol and because the dim lighting which Laban their father had deliberately set-up.

C.7 In some apocryphal books it states that Leah and Rachel were twin sisters. I guess twins ran in the family as Jacob also had a twin brother called Esau.

15 And my father deceived me, and removed me on that night, and did not suffer Jacob to see me; for had I been there, this had not happened to him.

C.8 Imagine the cruelty to the young woman Rachel who was in love with Jacob and she was promised in marriage to her boyfriend, when suddenly she was replaced by her sister in the night. Betrayed by her own father with the excuse that the elder has to marry before the younger, by local tradition.

---

16 Nevertheless, for the mandrakes I am hiring Jacob to thee for one night.

17 And Jacob knew Leah, and she conceived and bare me, and on account of the hire I was called Issachar.

C.9 The 'Love apples' were some sort of 'aphrodisiac', which would make them relevant to the situation mentioned here. In this scene in Genesis 30 we see Rachel fighting with her sister and other wife of Jacob Leah over which one of them will be with their husband for the night for the purpose of getting pregnant and having a child. It turns out that Rachel took the mandrakes and Leah got to be with Jacob that night and she became pregnant with her 5th son which was Issachar.

Genesis 30.16 And Jacob came out of the field in the evening, and Leah went out to meet him, and said, Thou must come in unto me; for surely I have hired thee with my son's mandrakes. And he lay with her that night. **Genesis 30.17** And God hearkened unto Leah, and she conceived, and bare Jacob the fifth son.

C.10 It appears that because Jacob loved Rachel but did not love Leah that God closed Rachel's womb

Genesis 29:31 And when the Lord saw that Leah was hated, he opened her womb: but Rachel was barren.

---

18 Then appeared to Jacob an angel of the Lord, saying: Two children shall Rachel bear, inasmuch as she hath refused company with her husband, and hath chosen continency.

19 And had not Leah my mother paid the two apples for the sake of his company, she would have borne eight sons; for this reason she bare six, and Rachel bare the two: for on account of the mandrakes the Lord visited her.

20 For He knew that for the sake of children she wished to company with Jacob, and not for lust of pleasure.

C.11 Apparently, according to this Testament, originally it was not God's plan for Rachel to have any children and that Leah should have had 8, but because of the sacrifice of the mandrakes with Rachel's sincere desire to have two children, God granted her wishes because she wasn't holding on to Jacob just for sexual pleasure but was willing to make a sacrifice before God in order to have children.

134

> 21 For on the morrow also she again gave up Jacob.

C.12 The very next day Rachel gave Jacob to be with Leah for another night proving to God that she was no longer 'holding on' selfishly to Jacob but was willing in her heart to let her sister Leah also be with her husband more frequently. This was counted unto Rachel as righteousness and God did eventually open her womb and she had the two sons Joseph and Benjamin who were very valuable sons indeed.

> 22 Because of the mandrakes, therefore, the Lord hearkened to Rachel.

C.13 This Testament reminds me of Hannah the mother of Samuel the prophet whose mother was also a sister wife. She was also barren was also a wife to Phennena the other wife of Elkanah. Because Hannah cried out to the Lord in great anguish of heart whilst in the temple when Eli was the High Priest – God also granted her wish, and she gave birth to Samuel who was one of the greatest leaders and prophets that Israel ever had. He it was that anointed the very first king of Israel – Saul and in fact the 2nd King David.

> 23 For though she desired them (mandrakes), she ate them not, but offered them in the house of the Lord, presenting them to the priest of the Most High who was at that time.

C.14 Who could have been priest before Levi was even High Priest and before Jerusalem even existed and before the Temple had been built? I: looked that up and this is what I got which again is very interesting when you know who Melchizedek is.

C.15 'Not only was **Melchizedek** not descended from the priestly tribe of Levi, but he was actually serving as priest of the Lord God long before Levi was even born! Melchizedek was a priest before the birth of Abraham's son Isaac, who later became the grandfather of Levi!'

C.16 If Melchizedek visited Abraham then why couldn't he have visited Abraham's grandson Jacob's wife? Verses 18 and 22 state that the Lord Himself blessed Rachel because she sacrificed the two mandrakes to for 'two children yet to be born', who was the high Priest at the time according to the Bible.

C.17 Since there was no high priest before the time of Levi, then it is also possible that it was Melchizedek to whom Rachel sacrificed the two mandrakes which was counted unto her for righteousness and she went on to have two children after a few more years.

C.18 Melchizedek is stated by some to have been Shem who in some apocryphal books even outlived Abraham. However if we study Hebrews chapter 7 we quickly find out that it was the creator Himself who was Melchizedek, and not a mortal person such as Shem.

C.19 According to Hebrews chapter 7, Melchizedek is Jesus our High Priest and King of Kings. It would seem that before the Levi priesthood came into existence that it was the Creator Himself

Hebrews 7.1-3 For this Melchizedek, king of Salem, priest of the Most High God, who met Abraham returning from the slaughter of the kings, and blessed him;

² To whom also Abraham gave a tenth part of all; first being by interpretation King of righteousness, and after that also King of Salem, which is, King of peace;

³ Without father, without mother, without descent, having <u>neither beginning of days, nor end of life</u>; but made like unto the <u>Son of God</u>; abides a priest continually.

C.20 I believe that Melchizedek the High Priest o the Most high God was Jesus the Messiah. He appeared to Abraham and also to Rachel as there was no High Priest of the Levites yet as Levi was but a small child at the time of this writing. I believe it very likely that it was Melchizedek who was the High Priest to whom Rachel gave the sacrifice of the two mandrakes and was thus blessed for her change of heart and her unselfishness towards her sister. She was directly blessed by the Lord Himself in the days before the Priesthood was established through Levi once he was grown up and his descendant tribe after him.

C.21 God's Hand in the Situation: I would further add that it looks like Jacob spoiled Rachel in comparison to Leah and therefore Jacob was mostly with Rachel and rarely with Leah. What changed Rachel was when she saw that in in spite of her withholding Jacob her husband from Leah as much as possible, that on the few occasions that Jacob was with Leah, that she always got pregnant, but Rachel in spite of being frequently with her husband did not bear any children. Once Rachel realized the 'error' of her own behaviour, she had a change of heart and started to let Leah be much more with her husband. This is reflected in the fact that soon after this situation with the mandrakes, Rachel gave her handmaiden also to her husband Jacob in the hope that she could bear children on Rachel's behalf. Rachel changed from being selfish with her husband to giving him away to Leah and her hand-maiden. This is very interesting, as a pivotal point in the life of Jacob. At the time of this 'mandrakes story', the family of Jacob had only 4 sons. I believe that because of Rachel changing her attitude, that was one of the reasons why Jacob ended up having 12 sons as was prophesied by Rebecca the wife of IsaaC. A later reflection of Rachel's change of heart was that her hand maiden had 2 children, then Leah stopped bearing children for a season and copied Rachel's idea of self-sacrifice and gave her handmaiden to Jacob also. She then bore another 2 children. Finally, God honoured Rachel herself with the last two children of Jacob as Joseph and Benjamin. God's plan was fulfilled even if initially the 'participants' of Jacob and Rachel were 'unwilling' to be unselfish and do things God's way - in order to fulfil God's plan of making the nation of Israel into the 12 Patriarchs who were also 12 different star signs, as prophesied by Rebecca of IsaaC. Wow! I praise God for His amazing foresight and managing us humans so well, even when we make a mess in our lives. He is able to bring good from bad. Praise His name.

Romans 8.28 'For all things work together for good to them who love God and to them who walk according to His purpose'.

C.22 Rachel gave her handmaiden to Jacob to wife for the purpose of having children by him.

Genesis 30.7-13, 19-24.

[7] And Bilhah Rachel's maid conceived again, and bare Jacob a second son.

[8] And Rachel said, 'With great wrestlings have I wrestled with my sister, and I have prevailed: and she called his name Naphtali.'

[9] When Leah saw that she had left bearing, she took Zilpah her maid, and gave her Jacob to wife.

[10] And Zilpah Leah's maid bare Jacob a son.

[11] And Leah said, A troop cometh: and she called his name Gad.

[12] And Zilpah Leah's maid bare Jacob a second son.

[13] And Leah said, Happy am I, for the daughters will call me blessed: and she called his name Asher.

[19] And Leah conceived again, and bare Jacob the sixth son.

[20] And Leah said, God hath endued me *with* a good dowry; now will my husband dwell with me, because I have born him six sons: and she called his name Zebulun.

[21] And afterwards she bare a daughter, and called her name Dinah.

[22] And God remembered Rachel, and God hearkened to her, and opened her womb.

[23] And she conceived, and bare a son; and said, God hath taken away my reproach:

[24] And she called his name Joseph; and said, The LORD shall add to me another son.

C.23 Finally Rachel gave birth to a 2nd child called Benjamin, which was the 12th son of Jacob but sadly she died in childbirth:

Genesis

C.24 Rachel was the mother of Benjamin, a woman passionately desirous of children, therefore the fittest person to have her name used to express the sorrow of all those mothers who had lost their children in the slaughter of innocents throughout the time from her death onwards. The slaughter of these children caused a lamentable mourning by tender mothers throughout the tribes of Benjamin and Judah, such as the former captivity caused to be mentioned in the Book of Jeremiah

Jeremiah 31.15 Thus saith the Lord; A voice was heard in Ramah, lamentation, and bitter weeping; Rachel weeping for her children refused to be comforted for her children, because they were not.

C.25 And also the massacre of the innocents at the time of the birth of the Messiah in the Book of Matthew by the hand of the monster Roman king Herod.

Matthew 2.18 'In Rama was there a voice heard, lamentation, and weeping, and great mourning, Rachel weeping for her children, and would not be comforted, because they are not'.

---

24 When, therefore, I grew up, my children, I walked in uprightness of heart, and I became a husbandman for my father and my brethren, and I brought in fruits from the field according to their season.

C.26 Issachar took on the responsibility of taking care of the fruit sowing and harvesting to take care of all of Jacob's family. Issachar was clearly an unselfish person.

---

25 And my father blessed me, for he saw that I walked in rectitude before him.

C.27 'Rectitude' - definition: uprightness, morally correct behaviour or thinking; righteousness.

---

26 And I was not a busybody in my doings, nor envious and malicious against my neighbour.

27 I never slandered anyone, nor did I censure the life of any man, walking as I did in singleness of eye.

28 Therefore, when I was thirty-five years old, I took to myself a wife, for my labour wore away my strength, and I never thought upon pleasure with women; but owing to my toil, sleep overcame me.

29 And my father always rejoiced in my rectitude, because I offered through the priest to the Lord all first-fruits; then to my father also.

30 And the Lord increased ten thousandfold His benefits in my hands; and also Jacob, my father, knew that God aided my singleness.

31 For on all the poor and oppressed I bestowed the good things of the earth in the singleness of my heart.

---

32 And now, hearken to me, my children, and walk in singleness of your heart, for I have seen in it all that is well-pleasing to the Lord. '

33 The single-minded man covets not gold, he overreaches not his neighbour, he longs not after manifold dainties, he delights not in varied apparel.

C.28 Being single-minded is unusual when one is young, as it the desire when you are a teenager generally speaking to try different things and even crazy and dangerous things, in the case of boys. It is easy to follow the wrong crowd when you are young and difficult to stick to the 'straight and narrow path'. However, God's idea of the 'straight and narrow' is often very different than that portrayed by organized religions, who use rules and regulations to 'control' and condemn rather than to give freedom of spirit. The cardinal rule whilst young would be 'Let your moderation be known unto all men' or don't be immoderate in all of your actions. It is the excess that leads to giving into temptations of Satan and to lusts and drunkenness and even violence and perversions. God is a God of both love and forgiveness. How are young people going to find out wrong is 'right and wrong' in a world that does not provide any godly or moral standards any more in the West.

34 He doth not desire to live a long life, but only waits for the will of God.

C.29 Perhaps because Issachar was born out of a situation of sorrow and desperate prayers on the part of Rachel, that Issachar became a sort of 'Holy' man and prophet like Samuel. In other words, Issachar could have been a man totally dedicated to God Himself like the child prophet Samuel at 5 years of age was talked to by God Himself.

35 And the spirits of deceit have no power against him, for he looks not on the beauty of women, lest he should pollute his mind with corruption.

C.30 Those who are very dedicated to God and the truth when very young normally have had a very good mentor. Like Samuel in the Bible who at five years old was serving in the temple together with Eli the high priest as his mother Hannah and one of the wives of Elkanah had dedicated Samuel unto the Lord from birth because God had granted her prayers to not remain barren. After she forsook Samuel to the Lord to serve in the temple from 5 years of age, God also heard her heartfelt and desperate prayers and she had another 6 children after the birth of Samuel.

36 There is no envy in his thoughts, no malicious person makes his soul to pine away, nor worry with insatiable desire in his mind.

> 37 For he walketh in singleness of soul, and beholds all things in uprightness of heart, shunning eyes made evil through the error of the world, lest he should see the perversion of any of the commandments of the Lord.

1 John 2.17 Love not the world neither all the things that are in the world.

C.31 The problem with being too 'religious' or dedicated to God is the sin of self-righteous or thinking one is better than others when it is only the grace of God that can cause any of us to be righteous. If righteousness came from the law and the 'adhering to the law' then are we all lost and of all men most miserable. *

C.32 Goodness of heart comes from God and not from self-works. God wants us to be humble in our service and dedication to Him and His Word.

C.33 The best way to stay humble is to have to give out God's word to others in humility whether they are willing to receive it or not. That keeps the dedicated person humble in having to care for others and tell others the truth of God's love and Salvation.

Mark 16.15 'Go Ye into all the world and preach the Gospel unto every creature.

> 38 Keep, therefore, my children, the law of God, and get singleness, and walk in guilelessness, not playing the busybody with the business of your neighbour, but love the Lord and your neighbour, have compassion on the poor and weak.
>
> 39 Bow down your back unto husbandry, and toil in labours in all manner of husbandry*, offering gifts to the Lord with thanksgiving.
>
> [***Husbandry:** Definition: the care, cultivation, and breeding of crops and animals."]
>
> 40 For with the first-fruits of the earth will the Lord bless you, even as He blessed all the saints from Abel even until now.
>
> 41 For no other portion is given to you than of the fatness of the earth, whose fruits are raised by toil.
>
> 42 For our father Jacob blessed me with blessings of the earth and of first-fruits.
>
> 43 And Levi and Judah were glorified by the Lord even among the sons

> of Jacob; for the Lord gave them an inheritance, and to Levi He gave the priesthood, and to Judah the kingdom.
>
> 44 And do ye therefore obey them and walk in the singleness of your father; for unto Gad hath it been given to destroy the troops that are coming upon Israel.? The following is what I found out:

C.34 Why does Issachar in his last Testament mention his brother Gad and what does this verse 44 have to do with this chapter? Verse 44 is indeed a mystery as to what it means and why is it inserted here in this chapter? Shouldn't verse 44 have been inserted in the Testament of Gad? Perhaps it was an oversight on the behalf of those who re-assembled the Testaments of the 12 Patriarchs in circa 100 BC. *See my comments about all this in the 'Testament of Gad'.*

C.35 In general, what Issachar the 'priest' says to his sons and daughters is certainly very good advice and is very helpful. We can see that in the past people lived much more from the ground, which was a very good idea, as it made them much healthier physically as well as spiritually. Unfortunately, in general for millions of people, modern life has taken man away from the land, where he belongs, and out of which he was created by God Himself from the dust.

CHAP. II.

> KNOW ye therefore, my children, that in the last times your sons will forsake singleness and will cleave unto insatiable desire.

C.1 The dictionary defines 'Insatiable desire' as meaning a 'desire that cannot be satisfied'. It is also defined as a craving. The dictionary does not do the subject justice, as it doesn't mention that the root cause of extreme cravings could be demonic, such as in the case of the insatiable woman in the Story of the Patriarch Joseph, which you will read about later on in this book, where Potiphar's wife had a 'craving for sex' with Joseph which was driving her crazy and made her irrational and violent.

> 2 And leaving guilelessness, will draw near to malice; and forsaking the commandments of the Lord, they will cleave unto Beliar.

C.2 Guilelessness - definition: without guile - honest and without being deceitful.

John 1.47 Jesus said of Nathaniel 'Behold an Israelite indeed in whom there is no guile'.

Malice - definition: - the desire to harm someone; ill will. From Latin word Mal = bad

C.3 In the Last Days Issachar is prophesying that his Tribe of Issachar will end up going astray and will be given over to evil things and following the Devil.

> 3 And leaving husbandry, they will follow after their own wicked devices, and they shall be dispersed among the Gentiles, and shall serve their enemies.

Ezekiel 36.19 And I scattered them among the heathen, and they were dispersed through the countries: according to their way and according to their doings I judged them.

> 4 And do you therefore give these commands to your children, that, if they sin, they may the more quickly return to the Lord; For He is merciful, and will deliver them, even to bring them back into their land.

Jeremiah 30.3 For, lo, the days come, saith the LORD, that I will bring again the captivity of my people Israel and Judah, saith the LORD: and I will cause them to return to the land that I gave to their fathers, and they shall possess it.

> 5 Behold, therefore, as ye see, I am a hundred and twenty-six years old and am not conscious of committing any sin.

C.4 Did Issachar actually say that he was sinless? I don't think it is likely, because he is so wise in every other way. What he probably meant to say was 'I try to please God to the best of my ability but I am not perfect' and unfortunately the religionists or scribes probably came later and altered what Issachar actually said to lift up piety and religious perfection.

Job 9:20 ²If I justify myself, mine own mouth shall condemn me: if I say, I am perfect, it shall also prove me perverse.

C.5' '*Not conscious of committing any sin*' That is a 'pious' religious statement and not possibly true. People sin in their thoughts probably every day and don't even know it. Sin is not just doing something 'terrible', but it is 'missing the mark' of God's will and His plan for each soul. It would seem that Issachar is comparing himself with the 'terrible sins' of rebellion mentioned in the Book of Enoch for which the Fallen angels, (who became the Devils), were guilty off, and were 'locked up for 10,000 years.

C.6 They that compare themselves among themselves are not wise' Better to be a sinner that desperately needs God than being so holy or pious or perfectionist as well as judgemental and self-righteous. Jesus preferred to spend time with the sinners and heal those who needed healing; but He was always buffeted by the self-righteous Pharisees and scribes following him around and trying to find fault with whatever he did.

C.7 On the other side of the coin, there is no such thing as a little sin. We either do what God says and His Spirit suggests, or we are doing our own thing, and being led astray by others. This is why early on in life, it is essential that each person has a good mentor or shepherd of their soul to set them on the right and godly path for their lives.

C.8 I am sure that Issachar was indeed a very good person, but he was not perfect, as no human can be! There is no such thing as 'sinless' perfection. That is the whole point, that God did not create us to be perfect. Why? - in order to 'test' us while we are on the earth. God gave us the majesty of choice to see what we would do with it?

C.9 I also question whether Issachar actually said that he was 'without sin'. Why? Only Christ came under that category. The original text has been tampered with in my opinion as a wise man would never proclaim himself perfect and sinless.

Even Jesus said of Himself 'Why do you call Me good. For none is good but your father which is in heaven'.

C.10 The idea of attaining to some sort of 'sinless perfection' is a perverted idea from the churches, who have mostly totally gone astray, in their mammon worship and desire for popularity and to 'be accepted, which is not what Christ said that it would be like for his disciples and followers.

C.11 The word disciple comes from the Latin word 'discipulos' and means one is a 'follower of the teaching'. In other words if we proclaim that we believe in the Messiah and thus Jesus the Christ, then we should be doing what his disciples did!

143

C.12 God never said to build church buildings and waste so much money on them, but to 'forsake all' and follow Jesus and go into all the world and preach the Gospel unto every creature. Not many Christians seem to be obeying that commandment by God Himself.

C.13 The churches and religions have got 'God all stuck in a box' when He likes to be out among the people.

C.14 We his followers have to take the message to the whole world and try and win them to Christ and His plan of Salvation. We are not here on earth to simply 'do our own thing' That is clearly the Devil's take on things. We are here to seek for the truth and in finding it spend our time telling others about it. Jesus said about Himself

Jn 14.6 'I am the Way and the Truth and the Life. No man cometh unto the Father but by Me.

C.15 'I have seen an end of all perfection but thy law is exceeding broad'. We are told in scripture that we will have to give an account for every idle word that we speak. I would also add to that verse 'and how we said each word'. No man will be able to utter a LIE before God or excuse themselves for their sins, iniquities and crimes, as they will have to give a totally honest account of themselves in the afterlife.

C.16 It is not sin that damns people to hell. We have a Saviour who can forgive all of our sins. The biggest sin is to be like Satan thinking that we don't need God and that we are our own boss to do what the hell we feel like and to act as if God simply does not exist. Rejecting Jesus and His Holy Spirit is very dangerous and puts people on the Devil's territory.

C.17 Unfortunately, many millions of people fall into this category in the West in modern times and don't see the grave danger that they are in because of the spiritual warfare. Satan is real and he is looking for his next meal. Don't let it be you. Tank up on God's Word daily and listen to the voice of His Spirit advising you what to do each day and you will be so much happier and totally fulfilled in Him.

---

6 Except my wife I have not known any woman. I never committed fornication by the uplifting of my eyes.

7 I drank not wine, to be led astray thereby.

8 I coveted not any desirable thing that was my neighbour's.

9 Guile arose not in my heart.

10 A lie passed not through my lips.

11 If any man were in distress, I joined my sighs with his,

144

> 12 And I shared my bread with the poor.
>
> 13 I wrought godliness, all my days I kept truth.
>
> 14 I loved the Lord. Likewise, also every man with all my heart.

C.18 Stating that we never did anything wrong is in itself a very big sin of self-righteous religious pride. I am convinced that verses 6-10 have been altered from what Issachar originally said to make him sound pious.

Definition of Pious: devoutly religious: · devout · devoted · dedicated · reverent · God-fearing · churchgoing · spiritual · prayerful · holy · godly · saintly · faithful · dutiful · righteous

Other definition of **pious**: making or constituting a hypocritical display of virtue:

C.19 I would say that pious can thus mean 'pretending' to be humble in order to deceive others, such as a corrupt Pope or what is called an Anti-Pope and we have had quite a few of those throughout the history of the Catholic church.

C.20 It is not sin that damns people to hell. We have a Saviour who can forgive all of our sins. The biggest sin is to be like Satan - thinking that we don't need God and that we are our own boss to do 'what the hell' we feel like doing, and to act as if God simply does not exist. Rejecting Jesus and His Holy Spirit is very dangerous and puts people on the Devil's territory.

> 15 So do you also these things, my children, and every spirit of Beliar (Satan) shall flee from you, and no deed of wicked men shall rule over you.
>
> 16 And every wild beast shall ye subdue, since you have with you the God of heaven and earth and walk with men in singleness of heart.

Mark 1:13 And he was there in the wilderness forty days, tempted of Satan; and was with the wild beasts; and the angels ministered unto him.

C.21 The beasts mentioned in verse 16 is probably talking about the spiritual beasts of demonic activity in putting thoughts of fear, worry, anguish and doubts into the minds of people.

C.22 We have to learn to face our fears and declare Satan as a liar by quoting the Word of God just as Jesus did.

Matthew 4.1-4 Then was Jesus led up of the Spirit into the wilderness to be tempted of the devil.

² And when he had fasted forty days and forty nights, he was afterward an hungry.

³ And when the tempter came to him, he said, If thou be the Son of God, command that these stones be made bread.

⁴ But he answered and said, 'It is written, Man shall not live by bread alone, but by every word that proceeds out of the mouth of God'.

> 17 And having said these things, he commanded his sons that they should carry him up to Hebron and bury him there in the cave with his fathers.
>
> 18 And he stretched out his feet and died, at a good old age; with every limb sound, and with strength unabated, he slept the eternal sleep.

Book of Jasher 62.3 And in the eighty-first year died Issachar the son of Jacob, in Egypt and Issachar was an hundred and twenty two years old at his death, and was put in a coffin in Egypt, and given in to the hands of his children.

THE TESTAMENT OF ZEBULUN

The Sixth Son of Jacob and Leah.

CHAP. I.

THE copy of the words of Zebulun, which he enjoined on his sons before he died in the hundred and fourteenth year of his life, two years after the death of Joseph.

2 And he said to them: Hearken to me, ye sons of Zebulun attend to the words of your father.

3 I, Zebulun, was born a good gift to my parents.

4 For when I was born my father was increased very exceedingly, both in flocks and herds, when with the straked rods he had his portion.

C.1 Zebulun is talking here about how Jacob used a very interesting method to influence the minds of the cattle so that they would produce cattle which were ringstraked, speckled and spotted. It was a sort of hypnotism or power over the minds of the animals. When the cattle came to mate in front of the watering troughs, the first thing they saw was the striped rods and somehow it influenced them to produce striped cattle. How is that possible? Well, that is a mystery, and how did Jacob know how to use such a method that is not even used today? I think the truth is that God was helping Jacob supernaturally, because He wanted Jacob to prosper and knew that Laban Jacob's uncle was totally corrupt, and not to be relied upon.

Genesis 35.37-39 And Jacob took him rods of green poplar, and of the hazel and chestnut tree; and pilled white strakes in them, and made the white appear which was in the rods. And he set the rods which he had pilled before the flocks in the gutters in the watering troughs when the flocks came to drink, that they should conceive when they came to drink. And the flocks conceived before the rods, and brought forth cattle ringstraked, speckled, and spotted. [SEE also Chapter-12: Jacob's Straked Rods (mostholyplace.com)]

5 I am not conscious that I have sinned all my days, save in thought.

6 Nor yet do I remember that I have done any iniquity, except the sin of ignorance which I committed against Joseph; for I covenanted with my brethren not to tell my father what had been done.

C.2 We are all sinners as Job brings out so well in stating that if we proclaim ourselves to be sinless our own words and actions will show us to be imperfect.

Job 9.20 If I justify myself, mine own mouth shall condemn me: if I say, I am perfect, it shall also prove me perverse.

7 But I wept in secret many days on account of Joseph, for I feared my brethren, because they had all agreed that if anyone should declare the secret, he should be slain.

8 But when they wished to kill him, I adjured them much with tears not to be guilty of this sin.

Genesis 37.17-20 So Joseph went after his brothers and found them at Dothan. They saw him from a distance. Before he reached them, they plotted to kill him. They said to each other, "Look, here comes that master dreamer! Let's kill him, throw him into one of the cisterns, and say that a wild animal has eaten him. Then we'll see what happens to his dreams." [See **Genesis 37** for the whole story of Joseph and his dreams of grandeur]

9 For Simeon and Gad came against Joseph to kill him, and he said unto them with tears: Pity me, my brethren, have mercy upon the bowels of Jacob our father: lay not upon me your hands to shed innocent blood, for I have not sinned against you.

10 And if indeed I have sinned, with chastening chastise me, my brethren, but lay not upon me your hand, for the sake of Jacob our father,

11 And as he spoke these words, wailing as he did so, I was unable to bear his lamentations, and began to weep, and my liver was poured out, and all the substance of my bowels was loosened.

12 And I wept with Joseph and my heart sounded, and the joints of my body trembled, and I was not able to stand.

13 And when Joseph saw me weeping with him, and them coming against him to slay him, he fled behind me, beseeching them.

14 But meanwhile Reuben arose and said: Come, my brethren, let us not slay him, but let us cast him into one of these dry pits, which our fathers digged and found no water.

15 For this cause the Lord forbade that water should rise up in them in order that Joseph should be preserved.

16 And they did so, until they sold him to the Ishmaelites.

17 For in his price I had no share, my children.

18 But Simeon and Gad and six other of our brethren took the price of Joseph, and bought sandals for themselves, and their wives, and their children, saying:

19 We will not eat of it, for it is the price of our brother's blood, but we will assuredly tread it under foot, because he said that he would be king over us, and so let us see what will become of his dreams.

C.3 What a childish thing to do, to not only sell their own brother to the Ishmaelites, but to use the money that they obtained for selling Joseph and buy sandals for themselves and their wives, thinking that Joseph's dreams could not come true, and that all his dreams were now beneath them.

20 Therefore it is written in the writing of the law of Moses, that whosoever will not raise up seed to his brother, his sandal should be unloosed, and they should spit in his face.

C.4 I have often wondered where the following tradition came from about the casting off of one sandal, and apparently it can be traced further back than the Laws of Moses. In fact, all the way back to the Patriarchs.

C.5 *'Law of Moses'* This last verse seems 'out of place' and was obviously written later than the original Testament of the 12 Patriarchs, as the Laws of Moses didn't come until some 200+ years later.

21 And the brethren of Joseph wished not that their brother should live, and the Lord loosed from them the sandal which they wore against Joseph their brother.

22 For when they came into Egypt they were unloosed by the servants of Joseph outside the gate, and so they made obeisance to Joseph after the fashion of King Pharaoh.

23 And not only did they make obeisance to him, but were spat upon also, falling down before him forthwith, and so they were put to shame before the Egyptians.

24 For after this the Egyptians heard all the evils that they had done to Joseph.

25 And after he was sold my brothers sat down to eat and drink.

26 But I, through pity for Joseph, did not eat, but watched the pit, since Judah feared lest Simeon, Dan, and Gad should rush off and slay him.

27 But when they saw that I did not eat, they set me to watch him, till he was sold to the Ishmaelites.

28 And when Reuben came and heard that while he was away, Joseph had been sold, he rent his garments, and mourning, said:

29 How shall I look on the face of my father Jacob? And he took the money and ran after the merchants but as he failed to find them he returned grieving.

30 But the merchants had left the broad road and marched through the Troglodytes by a short cut.

31 But Reuben was grieved and ate no food that day.

32 Dan therefore came to him and said: Weep not, neither grieve; for we have found what we can say to our father Jacob.

33 Let us slay a kid of the goats, and dip in it the coat of Joseph; and let us send it to Jacob, saying: Know, is this the coat of thy son?

34 And they did so. For they stripped off from Joseph his coat when they were selling him and put upon him the garment of a slave.

35 Now Simeon took the coat, and would not give it up, for he wished to rend it with his sword, as he was angry that Joseph lived and that he had not slain him.

36 Then we all rose up and said unto him: If thou give not up the coat, we will say to our father that thou alone didst this evil thing in Israel.

37 And so he gave it unto them, and they did even as Dan had said.

C.6 See Genesis Chapter 37 for the whole story of Joseph, his dreams of grandeur and his being sold into slavery in Egypt.

C.7 We read also about his father grieving over Joseph and refusing to be comforted. Imagine what that felt like hearing that one of your sons has disappeared or had suddenly died?

C.8 Jacob was totally devastated. It was a very cruel act by Joseph's brethren to a 17- year-old Joseph. Even if Joseph was arrogant and spoilt at the time this all happened.

C.9 God turned the tables upon Joseph's brethren as his dreams did all come true, and he ended up as Pharaoh in Egypt with his brethren 'bowing down' to him.

CHAP. II.

> AND now children, I urge you to keep the commands of the Lord, and to show mercy to your neighbours, and to have compassion towards all, not towards men only, but also towards beasts.

Deuteronomy 6.17 "Ye shall diligently keep the commandments of the LORD your God, and his testimonies, and his statutes, which he hath commanded thee."

> 2 For all this thing's sake the Lord blessed me, and when all my brethren were sick, I escaped without sickness, for the Lord knows the purposes of each.
>
> 3 Have, therefore, compassion in your hearts, my children, because even as a man doeth to his neighbour, even so also will the Lord do to him.

Galatians 6.7 Be not deceived for God is not mocked. For whatsoever a man soweth that shall he also reap.

> 4 For the sons of my brethren were sickening and were dying on account of Joseph, because they showed not mercy in their hearts; but my sons were preserved without sickness, as ye know.

Psalm 28.4 Give them according to their deeds, and according to the wickedness of their endeavours: give them after the work of their hands; render to them their desert.

> 5 And when I was in the land of Canaan, by the seacoast, I made a catch of fish for Jacob my father; and when many were choked in the sea, I continued unhurt.
>
> 6 I was the first to make a boat to sail upon the sea, for the Lord gave me understanding and wisdom therein.

C.1 'I was the first to make a boat to sail upon the sea'. I think that the writer is just stating that he was the first of all his brethren and thus of future Israel to be a fisherman.

> 7 And I let down a rudder behind it, and I stretched a sail upon another upright piece of wood in the midst.
>
> 8 And I sailed therein along the shores, catching fish for the house of my father until we came to Egypt.

9 And through compassion I shared my catch with every stranger.

10 And if a man were a stranger, or sick, or aged, I boiled the fish, and dressed them well, and offered them to all men, as every man had need, grieving with and having compassion upon them.

11 Wherefore also the Lord satisfied me with abundance of fish when catching fish; for he that shares with his neighbour receives manifold more from the Lord.

John 21:6-8 And he (Jesus) said unto them, Cast the net on the right side of the ship, and ye shall find. They cast therefore, and now they were not able to draw it for the multitude of fishes.

12 For five years I caught fish and gave thereof to every man whom I saw and sufficed for all the house of my father.

C.2 This is interesting as it is the only account of one of the sons of Jacob having become a fisherman for a season of five years. Is this supposed to be a reflection on Jesus and his disciples who were fishermen and went everywhere doing good and being kind to the poor. Was this story added much later in time from the original story? It would seem so. The big question is why would someone add this story of the fisherman to this Testament of Zebulon? Well, I was thinking about all this when I came upon the following very interesting material about the Tribe of Zebulon being a maritime tribe. Apparently, Jacob had prophesied in Genesis about this.

Genesis 49.13 'Zebulon will live by the seashore and become a haven for ships; his border will extend towards Sidon'

Deuteronomy 33:18-19 And of Zebulun he said, Rejoice, Zebulun, in thy going out; and, Issachar, in thy tents. They shall call the people unto the mountain; there they shall offer sacrifices of righteousness: for they shall suck of the abundance of the seas, and of treasures hid in the sand.

13 And in the summer, I caught fish, and in the winter, I kept sheep with my brethren.

C.3 Perhaps, it is true that Zebulon did learn to fish and that influenced his tribe in the generations that followed. For more on the territory of Zebulon see:

Conquest of Canaan: Zebulon by the Sea? Zebulon's Mysterious Borders - Associates for Biblical Research (biblearchaeology.org)

14 Now I will declare unto you what I did.

15 I saw a man in distress through nakedness in wintertime, and had compassion upon him, and stole away a garment secretly from my father's house and gave it to him who was in distress.

16 Do you, therefore, my children, from that which God bestows upon you, show compassion and mercy without hesitation to all men, and give to every man with a good heart.

17 And if ye have not the wherewithal to give to him that needs, have compassion for him in bowels of mercy.

18 I know that my hand found not the wherewithal to give to him that needed, and I walked with him weeping for seven furlongs, and my bowels yearned towards him in compassion.

19 Have, therefore, yourselves also, my children, compassion towards every man with mercy, that the Lord also may have compassion and mercy upon you.

Proverbs 19:17 "He that hath pity upon the poor lends unto the Lord ; and that which he hath given will he pay him again." Here's a word from GOD today; he that keeps the commandments will keep his own soul. The man that despises the commandments of the LORD will die.

20 Because also in, the last days God will send His compassion on the earth, and wheresoever He finds bowels of mercy He dwelleth in him.

Colossians 3.12 "Put on therefore, as the elect of God, holy and beloved, 'bowels of mercies', kindness, humbleness of mind, meekness, longsuffering;"

21 For in the degree in which a man hath compassion upon his neighbours, in the same degree hath the Lord also upon him.

Galatians 6.7 Be not deceived for God is not mocked. For whatsoever a man soweth that shall he also reap.

22 And when we went down into Egypt, Joseph bore no malice against us.

23 To whom taking heed, do ye also, my children, approve yourselves without malice, and love one another; and do not set down in account,

each one of you, evil against his brother.

24 For this breaks unity and divides all kindred, and troubles the soul, and wears away the countenance.

C.4 'Wears away the countenance' That is an interesting observation. Do people, as they grow older, show the type of person they really are on their countenance? Are the deeds of a man actually reflected in his face? It would appear to be true.

25 Observe, therefore, the waters, and know when they flow together, they sweep along stones, trees, earth, and other things.

26 But if they are divided into many streams, the earth swallows them up, and they vanish away.

27 So shall ye also be if ye be divided. Be not Ye, therefore, divided into two heads for everything which the Lord made hath but one head, and two shoulders, two hands, two feet, and all the remaining members.

1 Cor 1.10 "Now I beseech you, brethren, by the name of our Lord Jesus Christ, that ye all speak the same thing, and *that* there be no divisions among you; but *that* ye be perfectly joined together in the same mind and in the same judgment."

28 For I have learnt in the writing of my fathers, that ye shall be divided in Israel, and ye shall follow two kings, and shall work every abomination.

29 And your enemies shall lead you captive, and ye shall be evil entreated among the Gentiles, with many infirmities and tribulations.

Genesis 15.13-14 And he said unto Abram, 'Know of a surety that thy seed shall be a stranger in a land that is not theirs, and shall serve them; and they shall afflict them four hundred years; And also that nation, whom they shall serve, will I judge: and afterward shall they come out with great substance.'

Amos 6:7. Therefore now shall they go captive with the first that go captive, and the banquet ...

Jeremiah 13:19. The cities of the south shall be shut up, and none shall open them: Judah ...

Jeremiah 40:1. The word that came to Jeremiah from the LORD, after that Nebuzaradan the ...

> 30 And after these things ye shall remember the Lord and repent, and He shall have mercy upon you, for He is merciful and compassionate.

C.5 See the Books of Ezra and Nehemiah for the return of the Jews to Jerusalem after being in captivity for 70 years under the Babylonian Empire.

> 31 And He sets not down in account evil against the sons of men, because they are flesh, and are deceived through their own wicked deeds.
>
> 32 And after these things shall there arise unto you the Lord Himself, the light of righteousness, and ye shall return unto your land.
>
> 33 And ye shall see Him in Jerusalem, for His name's sake.
>
> 34 And again through the wickedness of your works shall ye provoke Him to anger,
>
> 35 And ye shall be cast away by Him unto the time of consummation.

C.6 Consummation means: the time of 'Judgment'

Micah 7:2 The good man is perished out of the earth: and there is none upright among men: they all lie in wait for blood; they hunt every man his brother with a net.

> 36 And now, my children, grieve not that I am dying, nor be cast down in that I am coming to my end.
>
> 37 For I shall rise again in the midst of you, as a ruler in the midst of his sons; and I shall rejoice in the midst of my tribe, as many as shall keep the law of the Lord, and the commandments of Zebulun their father.

Micah 7:8 For though I fall, I will rise again. Though I sit in darkness, the LORD will be my light.

> 38 But upon the ungodly shall the Lord bring eternal fire and destroy them throughout all generations.

Deuteronomy 9.3 "Understand therefore this day, that the LORD thy God *is* he which goes over before thee; *as* a consuming fire he shall destroy them, and he shall bring them down before thy face: so shalt thou drive them out, and destroy them quickly, as the LORD hath said unto thee."

39 But I am now hastening away to my rest, as did also my fathers.

40 But do ye fear the Lord our God with all your strength all the days of your life.

41 And when he had said these things he fell asleep, at a good old age.

42 And his sons laid him in a wooden coffin. And afterwards they carried him up and buried him in Hebron, with his fathers.

Jasher 61.3 And Zebulun the son of Jacob died in that year, that is the seventy-second year of the going down of the Israelites to Egypt, ad Zebulun died an hundred and fourteen years old, and was put in a coffin and given into the hands of his children.

THE TESTAMENT OF DAN

The Seventh Son of Jacob and Bilhah.

THE copy of the words of Dan, which he spake to his sons in his last days, in the hundred and twenty-fifth year of his life.

2 For he called together his family, and said: Hearken to my words, ye sons of Dan; and give heed to the words of your father.

3 I have proved in my heart, and in my whole life, that truth with just dealing is good and well pleasing to God, and that lying and anger are evil, because they teach man all wickedness.

1 Cor 3.3 For ye are yet carnal: for whereas there is among you envying, and strife, and divisions, are ye not carnal, and walk as men?

4 I confess, therefore, this day to you, my children, that in my heart I resolved on the death of Joseph my brother, the true and good man.

5 And I rejoiced that he was sold, because his father loved him more than us.

6 For the spirit of jealousy and vain glory said to me: Thou thyself also art his son.

Song of Solomon 8.6 Set me as a seal upon thine heart, as a seal upon thine arm: for love is strong as death; jealousy is cruel as the grave: the coals thereof are coals of fire, which hath a most vehement flame.

7 And one of the spirits of Beliar stirred me up, saying: Take this sword, and with it slay Joseph: so shall thy father love thee when he is dead.

C.1 It is just amazing what nonsense Satan will try and put into your head if he can get away with it. The best protection is getting in God's Word daily. When Satan tempted Jesus in the wilderness Jesus quoted scriptures saying,' The Lord rebuke thee Satan and 'get thee behind me Satan for thou savourest the things of man and not of God'.

8 Now this is the spirit of anger that persuaded me to crush Joseph as a leopard crushes a kid.

Ecclesiastes 7.9 Anger dwells in the bosom of fools

9 But the God of my fathers did not suffer him to fall into my hands, so

> that I should find him alone and slay him and cause a second tribe to be destroyed in Israel.

C.2 'A Second tribe to be destroyed in Israel'? What is this talking about. This has been added to the Testaments at a later date, as the destruction of one of the tribes didn't happen until the Book of Judges.

C.3 The tribe of Benjamin was destroyed save 600 young men and the tribe of Benjamin was destroyed by the other 11 tribes of Israel for a heinous crime.

Judges 20:21-25 records that the Benjaminites decimated the armies of the other tribes, killing 40,000 of them. The Israelite tribes had to fast and obtain God's divine help to defeat the Benjaminites. At the end of this needless war, the entire tribe of Benjamin was reduced to only 600 men

Judges 20.46-48 So that all which fell that day of Benjamin were twenty and five thousand men that drew the sword; all these were men of valour.

[47] But six hundred men turned and fled to the wilderness unto the rock Rimmon, and abode in the rock Rimmon four months.

[48] And the men of Israel turned again upon the children of Benjamin, and smote them with the edge of the sword, as well the men of every city, as the beast, and all that came to hand: also they set on fire all the cities that they came to.

> 10 And now, my children, behold I am dying, and I tell you of a truth, that unless ye keep yourselves from the spirit of lying and of anger, and love truth and longsuffering, ye shall perish.

C.4 The following dissertation on anger from verses 11 to the end of this chapter is excellent and thorough and really nails the source of uncontrollable anger right back to Satan the Devil.

> 11 For anger is blindness and does not suffer one to see the face of any man with truth.

Proverbs 14:29 He that is slow to wrath is of great understanding: but he that is hasty of spirit exalts folly.

> 12 For though it be a father or a mother, he behaves towards them as enemies; though it be a brother, he knows him not; though it be a prophet of the Lord, he disobeys him; though a righteous man, he regards him not; though a friend, he doth not acknowledge him.

> 13 For the spirit of anger encompasses him with the net of deceit, and blinds his eyes, and through lying darkens his mind, and giveth him its own peculiar vision.

Psalm 37.8 Cease from anger, and forsake wrath: fret not thyself in any wise to do evil.

Proverbs 14.29 He that is slow to wrath is of great understanding: but he that is hasty of spirit exalts folly.

James 1.20 For the wrath of man worketh not the righteousness of God.

Ephesians 4.26 Be ye angry, and sin not: let not the sun go down upon your wrath:

Proverbs 15.1 A soft answer turns away wrath: but grievous words stir up anger.

James 1.19 Wherefore, my beloved brethren, let every man be swift to hear, slow to speak, slow to wrath:

Ephesians 4.31 Let all bitterness, and wrath, and anger, and clamour, and evil speaking, be put away from you, with all malice:

Proverbs 19.11 The discretion of a man defers his anger; and it is his glory to pass over a transgression.

Ecclesiastes 7.9 Be not hasty in thy spirit to be angry: for anger rests in the bosom of fools.

James 1.19-20 Wherefore, my beloved brethren, let every man be swift to hear, slow to speak, slow to wrath:

Proverbs 29.11 A fool utters all his mind: but a wise man keeps it in till afterwards.

Proverbs 16.32 He that is slow to anger is better than the mighty; and he that rules his spirit than he that taketh a city.

Ephesians 4.26-27 Be ye angry, and sin not: let not the sun go down upon your wrath:

Proverbs 15.18 A wrathful man stirs up strife: but he that is slow to anger appeases strife.

Psalm 103.8 The LORD is merciful and gracious, slow to anger, and plenteous in mercy.

> 14 And wherewith encompasses it his eyes? With hatred of heart so as to be envious of his brother.
>
> 15 For anger is an evil thing, my children, for it troubles even the soul itself.

1 Corinthians 13.4-5 Charity suffers long, and is kind; charity envies not; charity vaunts not itself, is not puffed up, Doth not behave itself unseemly, seeks not her own, is not easily provoked, thinketh no evil.

162

16 And the body of the angry man it makes its own, and over his soul it gets the mastery, and it bestows upon the body power that it may work all iniquity.

17 And when the body does all these things, the soul justifies what is done, since it sees not aright.

18 Therefore he that is wrathful, if he be a mighty man, hath a three-fold power in his anger: one by the help of his servants; and a second by his wealth, whereby he persuades and overcomes wrongfully; and thirdly, having his own natural power he worketh thereby the evil.

19 And though the wrathful man be weak, yet hath he a power twofold of that which is by nature; for wrath ever aids such in lawlessness.

20 This spirit goes always with lying at the right hand of Satan, that with cruelty and lying his works may be wrought.

John 8.44 Ye are of your father the Devil, and the lusts of your father ye will do. He was a murderer from the beginning, and abode not in the truth, because there is no truth in him. When he speaks a lie, he speaks of his own: for he is a liar, and the father of it.

21 Understand ye, therefore, the power of wrath, that it is vain.

22 For it first of all giveth provocation by word; then by deeds it strengthens him who is angry, and with sharp losses disturbs his mind, and so stirs up with great wrath his soul.

23 Therefore, when anyone speaks against you, be not ye moved to anger, and if any man praises you as holy men, be not uplifted: be not moved either to delight or to disgust.

24 For first it pleases the hearing, and so makes the mind keen to perceive the grounds for provocation; and then being enraged, he thinketh that he is justly angry.

25 If ye fall into any loss or ruin, my children, be not afflicted; for this very spirit makes a man desire that which is perishable, in order that he may be enraged through the affliction.

> 26 And if ye suffer loss voluntarily, or involuntarily, be not vexed; for from vexation arises wrath with lying.
>
> 27 Moreover, a twofold mischief is wrath with lying; and they assist one another in order to disturb the heart; and when the soul is continually disturbed, the Lord departs from it, and Beliar rules over it.

1 Corinthians 13.4-5 Be ye angry, and sin not: let not the sun go down upon your wrath: Neither give place to the Devil. Let him that stole steal no more: but rather let him labour, working with his hands the thing which is good, that he may have to give to him that needs. Let no corrupt communication proceed out of your mouth, but that which is good to the use of edifying, that it may minister grace unto the hearers. And grieve not the Holy Spirit of God, whereby ye are sealed unto the day of redemption. Let all bitterness, and wrath, and anger, and clamour, and evil speaking, be put away from you, with all malice:

C.5 Well, it turns out that both Jacob and Moses prophesied about Gad and described him as like a lion. Jacob blessed Gad in Genesis chapter 49 and Moses in Deuteronomy chapter 33:

Genesis 49:19 "Gad will be attacked by a band of raiders, but he will attack them at their heels."

Deuteronomy 33: 20-21 And of Gad he said, Blessed be he that enlarges Gad: he dwelleth as a lion and tears the arm with the crown of the head. And he provided the first part for himself, because there, in a portion of the lawgiver, was he seated; and he came with the heads of the people, he executed the justice of the Lord, and his judgments with Israel.

Moses the prophet of the Lord blessed the tribe of Gad and said: 'Blessed be He who hath made wide the border of Gad. He reposes as a lion in his habitation; but when he goes out to battle against his adversaries, he slays kings and rulers, and his slaughtered ones are known from all the slain, for he strikes off the arm with the crown.' (of the head) - **Tg Pseudo-Jonathan**

CHAP. II.

OBSERVE, therefore, my children, the commandments of the Lord, and keep His law; depart from wrath, and hate lying, that the Lord may dwell among you, and Beliar may flee from you.

2 Speak truth each one with his neighbour. So shall ye not fall into wrath and confusion; but ye shall be in peace, having the God of peace, so shall no war prevail over you.

3 Love the Lord through all your life, and one another with a true heart.

4 I know that in the last days ye shall depart from the Lord, and ye shall provoke Levi unto anger, and fight against Judah; but ye shall not prevail against them, for an angel of the Lord shall guide them both; for by them shall Israel stand.

C.1 This did indeed happen in the days of Solomon as he went astray while he was old and followed after other gods:

1 Kings 11.4,11-13 For it came to pass, when Solomon was old, that his wives turned away his heart after other gods: and his heart was not perfect with the LORD his God, as was the heart of David his father. Therefore, the LORD said to Solomon, "Because you have done this, and have not kept My covenant and My statutes, which I have commanded you, I will surely tear the kingdom away from you and give it to your servant. Nevertheless, I will not do it in your days, for the sake of your father David; I will tear it out of the hand of your son. However, I will not tear away the whole kingdom; I will give one tribe to your son for the sake of My servant David, and for the sake of Jerusalem which I have chosen."

C.2 Unfortunately, after Israel became divided into the 10 Northern Tribes, it was only some 200 + years after the times of King Solomon that the 10 Northern Tribes disappeared into captivity into the hands of the Assyrians in around 730 BC, never to be seen again. At least that is what is often reported. The Tribe of Judah thus became known as Israel.

5 And whensoever ye depart from the Lord, ye shall walk in all evil and work the abominations of the Gentiles, going a-whoring after women of the lawless ones, while with all wickedness the spirits of wickedness work in you.

6 For I have read in the book of Enoch, the righteous, that your prince is Satan, and that all the spirits of wickedness and pride will conspire

> to attend constantly on the sons of Levi, to cause them to sin before the Lord.
>
> 7 And my sons will draw near to Levi, and sin with them in all things; and the sons of Judah will be covetous, plundering other men's goods like lions.

C.3 What a description of those who rule the world today through lying and stealing from the poor of the land to make the poor to fail.

Amos 8.4-6 ⁴ Hear this, 'O ye that swallow up the needy, even to make the poor of the land to fail,

⁵ Saying, 'When will the new moon be gone, that we may sell corn? and the sabbath, that we may set forth wheat, making the ephah small, and the shekel great, and falsifying the balances by deceit?'

⁶ That we may buy the poor for silver, and the needy for a pair of shoes; yea, and sell the refuse of the wheat?

> 8 Therefore shall ye be led away with them into captivity, and there shall ye receive all the plagues of Egypt, and all the evils of the Gentiles.

Amos 8.2-3 The end is come upon my people of Israel; I will not again pass by them anymore.

³ And the songs of the temple shall be howlings in that day, saith the Lord GOD: there shall be many dead bodies in every place; they shall cast them forth with silence.

C.4 Judah itself went astray and was led into captivity by Babylon, having been repeated warned by Jeremiah the prophet.

> 9 And so when ye return to the Lord ye shall obtain mercy, and He shall bring you into His sanctuary, and He shall give you peace.

C.5 Judah came back from 'captivity' in around 454 BC under the Medio-Persian world empire.

> 10 And there shall arise unto you from the tribe of Judah and of Levi the salvation of the Lord; and he shall make war against Beliar.

C.6 Here it is talking about the Messiah who brings Salvation to Israel and who ends up destroying Satan. It is Jesus the Messiah who will both bring down Satan and have him locked up in the Bottomless Pit along with all his devils and demons.

Revelation 20.1-3,7-10. And I saw an angel come down from heaven, having the key of the bottomless pit and a great chain in his hand.

166

² And he laid hold on the dragon, that old serpent, which is the Devil, and Satan, and bound him a thousand years,

³ And cast him into the bottomless pit, and shut him up, and set a seal upon him, that he should deceive the nations no more, till the thousand years should be fulfilled: and after that he must be loosed a little season.

> 11 And execute an everlasting vengeance on our enemies; and the captivity shall he take from Beliar the souls of the saints, and turn disobedient hearts unto the Lord, and give to them that call upon him eternal peace.
>
> 12 And the saints shall rest in Eden, and in the New Jerusalem shall the righteous rejoice, and it shall be unto the glory of God for ever.

Revelation 21.1-3 And I John saw the Holy City New Jerusalem coming down from God out of Heaven prepared as a Bride adorned for her husband.

> 13 And no longer shall Jerusalem endure desolation, nor Israel be led captive; for the Lord shall be in the midst of it [living amongst men], and the Holy One of Israel shall reign over it in humility and in poverty; and he who believeth on Him shall reign amongst men in truth.
>
> 14 And now, fear the Lord, my children, and beware of Satan and his spirits.
>
> 15 Draw near unto God and unto the angel that intercedes for you, for he is a mediator between God and man, and for the peace of Israel he shall stand up against the kingdom of the enemy.
>
> 16 Therefore is the enemy eager to destroy all that call upon the Lord.
>
> 17 For he knows that upon the day on which Israel shall repent, the kingdom of the enemy shall be brought to an end.
>
> 18 For the very angel of peace shall strengthen Israel, that it fall not into the extremity of evil.
>
> 19 And it shall be in the time of the lawlessness of Israel, that the Lord will not depart from them, but will transform them into a nation that doeth His will, for none of the angels will be equal unto him.

> 20 And His name shall be in every place in Israel, and among the Gentiles.

C.7 The good news is that all evil will get locked up for a season of 1000 years during the Golden Age of the Millennium. After that Satan is released out of his prison as he again leads the nations of the world in rebellion against the Lord and the Millennial saints. This time God burns up all of his forces and Satan and his demons are all cast into the Lake of Fire. After that there will never be evil again as we enter the Eternal Age!

Revelation 20.7 And when the thousand years are expired, Satan shall be loosed out of his prison,

[8] And shall go out to deceive the nations which are in the four quarters of the earth, Gog, and Magog, to gather them together to battle: the number of whom is as the sand of the sea.

[9] And they went up on the breadth of the earth, and compassed the camp of the saints about, and the beloved city: and fire came down from God out of heaven and devoured them. [10] And the devil that deceived them was cast into the lake of fire and brimstone, where the beast and the false prophet are, and shall be tormented day and night for ever and ever.

> 21 Keep, therefore, yourselves, my children, from every evil work, and cast away wrath and all lying, and love truth and long-suffering.
>
> 22 And the things which ye have heard from your father, do ye also impart to your children that the Saviour of the Gentiles may receive you; for he is true and long-suffering, meek and lowly, and teaches by his works the law of God.
>
> 23 Depart, therefore, from all unrighteousness, and cleave unto the righteousness of God, and your race will be saved for ever.

C.8 It is true that eventually Israel will be saved, and become a righteous nation forever, but not before 2/3 of the nation is totally destroyed, according to the Bible in the time of the End. It is called the 'time of Jacob's trouble'. It is mentioned in Zechariah and the book of Ezekiel 38-39.

> 24 And bury me near my fathers.
>
> 25 And when he had said these things he kissed them and fell asleep at a good old age.
>
> 26 And his sons buried him, and after that they carried up his bones,

and placed them near Abraham, and Isaac, and Jacob.

Book of Jasher 62.2 And in the eightieth year died his brother Dan; he was an hundred and twenty years old at his death, and he was put in a coffin and given into the hands of his children.

27 Nevertheless, Dan prophesied unto them that they should forget their God and should be alienated from the land of their inheritance and from the race of Israel, and from the family of their seed.

C.9 That was a true prophecy, as Israel was kicked out of its own country in 70 A.D by the Romans under the legions of general Titus in what is known as the Diaspora. It was the final judgment against the nation of Israel, (40 years after they crucified their own Messiah), for its blatant rebellion against God in murdering his Only Begotten Son the Messiah, which also seems to have been prophesied by the Patriarchs in their Testaments.

THE TESTAMENT OF NAPHTALI

The Eighth Son of Jacob and Bilhah.

CHAP. I.

THE copy of, the testament of Naphtali, which he ordained at the time of his death in the hundred and thirtieth year of his life.

2 When his sons were gathered together in the seventh month, on the first day of the month, while still in good health, he made them a feast of food and wine.

C.1 This is not the first time that we have heard of a person who was in perfect health, and yet died suddenly. There seems to be a 'cut-off' point for people's lives. In other words, the length of our lives is planned by God - overall. I find it amazing that the Patriarchs all knew that they were about to die when some of them were actually still in perfect health.

C.2 The modern idea of Western medicine that 'this or that organ failed.' In modern times, the doctor calls in the pathologist to open up the body and decide what killed the person, which seems totally unnecessary. It also appears that people can 'will themselves to die, according to this Book the Testament of the 12 Patriarchs. However, it seems to be more than that. God is the One telling the Patriarchs that their time is up, and they need to call all the relatives to themselves, and say 'goodbye'.

C.3 Are those who are about to die visited by the angel of God or even by the spirit of a relative who has already passed away? There is evidence of this from doctors and carers today. **Hospice caregivers claim patients experience visions of loved ones before death:** https://youtu.be/KPnzY8164_o?t=10

C.4 I remember the night before my father died. He claimed to be an atheist, but the very night before he died for some strange reason to phoned all his adult children and friends and simply said 'Goodbye' and 'Thanks for everything'. My whole family wondered what was going on? Well, the next morning we all found out that our father had died. It was as if a messenger of God got through to him and told him that he was about to pass on and to say his 'Goodbyes'. My wife and I had prayed that he would come to believe in God.

3 And after he was awake in the morning, he said to them, I am dying; and they believed him not.

4 And as he glorified the Lord, he grew strong and said that after yesterday's feast he should die.

5 And he began then to say: Hear, my children, ye sons of Naphtali, hear the words of your father.

> 6 I was born from Bilhah, and because Rachel dealt craftly, and gave Bilhah in place of herself to Jacob, and she conceived and bare me upon Rachel's knees, therefore she called my name Naphtali.

C.5 Why does Naphtali state that Rachel dealt craftly? Well, I suppose that it was unusual for a wife to give another woman to her husband that he might have children by that women, and that the wife might enjoy having that baby. It also happens in modern times, and we call such women surrogate mothers. Does the word crafty mean craftily, or as in modern terms – cleverly, or is this word craftly a much more sinister word such as witchcraft.

C.6 We know that Jacob's father-in-law Laban was a trickster and an idol worshipper and certainly was not a good person. If Rachel's intent was evil, how was it manifested?

C.7 Personally, I can't see any evil in the situation. Rachel was desperate to be a mother and she did what she thought was best, and what could help her to attain the goal of having a baby. Simple as that. I don't think there was any witchcraft involved, as suggested by some people.

[*Craftily* – definition: Deceitful, underhanded, clever at achieving one's aims by indirect or deceitful methods.

Craftly (very old English) definition: Skilfully, cleverly; in a manner requiring or demonstrating skill, knowledge, or expertise;]

> 7 For Rachel loved me very much because I was born upon her lap; and when I was still young she was wont to kiss me, and say: May I have a brother of thine from mine own womb, like unto thee.
>
> 8 Whence also Joseph was like unto me in all things, according to the prayers of Rachel.
>
> 9 Now my mother was Bilhah, daughter of Rotheus the brother of Deborah, Rebecca's nurse, who was born on one and the self-same day with Rachel.
>
> 10 And Rotheus was of the family of Abraham, a Chaldean, God-fearing, free-born, and noble.

C.8 New information about Rebecca, the wife of Isaac's nurse. So, Deborah, the nurse of Rebecca was a relative of Rebecca and related to Abraham's family which was originally Chaldean, or from the area of Babel and Babylon. The Babylonians were renowned as astronomers and astrologers.

> 11 And he was taken captive and was bought by Laban; and he gave him Euna his handmaid to wife, and she bore a daughter, and called

her name Zilpah, after the name of the village in which he had been taken captive.

12 And next she bore Bilhah, saying: My daughter hastens after what is new, for immediately that she was born she seized the breast and hastened to suck it.

C.9 It is stating here that all of Jacobs 4 wives were closely related. Rachel was the sister and even the twin sister of Leah according to one of apocryphal books. Rachel's handmaid was Bilhah, born the very same day as Rachel, who was a close relative. Leah's handmaid Zilpah was the sister of Bilhah. It just stated above in verse 10 that the father of Zilpah and Bilhah, who was called Rotheus, was a relative of Abraham, and noble born. Abraham had lived at Babel/Babylon with his father and two brothers. Abraham moved away from Babylon and Rotheus, it appears must have been one of the sons of his brothers. Jacob and his 4 wives were literally keeping marriage 'in the family' of Abraham.

13 And I was swift on my feet like the deer, and my father Jacob appointed me for all messages, and as a deer did he give me his blessing.

14 For as the potter knows the vessel, how much it is to contain, and bringeth clay accordingly, so also doth the Lord make the body after the likeness of the spirit, and according to the capacity of the body doth He implant the spirit.

15 And the one does not fall short of the other by a third part of a hair; for by weight, and measure, and rule was all the creation made.

C.10 Naphtali is stating in the last 3 verses, that he was a very fast runner and God had created him specifically to be a very fast runner and he was appointed to 'run messages' for his father which would have been very useful in the olden times when there were no cars, trains, telephone etc.

16 And as the potter knows the use of each vessel, what it is meet for, so also doth the Lord know the body, how far it will persist in goodness, and when it begins in evil.

17 For there is no inclination or thought which the Lord knows not, for He created every man after His own image.

18 For as a man's strength, so also in his work; as his eye, so also in his sleep; as his soul, so also in his word either in the law of the Lord or in

the law of Beliar.

C.11 It would appear that Naphtali is talking about doing things God's way and at the right time. As has been said by the wise: 'Knowing what God's will is important, but equally important is to know 'when' to perform it, as God has His perfect timing for His will. The Patriarch is warning his sons to walk in the spirit listening to God's guidance and not to lean to their own fleshly understanding.

19 And as there is a division between light and darkness, between seeing and hearing, so also is there a division between man and man, and between woman and woman; and it is not to be said that the one is like the other either in face or in mind.

20 For God made all things good in their order, the five senses in the head, and He joined on the neck to the head, adding to it the hair also for comeliness and glory, then the heart for understanding, the belly for excrement, and the stomach for grinding, the windpipe for taking in the breath, the liver for wrath, the gall for bitterness, the spleen for laughter, the reins for prudence, the muscles of the loins for power, the lungs for drawing in, the loins for strength, and so forth.

21 So then, my children, let all your works be done in order with good intent in the fear of God, and do nothing disorderly in scorn or out of its due season.

22 For if thou bid the eye to hear, it cannot; so, neither while ye are in darkness can ye do the works of light.

23 Be ye, therefore, not eager to corrupt your doings through covetousness or with vain words to beguile your souls; because if ye keep silence in purity of heart, ye shall understand how to hold fast the will of God, and to cast away the will of Beliar.

24 Sun and moon and stars, change not their order; so, do ye also change not the law of God in the disorderliness of your doings.

25 The Gentiles went astray, and forsook the Lord, and changed their order, and obeyed stocks and stones, spirits of deceit.

Deuteronomy 28.64 "And the LORD shall scatter thee among all people, from the one end of the earth even unto the other; and there thou shalt serve other gods, which neither thou nor thy fathers have known, *even* wood and stone."

Romans 1.20 For the invisible things of him from the creation of the world are clearly seen, being understood by the things that are made, *even* his eternal power and Godhead; ‖so that they are without excuse:

C.12 It is mentioned in the Book of Jubilees and the Book of Enoch that the Fallen angels had changed their orders in cohabiting with human woman and having gotten Giants for their sons.

C.13 It also says that they will change the seasons and the times. This will happen in the days of the Anti-Christ according to the Book of Daniel. They along with the influence of the demons and devils will try to change the order that God has put in the nature.

Daniel 7:25 And he shall speak great words against the Most High and shall wear out the saints of the most High, and think to change times and laws: and they shall be given into his hand until a time and times and the dividing of time.

C.14 The book of Enoch mentions in chapters 2-4 how God has created order in all His creation but goes on to expose the Fallen angels in Enoch chapter 5 for bringing chaos and disorder to the Creation with all of their DNA splicing aberrations, whilst creating creatures that God had not created such as chimeras and giants and monsters.

C.15 What does it mean that they obeyed 'stocks and stones and spirits of deceit'? That is a exact nature of what science falsely so-called worships today with their 'Theory' of Evolution which is sacrosanct to them. Woe betide anyone who speaks against their lying doctrine of Evolution. In analysing what evolution states it says that we evolved essentially from a rock or a stone. The modern gods of the wicked are rocks and stones.

> 26 But ye shall not be so, my children, recognizing in the firmament, in the earth, and in the sea, and in all created things, the Lord who made all things, that ye become not as Sodom, which changed the order of nature.

Romans 1.25 Who changed the truth of God into a lie and worshipped and served the creature more than the Creator, who is blessed for ever. Amen.

> 27 In like manner the Watchers also changed the order of their nature, whom the Lord cursed at the flood, on whose account He made the earth without inhabitants and fruitless.
>
> 28 These things I say unto you, my children, for I have read in the writing of Enoch that ye yourselves also shall depart from the Lord, walking according to all the lawlessness of the Gentiles, and ye shall do

according to all the wickedness of Sodom.

C.16 '*Watchers*' are mentioned. What are they? This expression is mentioned in the Book of Enoch and also in the Book of Daniel. They were a specific class of angels who were supposed to know the thoughts of mankind and designed to help mankind. Daniel saw a good Watcher but Enoch had an experience with evil watchers or better know as 'Fallen Angels.'

Book of Daniel 4 'I saw in the visions of my head upon my bed, and, behold, a Watcher and an holy one came down from heaven.'

Book of Enoch 10.3: And on the day of the Great Judgment he shall be cast into the fire.

And heal the earth which the angels have corrupted themselves, and proclaim the healing of the earth, that they may heal the plague. And that all the children of men may not perish through all the secret things that the Watchers have disclosed and have taught their sons.

[See my books ENOCH INSIGHTS, JASHER INSIGHTS, JUBILEES INSIGHTS about the Fallen angels]

29 And the Lord shall bring captivity upon you, and there shall ye serve your enemies, and ye shall be bowed down with every affliction and tribulation, until the Lord have consumed you all.

30 And after ye have become diminished and made few, ye return and acknowledge the Lord your God; and He shall bring you back into your land, according to His abundant mercy.

Isaiah 64 And they shall build the old wastes, they shall raise up the former desolations, and they shall repair the waste cities, the desolations of many generations.

31 And it shall be, that after that they come into the land of their fathers, they shall again forget the Lord and become ungodly.

Deuteronomy 28.62 "And ye shall be left few in number, whereas ye were as the stars of heaven for multitude; because thou would not obey the voice of the LORD thy God."

32 And the Lord shall scatter them upon the face of all the earth, until the compassion of the Lord shall come, a man working righteousness and working mercy unto all them that are afar off, and to them that are near.

Titus 3.5 Not by works of righteousness which we have done but according to his mercy he saved us.

C.17 Israel was scattered to the four winds of heaven in 70 AD by the Romans and didn't come back as a nation until 1949. Once the Lord returns he will rescue the 'remnant 'in Israel. From that time on Israel shall become upright and godly forever more according to scriptures. Sadly, 2/3 of Israel will be destroyed in the 'Wars of the Anti-Christ.'

Ezekiel 39.25-26 Therefore thus saith the Lord GOD; Now will I bring again the captivity of Jacob, and have mercy upon the whole house of Israel, and will be jealous for my holy name.

[26] After that they have borne their shame, and all their trespasses whereby they have trespassed against me, when they dwelt safely in their land, and none made them afraid.

CHAP. II.

C.1 Naphtali has a vision of the future in the which he sees a Chimera of sorts. Chimeras became popular images for the coming Assyrian and Babylonian 2nd and 3rd World Empires that followed 500-1000 years after the Patriarchs as they also did for the Ist World Empire of Egypt in the time of Moses some 250 years after the Patriarchs.

C.2 It is interesting how God uses chimeras as illustrations in the books of his prophets such as Daniel and John in the Book of revelations to describe the World empires of man. Since God did not create most chimeras why would he use chimeras to depict the world governments of man?

> FOR in the fortieth year of my life, I saw a vision on the Mount of Olives, on the east of Jerusalem, that the sun and the moon were standing still.

C.3 What is the significance of the Mount of Olives? What is its history?

'The Mount of Olives is one of the most fascinating places found in Scripture. Regarded as sacred, it is mentioned in both the Old and New Testaments. Horror and hope collide on the Mount of Olives. There, Jesus prayed before His betrayal and crucifixion, however, it is also from there that Jesus triumphantly ascended into Heaven (Luke 22.39-44, Acts 1.11.) The Mount of Olives also holds the hope of His victorious second coming (Zechariah 14.4.) It is a sacred Biblical location that still exists today and is central to God's plan of redemption.'- What Is the Mount of Olives in the Bible - Importance (crosswalk.com)

> 2 And behold Isaac, the father of my father, said to us; Run and lay hold of them, each one according to his strength; and to him that seizes them will the sun and moon belong.
>
> 3 And we all of us ran together, and Levi laid hold of the sun, and Judah outstripped the others and seized the moon, and they were both of them lifted up with them.
>
> 4 And when Levi became as a sun, lo, a certain young man gave to him twelve branches of palm; and Judah was bright as the moon, and under their feet were twelve rays.
>
> 5 And the two, Levi and Judah, ran, and laid hold of them.
>
> 6 And lo, a bull upon the earth, with two great horns, and an eagle's wings upon its back; and we wished to seize him but could not.

C.4 I found a chimera that sounds somewhat like the above description and the Assyrian empire used this chimera as a symbol of power for the Assyrian empire which came some 900 years after the times of the Patriarchs. The chimera described above had the body of a bull and two large horns and also had the wings of an eagle. Add to that the head of a human and you have what is called a Lamassu:

Revision history of "Lamassu" - The Authentic D&D Wiki (alexissmolensk. com)

> 7 But Joseph came, and seized him, and ascended up with him on high.

C.5 Paintings, statues, emblems, and paintings of chimeras were used by all the World Empires of man starting with Egypt, so it is not surprising that it mentions Joseph ascending on the Chimera as he became 2nd to Pharaoh in the 1st World Empire.

> 8 And I saw, for I was there, and behold a holy writing appeared to us, saying: Assyrians, Medes, Persians, Chaldeans, Syrians, shall possess in captivity the twelve tribes of Israel.

C.6 This verse above is showing clearly how the chimeras would influence all the cultures which would arise and form world governments one after the other starting with 1) Egypt in the time of Joseph around 1700 BCE 2) Assyria in the time of Jonah the Prophet circa 900 BCE 3) Babylon circa 600 BCE in the time of Daniel the prophet 4) Medio-Persia circa 538 BCE in the times of Esther 5) Grecian Empire 333 BCE and later the Maccabee brothers. 6) Roman Empire 43 BCE and the coming of Christ the Messiah.

> 9 And again, after seven days, I saw our father Jacob standing by the sea of Jamnia, and we were with him.
>
> 10 And behold, there came a ship sailing by, without sailors or pilot; and there was written upon the ship, The Ship of Jacob.
>
> 11 And our father said to us: Come, let us embark on our ship.
>
> 12 And when he had gone on board, there arose a vehement storm, and a mighty tempest of wind; and our father, who was holding the helm, departed from us.
>
> 13 And we, being tost with the tempest, were borne along over the sea; and the ship was filled with water, and was pounded by mighty waves, until it was broken up.

14 And Joseph fled away upon a little boat, and we were all divided upon nine planks, and Levi and Judah were together.

15 And we were all scattered unto the ends of the earth.

16 Then Levi, girt about with sackcloth, prayed for us all unto the Lord.

17 And when the storm ceased, the ship reached the land as it were in peace.

18 And, lo, our father came, and we all rejoiced with one accord.

C.7 This dream it would appear seems to be showing that the times would come in the far future that Israel would become a righteous nation after the storm had passed. What storm are we think it is talking about? I believe that it is talking about the 'storm of evil' that has taken over the whole world because of Satan and the Fall of man and the Fallen angels, and there will only come true peace to this world when the Messiah returns and peace for 1000 years will begin in the Golden Age of the Millennium as described so well in the Bible in the book of Isaiah and the Book of Revelation.

19 These two dreams I told to my father; and he said to me: These things must be fulfilled in their season, after that Israel hath endured many things.

C.8 This is a very intriguing chapter as Naphtali had a dream about Joseph when Joseph was a captive down in Egypt, and long before Jacob and his family had moved down to Egypt.

20 Then my father saith unto me: I believe God that Joseph lives, for I see always that the Lord numbers him with you.

C.9 Naphtali's dreams were an encouragement to Jacob his father because he still believed that his son Joseph was still alive and thus was shown in the dream as still being alive tough having fled on a boat. Meaning he had become separated from his family but that he was definitely still alive.

21 And he said, weeping: Ah me, my son Joseph, thou lives, though I behold thee not, and thou see not Jacob that begat thee.

22 He caused me also, therefore, to weep by these words, and I burned in my heart to declare that Joseph had been sold, but I feared my brethren.

C.10 Naphtali wanted to tell his father the truth concerning Joseph his brother having been sold into slavery by his brothers, but he was afraid of them so he didn't tell his father the truth, as they had sworn to kill anyone of them that told the truth.

> 23 And lo! my children, I have shown unto you the last times, how everything shall come to pass in Israel.

C.11 Naphtali is declaring that he shown them what will pass in the future as in regards to Israel.

> 24 Do ye also, therefore, charge your children that they be united to Levi and to Judah; for through them shall salvation arise unto Israel, and in them shall Jacob be blessed.

C.12 Salvation did indeed come through the tribe of Judah in the form of Jesus the Messiah. The tribe of Levi in the form of the Pharisees the high priests had gone astray, and they killed their own Messiah, which was also prophesied by the Patriarchs as being the reason Israel was finally thrown out into all the world in what is called the Diaspora in 70 AD.

> 25 For through their tribes shall God appear dwelling among men on earth, to save the race of Israel, and to gather together the righteous from amongst the Gentiles.

C.13 Of course many from Israel would have testified of their faith in God after they had been scattered into all the nations of the earth by the Romans in 70 AD. As I have mentioned several times eventually Israel will be forgiven their blasphemous sins of having rejected their own Messiah when they repent and acknowledge their crimes and sins against God. It is stated in the Book of Zechariah that when Israel finally realizes that Jesus was the Messiah they shall mourn for Him as for an only son. The end of the story is good!

Zechariah 12.10 'And I will pour upon the house of David, and upon the inhabitants of Jerusalem, the spirit of grace and of supplications: and they shall look upon me whom they have pierced, and they shall mourn for him, as one mourns for *his* only *son*, and shall be in bitterness for him, as one that is in bitterness for *his* firstborn."

> 26 If ye work that which is good, my children, both men and angels shall bless you; and God shall be glorified among the Gentiles through you, and the devil shall flee from you, and the wild beasts shall fear you, and the Lord shall love you, and the angels shall cleave to you.
>
> 27 As a man who has trained a child well is kept in kindly remembrance; so also for a good work there is a good remembrance before God.

> 28 But him that doeth not that which is good, both angels and men shall curse, and God shall be dishonoured among the Gentiles through him, and the devil shall make him as his own peculiar instrument, and every wild beast shall master him, and the Lord shall hate him.
>
> 29 For the commandments of the law are twofold, and through prudence must they be fulfilled.
>
> 30 For there is a season for a man to embrace his wife, and a season to abstain therefrom for his prayer.
>
> 31 So, then, there are two commandments; and, unless they be done in due order, they bring very great sin upon men.

Deuteronomy 6:4-9 'Hear, O Israel: The Lord our God is one Lord: 5 And thou shalt love the Lord thy God with all thine heart, and with all thy soul, and with all thy might.'

Leviticus 19:20 'Thou shalt not hate thy brother in thine heart: thou shalt in any wise rebuke thy neighbour, and not suffer sin upon him. 18 Thou shalt not avenge, nor bear any grudge against the children of thy people, but thou shalt love thy neighbour as thyself: I am the LORD. 19 Ye shall keep my statutes.'

C.14 Why is the word God in Hebrew in Deuteronomy 6.4 in the plural form of Elohim and not the singular form of El or Eloah? Is it a mistranslation or is it hiding something? - Meaning: El and Eloah mean "mighty One," "strong One," or "powerful One" according to Brown, Driver, and Briggs. Elohim is a Hebrew word meaning "gods". Although the word is plural in form, in the Hebrew Bible it usually refers to a single deity, particularly (but not always) the God of Israel. At other times it refers to deities in the plural. Morphologically, the word is the plural form of the word Eloah and related to El. Source: Daily Verse and Comment for Deuteronomy 6:4 (theberean.org)

C.15 According to both the Book of Enoch and the Book of Daniel there are several Gods. Both the Book of Daniel and the Book of Enoch shows Jesus the Son of God together with God the Father. According to the New Testament there are 3 Gods: God the Father, and God the Son, and God the Holy Spirit.

Daniel 7.13-14 I in the night visions, and, behold, one like the Son of man came with the clouds of heaven, and came to the Ancient of days, and they brought him near before him.[14] And there was given him dominion, and glory, and a kingdom, that all people, nations, and languages, should serve him: his dominion is an everlasting dominion, which shall not pass away, and his kingdom that which shall not be destroyed.

Book of Enoch Chapter 105 For I (God the Father), and My Son, will be united with them forever in the paths of righteousness in their lives and ye shall have peace. Rejoice ye children of uprightness. Amen

1 John 5.5-7 Who is he that overcomes the world, but he that believeth that Jesus is the Son of God?

⁶ This is he that came by water and blood, even Jesus Christ; not by water only, but by water and blood. And it is the Spirit that bears witness, because the Spirit is truth.

⁷ For there are three that bear record in heaven, the Father, the Word, and the Holy Ghost: and these three are one. ⁸ And there are three that bear witness in earth, the Spirit, and the water, and the blood: and these three agree in one.

C.16 Another mystery! It is just possible that the Holy Spirit is actually female and not male, so that we have God the Father and God the Holy Spirit Mother and Jesus their Son? See my book '**Enoch Insights**' for more info on this interesting topiC.

See also: The Holy Spirit/Holy Ghost was viewed as **Female** by early Jewish-Christians. This is indisputable: The Earliest Christians Viewed the Holy Spirit as Female! - Jason's Voyage (jasonsvoyage.com)

C.17 'The earliest Christians – all of whom were Jews – spoke of the Holy Spirit as a feminine figure'. An essential background to the occurrence of the Holy Spirit as Mother is, of course, the fact that the Hebrew word for Spirit, Ruach, is in nearly all cases feminine. The first Christians, all of whom were Jews, took this over. Also in Aramaic the word for Spirit, Rucha, is feminine.

(PDF) The Holy Spirit as feminine: Early Christian testimonies and their interpretation (researchgate.net)

---

32 So also is it with the other commandments.

33 Be ye therefore wise in God, my children, and prudent, understanding the order of His commandments, and the laws of every word, that the Lord may love you,

34 And when he had charged them with many such words, he exhorted them that they should remove his bones to Hebron, and that they should bury him with his fathers.

35 And when he had eaten and drunken with a merry heart, he covered his face and died.

Jasher 62.24 And in the eighty-ninth year died Naphtali, he was an hundred and thirty-two years old, and he was put in a coffin, and given into the hands of his children.

36 And his sons did according to all that Naphtali their Father had commanded them.

THE TESTAMENT OF GAD

The Ninth Son of Jacob and Zilpah.

CHAP. I.

THE copy of the testament of Gad, what things he spake unto his sons, in the hundred and twenty-fifth year of his life, saying unto them:

2 Hearken, my children, I was the ninth son born to Jacob, and I was valiant in keeping the flocks.

3 Accordingly I guarded at night the flock; and whenever the lion came, or the wolf, or any wild beast against the fold, I pursued it, and overtaking it I seized its foot with my hand and hurled it about a stone's throw, and so killed it.

4 Now Joseph my brother was feeding the flock with us for upwards of thirty days, and being young, he fell sick by reason of the heat.

5 And he returned to Hebron to our father, who made him lie down near him, because he loved him greatly.

6 And Joseph told our father that the sons of Zilpah and Bilhah were slaying the best of the flock and eating them against the judgement of Reuben and Judah.

7 For he saw that I had delivered a lamb out of the mouth of a bear and put the bear to death; but had slain the lamb, being grieved concerning it that it could not live, and that we had eaten it.

8 And regarding this matter I was wroth with Joseph until the day that he was sold.

9 And the spirit of hatred was in me, and I wished not either to hear of Joseph with the ears, or see him with the eyes, because he rebuked us to our faces saying that we were eating of the flock without Judah.

C.1 Notice how it mentions 'the spirit of hatred'.

1 John 3.15 "Whosoever hates his brother is a murderer: and ye know that no murderer hath eternal life abiding in him."

1 Samuel 16:14,23. But the Spirit of the Lord departed from King Saul, and an evil spirit from the Lord troubled him. [23] And it came to pass, when the evil spirit from

God was upon Saul, that David took an harp, and played with his hand: so Saul was refreshed, and was well, and the evil spirit departed from him.

> 10 For whatsoever things he told our father, he believed him.
>
> 11 I confess now my gin, my children, that oftentimes I wished to kill him, because I hated him from my heart. (Gin definition: snare)

Psalm 140:4-5 Keep me, O LORD, from the hands of the wicked; preserve me from the violent man; who have purposed to overthrow my goings. The proud have hid a snare for me, and cords; they have spread a net by the wayside; they have set gins for me.

> 12 Moreover, I hated him yet more for his dreams; and I wished to lick him out of the land of the living, even as an ox licks up the grass of the field.

C.2 In modern times the word 'lick' in the above sense is still used. Example: the amateur boxer totally 'licked' the reigning world champion.

> 13 And Judah sold him secretly to the Ishmaelites.
>
> 14 Thus the God of our fathers delivered him from our hands, that we should not work great lawlessness in Israel.

C.3 *Lawlessness:* It would appear that God's angels prevented Joseph's brothers from killing him when he was 17, arrogant and boasting that he was much greater than them. He was indeed asking for a clobbering! God didn't want Jacob's sons to end up being lawless, so He limited the damage that they could do to Joseph by 'preventing' their most wicked intent of killing him.

> 15 And now, my children, hearken to the words of truth to work right-eousness, and all the law of the Most High, and go not astray through the spirit of hatred, for it is evil in all the doings of men.

C.4 The 'Spirit of Hatred' is apparently very dangerous and drags a whole lot of other evil spirits or demons with it.

C.5 It is dangerous to give oneself over to the spirit of Hatred which brings along the spirit of anger and spitefulness, and even the spirits of violence and murder.

> 16 Whatsoever a man doeth the hater abominates him: and though a man worketh the law of the Lord, he praises him not; though a man fears the Lord, and taketh pleasure in that which is righteous, he loveth

him not.

C.6 It is said that when a person is taken over by hatred that the person they hate cannot even walk across the floor without the 'hater' finding something wrong with the way they did it. It is also said that 'Hatred blinds the person who harbours it.'

17 He dispraises the truth, he envies him that prospers, he welcomes evil-speaking, he loveth arrogance, for hatred blinds his soul; as I also then looked on Joseph.

C.7 What does *dispraise* mean? 'To say bad things about another person.' Example:- John could not 'speak well' of or (praise) one person without mentioning *'how bad'* another person was. (dispraise)

C.8 This definition of *dispraise* is exactly what the ungodly wicked merchant rulers of the world today are like. They are always dispraising the Truth in every form. They speak arrogantly against God and believers and lift themselves up as great ones to whom all mankind would submit themselves showing that in fact demons and devils are ruling the planet earth at the present time. Transhumanism is their agenda as well as 'eugenics' to get rid of most of the human population, one way or the other.

18 Beware, therefore, my children of hatred, for it worketh lawlessness even against the Lord Himself.

19 For it will not hear the words of His commandments concerning the loving of one's--neighbour, and it sins against God.

1 Samuel 15.23 For rebellion is as the sin of witchcraft, and stubbornness is as iniquity and idolatry. Because you have rejected the Word of the Lord, He has also rejected you from being king.

20 For if a brother stumble, it delights immediately to proclaim it to all men, and is urgent that he should be judged for it and be punished and be put to death.

C.9 Watch out about the 'spirit of gossiping' as it sows many bad seeds of evil.

Proverbs 16:28 A froward man soweth strife: and a whisperer separates chief (the best of) friends.

21 And if it be a servant, it stirs him up against his master, and with every affliction it devises against him, if possibly he can be put to death.

> 22 For hatred worketh with envy also against them that prosper: so long as it heareth of or sees their success it always languishes.

Proverbs 6:34 For jealousy is the rage of a man: therefore, he will not spare in the day of vengeance.

> 23 For as love would quicken even the dead and would call back them that are condemned to die, so hatred would slay the living, and those that had sinned venially it would not suffer to live.
>
> **Definition** of **venial** sin: Venial sins are slight sins. They do not break our friendship with God, although they injure it. They involve disobedience of the law of God in slight (venial) matters. If we gossip and destroy a person's reputation it would be a mortal sin. However, normally gossip is about trivial matters and only venially sinful.

C.10 You could be wondering why a 'Catholic' word such as 'venial' has been used in this text? The answer is simple. The Testament of the Patriarchs was first translated into Latin from the original Hebrew by the Catholic Bishop of Lincoln in the 13th century, and from Latin into English by Canon R.H.Charles who was also Catholic just over 100 years ago.

> 24 For the spirit of hatred worketh together with Satan, through hastiness of spirits, in all things to men's death; but the spirit of love worketh together with the law of God in long-suffering unto the salvation of men.

C.11 *Salvation*. The word 'salvation' mentioned in the Old Testament, was mostly talking about 'deliverance' physically, such as Moses delivering the Children of Israel from Pharoah and Egypt. Spiritual Salvation has always been by Grace and by Faith. See Hebrews chapter 11 the Faith chapter, which also mentions that in the Old Testament they looked ahead to the Messiah and His sacrifice for their Salvation just as we look backwards to Jesus having paid the price for our sin on the cross 2000 years ago.

C.12 Here is a list of some 47 prophecies in the Old Testament out of a total of 300 talking about the Messiah: 47 Old Testament Prophecies About Jesus (learnreligions.com)

> 25 Hatred, therefore, is evil, for it constantly mates with lying, speaking against the truth; and it makes small things to be great, and causes the light to be darkness, and calleth the sweet bitter, and teaches slander, and kindles wrath, and stirs up war, and violence and all covetousness; it fills the heart with evils and devilish poison.

191

1 Peter 5:8 —Be sober, be vigilant; because your adversary the devil walks about like a roaring lion, seeking whom he may devour.

C.13 Verse 25 is a descriptive verse and gives a lot of information about the evil spirit world and spiritual warfare. It also shows how powerful evil spirits work together to destroy mankind.

> 26 These things, therefore, I say to you from experience, my children, that ye may drive forth hatred, which is of the devil, and cleave to the love of God.

John 8.44 'Ye are of your father the devil, and the lusts of your father ye will do. He was a murderer from the beginning, and abode not in the truth, because there is no truth in him'.

> 27 Righteousness casts out hatred, humility destroys envy.
>
> 28 For he that is just and humble is ashamed to do what is unjust, being reproved not of another, but of his own heart, because the Lord looks on his inclination.
>
> 29 He speaks not against a holy man, because the fear of God over-comes hatred.
>
> 30 For fearing lest he should offend the Lord, he will not do wrong to any man, even in thought.
>
> 31 These things I learnt at last, after I had repented concerning Joseph.
>
> 32 For true repentance after a godly sort destroys ignorance, and drives away the darkness, and enlightens the eyes, and giveth knowledge to the soul, and leadeth the mind to salvation.

C.14 As has been wisely said, 'Let the Light in and the Darkness will flee of itself. Jesus said that He is the Light of the world.

John 8:12 Then spake Jesus again unto them, saying, I am the light of the world: he that follows me shall not walk in darkness, but shall have the light of life.

> 33 And those things which it hath not learnt from man, it knows through repentance.
>
> 34 For God brought upon me a disease of the liver; and had not the

prayers of Jacob my father succoured me, it had hardly failed but my spirit had departed.

C.15 Could hatred and anger possibly bring disease to the liver and even to other organs of the body? It would appear that our thoughts and feelings and resultant emotions do affect our health. See below for more on the effects of hatred and anger on the body. This is called psychosomatic by psychologists - or the effect of the mind over the body.

35 For by what things a man transgresses by the same also is he punished.

Galatians 6.7 Be not deceived; God is not mocked: for whatsoever a man soweth, that shall he also reap

36 Since, therefore, my liver was set mercilessly against Joseph, in my liver too I suffered mercilessly, and was judged for eleven months, for so long a time as I had been angry against Joseph.

C.16 Your emotions can affect the health of your liver. Most of our organs are connected to an emotion, and your liver is the organ connected to anger.

The majority of people are unaware of the correlation between their anger and the effect it has on their liver because they don't understand the depth of the connection. The state of the liver is actually fundamental to how we will feel the emotion, which could directly shape how we will act or react to what life dishes out.

Source: Your emotions can affect the health of your liver | Liver Doctor

RELATED: Your inner warrior - why the liver is associated with anger: Your inner warrior - why the liver is associated with anger (kimiyahealing.co.uk)

CHAP. II.

AND now, my children, I exhort you, love ye each one his brother, and put away hatred from your hearts, love one another in deed, and in word, and in the inclination of the soul.

2 For in the presence of my father I spake peaceably to Joseph; and when I had gone out, the spirit of hatred darkened my mind, and stirred up my soul to slay him.

C.1 This whole discourse on Hatred is quite remarkable. Why? Because in modern times mankind has forgotten the spiritual warfare that is going on all around him and even in him at times. Our life is not just a big of chemicals as told us by unbelieving sceptical and ungodly science 'falsely so-called'. Man has a spirit which is affected by the spirit world which is all around him which he simply cannot see at least in this present time period. We must be careful that our emotions are moderate and not extreme. It is 'being out of control' that is dangerous and invites evil spirits to affect our minds and even our spirits, if we are not seriously watchful, and on guard.

C.2 It would appear that the Patriarchs were a lot wiser than most people today. They had a lot of wisdom about many things from a godly perspective which is quite refreshing in this present 'spiritually'- disconnected Western world.

3 Love ye one another from the heart; and if a man sin against thee, speak peaceably to him, and in thy soul hold not guile; and if he repent and confess, forgive him.

Luke 17:3-4 Take heed to yourselves: If thy brother trespass against thee, rebuke him; and if he repent, forgive him. And if he trespass against thee seven times in a day, and seven times in a day turn again to thee, saying, I repent; thou shalt forgive him.

4 But if he deny it, do not get into a passion with him, lest catching the poison from thee he take to swearing and so thou sin doubly.

5 Let not another man hear thy secrets when engaged in legal strife, lest he come to hate thee and become thy enemy and commit a great sin against thee; for ofttimes he addresses thee guilefully or busy himself about thee with wicked intent.

6 And though he denies it and yet have a sense of shame when reproved, give over reproving him.

> 7 For be who denies may repent so as not again to wrong thee; yea, he may also honour thee, and fear and be at peace with thee.
>
> 8 And if he be shameless and persist in his wrongdoing, even so forgive him from the heart, and leave to God the avenging.

Romans 12.19 "Dearly beloved, avenge not yourselves, but *rather* give place unto wrath: for it is written, Vengeance *is* mine; I will repay, saith the Lord."

Ephesians 6:12 - For we wrestle not against flesh and blood, but against principalities, against powers, against the rulers of the darkness of this world, against spiritual wickedness in high places.

> 9 If a man prospers more than you, do not be vexed, but pray also for him, that he may have perfect prosperity.

C.3 Clearly the Patriarch is merely wishing others well and not to be jealous of their prosperity, if that person is richer than you are.

C.4 On the other side of the coin, I personally don't believe in the 'prosperity' doctrine that many of the churches follow - that favour the rich as being more blessed. This simply is false doctrine.

C.5 Jesus did not encourage his disciples to 'get rich' but the opposite. To told Christians for 'forsake all' and to live by faith and to give their extra that they did not need to the poor. Then He said you will have riches in heaven but not necessarily here on earth.

C.6 Most of the churches and established religions have lost the spiritual side of their original nature, because they compromised with the spirit of wealth or mammon.

C.7 Like the Catholic church with such wealth and fancy glamourous buildings full of gold and silver, treasures, idols and statues. Look at the corruption in that church. What the last verse should state is pray for others to find the truth in finding Jesus the Messiah and eternal salvation - not to find material prosperity.

Revelation 3.14-19 And unto the Angel of the Church of the Laodiceans, write, These things saith the Amen, the faithful and true witness, the beginning of the creation of God:

I know thy works, that thou art neither cold nor hot, I would thou wert cold or hot.

So then because thou art lukewarm, and neither cold nor hot, I will spew thee out of my mouth:

Because thou sayest, I am rich, and increased with goods, and have need of nothing: and knows not that thou art wretched, and miserable, and poor, and blind, and naked.

I counsel thee to buy of me gold tried in the fire, that thou mayest bee rich, and white raiment, that thou mayest be clothed, and that the shame of thy nakedness does not appear, and anoint thine eyes with eye salve, that thou mayest see.

As many as I love, I rebuke and chasten, be zealous therefore, and repent.

1 John 2.15-17 Love not the world, neither the things that are in the world. If any man love the world, the love of the Father is not in him. For all that is in the world, the lust of the flesh, and the lust of the eyes, and the pride of life, is not of the Father, but is of the world. And the world passes away, and the lust thereof: but he that doeth the will of God abides for ever.

Luke 14.26 So likewise whosoever of you that forsakes not all that he has he cannot be my disciple.

---

10 For so it is expedient for you.

11 And if he be further exalted, be not envious of him, remembering that all flesh shall die; and offer praise to God, who giveth things good and profitable to all men.

12 Seek out the judgments of the Lord, and thy mind will rest and be at peace.

13 And though a man become rich by evil means, even as Esau, the brother of my father, be not jealous; but wait for the end of the Lord.

14 For if he taketh away from a man wealth gotten by evil means He forgives him if he repents, but the unrepentant is reserved for eternal punishment.

---

1 John 1:9 - If we confess our sins, he is faithful and just to forgive us our sins, and to cleanse us from all unrighteousness

---

15 For the poor man, if free from envy he pleases the Lord in all things, is blessed beyond all men, because he hath not the travail of vain men.

16 Put away, therefore, jealousy from your souls, and love one another with uprightness of heart.

17 Do ye also therefore tell these things to your children, that they honour Judah and Levi, for from them shall the Lord raise up salvation to Israel.

---

18 For I know that at the last your children shall depart from Him, and shall walk in wickedness, and affliction and corruption before the Lord.

19 And when he had rested for a little while, he said again; My children, obey your father, and bury me near to my fathers.

20 And he drew up his feet and fell asleep in peace.

Jasher 62.5 And in the eighty-third year died Gad, he was an hundred and twenty-five years old, and he was put in a coffin in Egypt, and given into the hands of his children.

21 And after five years they carried him up to Hebron and laid him with his fathers.

THE TESTAMENT OF ASHER

The Tenth Son of Jacob and Zilpah.

CHAP. I.

THE copy of the Testament of Asher, what things he spake to his sons in the hundred and twenty-fifth year of his life.

2 For while he was still in health, he said to them: Hearken, ye children of Asher, to your father, and I will declare to you all that is upright in the sight of the Lord.

3 Two ways hath God given to the sons of men, and two inclinations, and two kinds of action, and two modes of action, and two issues.

4 Therefore all things are by twos, one over against the other.

5 For there are two ways of good and evil, and with these are the two inclinations in our breasts discriminating them.

C.1 These first few verses are stating that God gave us the choice to do good or evil.

C.2 This following discourse is excellent as it brings out how deceptive spirits work in conjunction with Satan to both deceive and lead away souls into perdition and darkness through seeming good works. Satan is a trickster, and it is clearly shown in this discourse.

6 Therefore if the soul take pleasure in the good inclination, all its actions are in righteousness; and if it sin it straightway repents

1 Timothy 2.15 Study to show thyself approved unto God a workman who needs to be ashamed rightly dividing the word of truth

7 For, having its thoughts set upon righteousness, and casting away wickedness, it straightway overthrows the evil, and uproots the sin.

1 John 2.15-20 Love not the world, neither the things that are in the world. If any man love the world, the love of the Father is not in him. For all that is in the world, the lust of the flesh, and the lust of the eyes, and the pride of life, is not of the Father, but is of the world. And the world passes away and the lust thereof.

1 Timothy 4.15 Meditate upon these things give thyself wholly unto them that thy profiting might appear unto all.

8 But if it incline to the evil inclination, all its actions are in wickedness, and it drives away the good, and cleaves to the evil, and is ruled by

Beliar; even though it work what is good, he perverts it to evil.

9 For whenever it begins to do good, he forces the issue of the action into evil for him, seeing that the treasure of the inclination is filled with an evil spirit.

10 A person then may with words help the good for the sake of the evil, yet the issue of the action leadeth to mischief.

Romans 7.21 I find a law that when I would do good evil is present with me.

C.3 See at the end of this chapter a comparison with the writings of the apostle Paul in Romans chapter 7.

11 There is a man who shows no compassion upon him who serves his turn in evil; and this thing hath two aspects, but the whole is evil.

12 And there is a man that loveth him that worketh evil, because he would prefer even to die in evil for his sake; and concerning this it is clear that it hath two aspects, but the whole is an evil work.

13 Though indeed he have love, yet is he wicked who conceals what is evil for the sake of the good name, but the end of the action tends unto evil.

14 Another steals, doeth unjustly, plunders, defrauds, and withal pity the poor: this too hath a twofold aspect, but the whole is evil.

15 He who defrauds his neighbour provokes God, and swears falsely against the Most High, and yet pity the poor: the Lord who commanded the law he sets at nought and provokes, and yet he refreshes the poor.

16 He defiles the soul, and makes gay the body; he kills many, and pities a few: this, too, hath a twofold aspect, but the whole is evil.

17 Another commits adultery and fornication, and abstains from meats, and when he fasts he doeth evil, and by the power of his wealth overwhelms many; and notwithstanding his excessive wickedness he doeth the commandments: this, too, hath a twofold aspect, but the whole is evil.

C.4 This reminds of the sad condition of some of the organized established religions who pretend to be pious and good and even abstain from marriage and fast and pray to be seen to be good in public and yet secretly they are paedophiles abusing young boys.

C.5 I have also seen reports of Catholic churches of the past forbidding people to marry among their priesthood and yet nuns and monks secretly came together for sexual intercourse which is not a sin or crime unless you think it is. The sad thing is that when babies would result, they would be killed and buried in the graveyard of the church. Some religions have a lot to answer for before God one of these days.

18 Such men are hares; clean - like those that divide the hoof, but in very deed are unclean.

Proverbs 17:15 He that justifies the wicked, and he that condemns the just, even they both are abomination to the LORD.

19 For God in the tables of the commandments hath thus declared.

20 But do not ye, my children, wear two faces like unto them, of goodness and of wickedness; but cleave unto goodness only, for God hath his habitation therein, and men desire it.

James 1.8 A double-minded man is unstable in all of his ways.

21 But from wickedness flee away, destroying the evil inclination by your good works; for they that are double-faced serve not God, but their own lusts, so that they may please Beliar and men like unto themselves.

Psalms 101:7 - He that worketh deceit shall not dwell within my house: he that tells lies shall not tarry in my sight.

Proverbs 6:16-19 - These six things doth the LORD hate: yea, seven are an abomination unto him: A proud look, a lying tongue, and hands that shed innocent blood; An heart that devises wicked imaginations, feet that be swift in running to mischief, A false witness that speaks lies, and he that soweth discord among brethren.

22 For good men, even they that are of single face, though they be thought by them that are double-faced to sin, are just before God.

23 For many in killing the wicked, do two works of good and evil; but the whole is good, because he hath uprooted and destroyed that which is evil.

24 One man hates the merciful and unjust man, and the man who commits adultery and fasts: this, too, hath a twofold aspect, but the whole work is good, because he follows the Lord's example, in that he accepts not the seeming good as the genuine good.

25 Another, desires not to see good day with them that not, lest he defile his body and pollute his soul; this, too, is double-faced, but the whole is good.

26 For such men are like to stags and to hinds, because in the manner of wild animals they seem to be unclean, but they are altogether clean; because they walk in zeal for the Lord and abstain from what God also hates and forbids by His commandments, warding off the evil from the good.

27 Ye see, my children, how that there are two in all things, one against the other, and the one is hidden by the other: in wealth is hidden covetousness, in conviviality drunkenness, in laughter grief, in wedlock profligacy.

28 Death succeeds to life, dishonour to glory, night to day and darkness to light; and all things are under the day, just things under life, unjust things under death; wherefore also eternal life awaits death.

29 Nor may it be said that truth is a lie, nor right wrong; for all truth is under the light, even as all things are under God.

30 All these things, therefore, I proved in my life, and I wandered not from the truth of the Lord, and I searched out the commandments of the Most High, walking according to all my strength with singleness of face unto that which is good.

31 Take heed, therefore, ye also, my children, to the commandments of the Lord, following the truth with singleness of face.

Isaiah 5:20-23 Woe unto them that call evil good, and good evil; that put darkness for light, and light for darkness; that put bitter for sweet, and sweet for bitter! Woe unto them that are wise in their own eyes, and prudent in their own sight!

> 32 For they that are double-faced are guilty of a twofold sin; for they both do the evil thing and they have pleasure in them that do it, following the example of the spirits of deceit, and striving against mankind.
>
> 33 Do ye, therefore, my children, keep the law of the Lord, and give not heed unto evil as unto good; but look unto the thing that is really good, and keep it in all commandments of the Lord, having your conversation therein, and resting therein.
>
> 34 For the latter ends of men do show their righteousness or unrighteousness, when they meet the angels of the Lord and of Satan.

Ezekiel 18.20 The soul that sins, it shall die. The son shall not bear the iniquity of the father, neither shall the father bear the iniquity of the son: the righteousness of the righteous shall be upon him, and the wickedness of the wicked shall be upon him.

Matthew 25.41 Then shall he say also unto them on the left hand, Depart from me, ye cursed, into everlasting fire, prepared for the devil and his angels.

> 35 for when the soul departs troubled, it is tormented by the evil spirit which also it served in lusts and evil works.

John 5.29 "And shall come forth; they that have done good, unto the resurrection of life; and they that have done evil, unto the resurrection of damnation.

> 36 But if he is peaceful with joy he meets the angel of peace, and he leadeth him into eternal life.
>
> 37 Become not, my children, as Sodom, which sinned against the angels of the Lord, and perished for ever.

Genesis 19:24-25,27-28 Then the Lord rained upon Sodom and upon Gomorrah brimstone and fire from the Lord out of heaven; And he overthrew those cities, and all the plain, and all the inhabitants of the cities, and that which grew upon the ground. And Abraham got up early in the morning to the place where he stood before the Lord: And he looked toward Sodom and Gomorrah, and toward all the land of the plain, and beheld, and, lo, the smoke of the country went up as the smoke of a furnace.

> 38 For I know that ye shall sin and be delivered into the hands of your enemies; and your land shall be made desolate, and your holy places

> destroyed, and ye shall be scattered unto the four corners of the earth.
>
> 39 And ye shall be set at nought in the dispersion vanishing away as water.

C.6 Dispersion. This sounds like the Diaspora of 70 AD when the Romans destroyed Jerusalem and Israel because they killed their own Messiah 40 years earlier.

> 40 Until the Most High shall visit the earth, coming Himself as man, with men eating and drinking, and breaking the head of the dragon in the water.

C.7 Most High shall visit the earth – this is most definitely talking about Jesus the Messiah. And breaking the head of the dragon in the water. Is the dragon physical or spiritual or both? These next two verses would show that the dragon or Leviathan is physical as in Isaiah 27.1 and Job chapter 41.

Isaiah 27:1 - In that day the LORD with his sore and great and strong sword shall punish leviathan the piercing serpent, even leviathan that crooked serpent; and he shall slay the dragon that is in the sea.

Job.41.1,10,19,21,31,33-34 Can you draw out leviathan with a hook? Non is so fierce, that dare stir him up. Out of his mouth go burning lamps. His breath kindles coals and a flame goes out of his mouth. He makes the deep sea to boil. Upon earth there is not his like. He is made without fear. He beholds all things, and is the king over all the children of pride.

C.8 Who is the dragon? It is talking about Satan as mentioned in Revelation chapter 12. Is the dragon also Satan and thus Satan has the ability to change form at will?

Revelation 12.3-5 And there appeared another wonder in heaven; and behold a great red dragon, having seven heads and ten horns, and seven crowns upon his heads. And his tail drew the third part of the stars of heaven, and did cast them to the earth: and the dragon stood before the woman which was ready to be delivered, for to devour her child as soon as it was born. And she brought forth a man child, who was to rule all nations with a rod of iron: and her child was caught up unto God, and to his throne.

C.9 This last verse of Revelation 12.5 talks about Mary who represents of true church of God from all time who gave birth to Jesus the Messiah who was caught up to heaven and who will return to rule all nations with a rod of Iron. No more wicked people or liars and merchants of deceit but Jesus will rule the whole earth with love and kindness to those who deserve it and all the wicked shall be gotten rid of. The dragon being Satan and his Fallen angels, devils and demons will be locked up in the Bottomless Pit for the1000 year Golden Age of the Millennium.

Revelation 20:1-3 And I saw an angel come down from heaven, having the key of the bottomless pit and a great chain in his hand. And he laid hold on the dragon, that old serpent, which is the Devil, and Satan, and bound him a thousand years. And cast him into the bottomless pit, and shut him up, and set a seal upon him, that he should deceive the nations no more, till the thousand years should be fulfilled: and after that he must be loosed a little season.

C.10 The dragon being Satan gets locked up for the 1000-year reign of Christ during the Millennium. The dragon is finally released to try to deceive the nations unto directly following him against Christ and His millennial saints. This time the Dragon is thrown into the Lake of Fire as being totally incorrigible.

Revelation 20.7-10 When the thousand years are expired, Satan shall be loosed out of his prison,

And shall go out to deceive the nations which are in the four quarters of the earth, Gog, and Magog, to gather them together to battle: the number of whom is as the sand of the sea.

And they went up on the breadth of the earth, and compassed the camp of the saints about, and the beloved city: and fire came down from God out of heaven and devoured them.

And the devil that deceived them was cast into the lake of fire and brimstone, where the beast and the false prophet are, and shall be tormented day and night for ever and ever.

---

41 He shall save Israel and all the Gentiles, God speaking in the person of man.

42 Therefore do ye also, my children, tell these things to your children, that they disobey Him not.

43 For I have known that ye shall assuredly be disobedient, and assuredly act ungodly, not giving heed to the law of God, but to the commandments of men, being corrupted through wickedness.

44 And therefore shall ye be scattered as Gad and Dan my brethren, and ye shall know not your lands, tribe, and tongue.

45 But the Lord will gather you together in faith through His tender mercy, and for the sake of Abraham, Isaac, and Jacob.

46 And when he had said these things unto them, he commanded them,

> saying: Bury me in Hebron.
>
> 47 And he fell asleep and died at a good old age.

Jasher 62.4 And in the eighty-second year died Asher his brother, he was an hundred and twenty-three years old at his death, and he was placed in a coffin in Egypt, and was given into the hands of his children.

> 48 And his sons did as he had commanded them, and they carried him up to Hebron, and buried him with his fathers.

C.11 It is reported by those who translated these Testaments of the 12 Patriarchs that the apostle Paul carried a copy of them around with him all the time. I think we can definitely see evidence of this in Romans chapter 7. I will quote some of his amazing verses on the duality of life or good and evil which would appear to be talking about the same concept as mentioned by the Patriarch Asher.

C.12 Both the Patriarch Asher and the apostle Paul bring out the concept that evil is always trying to usurp the good and take it away from people's hearts and is always trying to make people evil and godless instead of good and godly:

Romans 7.10-25 And the commandment, which *was ordained* to life, I found *to be* unto death.

For sin, taking occasion by the commandment, deceived me, and by it slew *me*.

Wherefore the law *is* holy, and the commandment holy, and just, and good. Was then that which is good made death unto me? God forbid. But sin, that it might appear sin, working death in me by that which is good; that sin by the commandment might become exceeding sinful. We know that the law is spiritual: but I am carnal, sold under sin. For that which I do I allow not: for what I would, that do I not; but what I hate, that do I. If then I do that which I would not, I consent unto the law that *it is* good. Now then it is no more I that do it, but sin that dwelleth in me. For I know that in me (that is, in my flesh,) dwelleth no good thing: for to will is present with me; but *how* to perform that which is good I find not. For the good that I would I do not: but the evil which I would not, that I do. Now if I do that I would not, it is no more I that do it, but sin that dwelleth in me. I find then a law, that, when I would do good, evil is present with me. For I delight in the law of God after the inward man: But I see another law in my members, warring against the law of my mind, and bringing me into captivity to the law of sin which is in my members. O wretched man that I am! who shall deliver me from the body of this death? I thank God through Jesus Christ our Lord. So then with the mind I myself serve the law of God; but with the flesh the law of sin.

THE TESTAMENT OF JOSEPH

The Eleventh Son of Jacob and Rachel.

CHAP. I.

THE copy of the Testament of Joseph.

C.1 Joseph is referred to here as 'beloved'. Only a few people in the whole Bible have gained that title. Two of the Patriarchs were called beloved – one was Joseph and the other was Joseph's mother Rachel's handmaiden Bilhah's son Naphtali who was born on Rachel's lap and became a priest or holy man. He was also called 'beloved'. Daniel the prophet was also called 'beloved' as was John who wrote the Book of Revelations. King David was called 'A man after God's own heart' which essentially means – 'beloved'

Acts 13.2 God said, 'I have found David, the son of Jesse, a man after my own heart, and he will do everything that I want him to do.

C.2 What is the definition of 'Beloved of God' if not a person who depends totally on God. It has nothing to do with being religious and perfect by abstaining from meats or fasting and praying incessantly or going to a church building. Fasting can be a blessing at times and good for both our physical and spiritual health. The point being that only Jesus the Son of God can take away our sins.

C.3 Sins are not just doing something bad or evil, but sin is 'missing the mark' of God's will in our lives. Sin is refusing to listen to God's Holy Spirit, and instead deliberately doing our 'own thing' and going our own way and not following what God has said to do in His Word.

C.4 The word 'Beloved' has been assigned to those who truly loved God's word and tried to obey His instructions and made a constant attempt to listen to the voice of His Spirit. Those who truly did what God asked of them and did not just flow with the tide of public opinion. None of those who were called 'beloved' had an easy and cushy life. It took sacrifice and dedication to listening to God's voice that earned them the title of 'Beloved'.

2 When he was about to die, he called his sons and his brethren together, and said to them:

C.5 It is my conviction that when Joseph is mentioning talking to his sons and brethren that the women were also there such as the wives of the Patriarchs who were still alive and their daughters and granddaughters. Unfortunately, it seems to have been the habit of the Jews in the Old Testament repeatedly to mention the men only and not the women. Why?

3 My brethren and my children, hearken to Joseph the beloved of Israel; give ear, my sons, unto your father.

C.6 Joseph was the first to die of the 12 Patriarch sons of Jacob at 110 years old. He therefore had his 11 brethren there at his death. I think that was a good choice of God to do things that way as Joseph died it was a reminder to this brethren that they had all been forgiven in spite of their heinous crimes against their brother Joseph when he was but 17 years old.

C.7 I really believe that God is a loving God, and He took Joseph first back to the spirit world because as a good leader and a humble person the paved the way for his brethren just like the vision he had when 17- years old that he would be a leader of his brethren.

C.8 Apart from Christ himself, Joseph was the best example of forgiveness in the entire Bible in my opinion. That is what we are supposed to learn whilst on earth: To Love God and to love others. To learn to forgive even when everything goes all wrong and things done against us seem even cruel sometimes. As the Patriarchs have clearly stated getting angry and full of hatred is Satan's answer to having problems but it is not God's. Joseph was an unusually good sample. How did he become such a good sample of love and humility and forgiveness?

> 4 I have seen in my life envy and death, yet I went not astray, but persevered in the truth--of the Lord.

C.9 What does it mean to persevere in the truth of the Lord? Seek the Lord first and find out what the Lord's will is for you each day.

> 5 These my brethren hated me, but the Lord loved me:

C.10 Imagine how convicting this story was as Joseph had a captive audience of all of his 11 brethren and all their children. In the next verse Joseph is also telling all of their children and grand-children and even great grandchildren the whole story of what had happened to him when he was but 17 years old, but how God brought a miraculous victory and deliverance for Israel through his sufferings and final exaltation to the right hand of Pharaoh. A position where he could help his brethren and their families. Egypt was the 'womb' for the nurturing the budding nation of Israel.

> 6 They wished to slay me, but the God of my fathers guarded me:

C.11 As good a leader like Joseph and as kind as we know he was, I am sure that he would have asked permission from his brethren to tell the story of his life so that all the younger relatives could benefit from all the lessons involved and to fear God. To learn that what one sows you will reap. Joseph when he gave his last Testament was an excellent sample to his other 11 brothers, and that is probably why they all came clean in their own Testaments a few years later when they themselves in turn were on their deathbeds. They were being totally honest and forthright about their sins and mistakes in life. That was outstanding and convicting. To me the Testaments of the 12 Patriarchs is electrifying and alive and so different from today's society where very few people are honest with themselves and give a true account of their lives before both God and man or relatives. Most people seem to think that it is ok to hide the truth and not confess their mistakes and sins which in turn keeps them from being close to God and His love.

> 7 They let me down into a pit, and the Most High brought me up again.
>
> 8 I was sold into slavery, and the Lord of all made me free:
>
> 9 I was taken into captivity, and His strong hand succoured me.
>
> 10 I was beset with hunger, and the Lord Himself nourished me.
>
> 11 I was alone, and God comforted me:

Isaiah 41.10 Fear thou not for I am with thee, be not dismayed for I am thy God I will comfort thee Yea I will uphold thee with the right hand of My righteousness

> 12 I was sick, and the Lord visited me.
>
> 13 I was in prison, and my God showed favour unto me.
>
> 14 In bonds, and He released me.

Matthew 25.35-36 For I was an hungred, and ye gave me meat: I was thirsty, and ye gave me drink: I was a stranger, and ye took me in: "Naked, and ye clothed me: I was sick, and ye visited me: I was in prison, and ye came unto me."

> 15 Slandered, and He pleaded my cause.
>
> 16 Bitterly spoken against by the Egyptians, and He delivered me.
>
> 17 Envied by my fellow-slaves, and He exalted me.
>
> 18 And this chief captain of Pharaoh entrusted to me his house.

Genesis 39.5-6 And it came to pass from the time that he had made him overseer in his house, and over all that he had, that the Lord blessed the Egyptian's house for Joseph's sake; and the blessing of the Lord was upon all that he had in the house, and in the field. And he left all that he had in Joseph's hand; and he knew not ought he had, save the bread which he did eat. And Joseph was a goodly person, and well favoured.

C.12 When Joseph was brought into the house of Potiphar all was going very well and smoothly for a while, but Satan had other plans, in trying to tempt Joseph to go astray and thus not fulfil God's plan to deliver His people.

> 19 And I struggled against a shameless woman, urging me to transgress with her; but the God of Israel my father delivered me from the burning flame.

C.13 The burning flame of lust.

James 1.14-15 "But every man is tempted, when he is drawn away of his own lust, and enticed." Then, when lust hath conceived it brings forth sin; and sin when hath finished brings death.

C.14 Lust can be a very dangerous and beguiling spirit, just like the snake in the Garden of Eden. Lust comes in many forms and the definition of lust is 'having an inordinate and compulsive desire for something'.

C.15 These lusts can become devilish as happened to Eve in the Garden of Eden. Lust for flesh, or lust for Power and wealth and position and the praise of men. This is why Jesus stated about this physical world:

1 John 2.15-17 Love not the world, neither the things that are in the world. If any man love the world, the love of the Father is not in him. For all that is in the world, the lust of the flesh, and the lust of the eyes, and the pride of life, is not of the Father, but is of the world. And the world passes away, and the lust thereof: but he that doeth the will of God abides for ever.

Genesis 39.7-9 And it came to pass after these things, that his master's wife cast her eyes upon Joseph; and she said, Lie with me.

⁸ But he refused, and said unto his master's wife, Behold, my master wot not what is with me in the house, and he hath committed all that he hath to my hand;

⁹ There is none greater in this house than I; neither hath he kept back anything from me but thee, because thou art his wife: how then can I do this great wickedness, and sin against God?

C.16 There is a very dramatic account of Potiphar's wife in the Book of Jasher Chapter 44. [See my book Jasher Insights Book II]

> 20 I was cast into prison, I was beaten, I was mocked; but the Lord granted me to find mercy, in the sight of the keeper of the prison.

Genesis 39.20-21 And Joseph's master took him, and put him into the prison, a place where the king's prisoners were bound: and he was there in the prison. But the Lord was with Joseph, and shewed him mercy, and gave him favour in the sight of the keeper of the prison.

> 21 For the Lord doth not forsake them that fear Him, neither in darkness, nor in bonds, nor in tribulations, nor in necessities.

> 22 For God is not put to shame as a man, nor as the son of man is he

afraid, nor as one that is earth-born is He weak or affrighted.

C.17 Is verse 22 stating 'nor as the son of man - meaning the Patriarch Joseph' or is the verse actually stating 'For God ... as the 'Son' of Man. That is very interesting. Jesus is mentioned as the 'Son of Man' over 140 times in the Gospels. When a small 's' was used, it was normally talking about one of God's prophets, but when a Capital 'S' was used, it was clearly talking about Jesus the Messiah or the Son of God.

C.18 The expression 'Son of Man is also mentioned in the book of Daniel chapter 7.13-14 and furthermore in the book of Enoch both as the 'Son of Man' and the 'Elect One' walking together with God the Father.

C.19 Most times in the Old Testament the expression 'son of man' was referring to one of God's prophets such as in the Book of Ezekiel. However, both Enoch and Daniel mention the son of man in capitals or 'Son of Man' as referring to Jesus the Christ.

C.20 Why did Jesus Himself refer to Himself as the 'Son of Man' and not his complete title as the Son of God? Jesus referred to Himself as the Son of Man because it was written in the books of the prophets and in particular the Book of Daniel chapter 7.13-14 and in the Book of Enoch in many places.

C.21 Christ is also referred to as the Son of Man, because it was prophesied that the Messiah or God the Son would be born of mankind in the flesh of a woman.

C.22 Both the Book of Daniel and the Book of Enoch show the Son of Man walking together with God the Father.

C.23 Who is this 'son of man' in the above verse 22? Is it talking about a prophet as 'son of God' or is it referring to 'Son of Man which is the Son of God? See my video on YOUTUBE about the 'Son of Man': THE BOOK OF ENOCH – Unpacking its Powerful Prophecies! – with Stephen Strutt - YouTube

C.24 Have we stumbled across an amazing verse in verse 22 of Chapter 1 of the Patriarch Joseph. As far as I know the Son of Man is only mentioned in the Old Testament in Daniel 7.13-14 and many times in the Book of Enoch and over 100 times in the New Testament by the Messiah Himself.

C.25 Have we found yet another verse in the patriarch Joseph talking about God as the 'Son of Man' or Jesus the Messiah? If I am right, then verse 22 has been deliberately obscured and made to be ambiguous. Of course, verse 22 could be arguably just comparing God to man and the son of man – the Patriarch and the earthborn that God unlike them is not afraid. Maybe that is all it means. I would like to see the original text in Hebrew to be sure of the original meaning with verse 22.

C.26 Even if verse 22 is just referring to the 'son of man' as the Patriarch Joseph, this reference to the 'son of man' is the furthest back in time or 3700 years ago or 1700 BC, where the expression 'son of man' is used in referring to the prophet of God, or this case the Patriarch Joseph. I have also seen verses in the Bible about the 'son of man' in the psalms circa 1100 BC, and in the Book of Job circa 1500 BC.

> 23 But in all those things He gives protection, and in divers ways doth He comfort, though for a little space He departs to try the inclination of the soul.

Psalm 11.5 "The LORD tries the righteous: but the wicked and him that loveth violence his soul hates."

> 24 In ten temptations He showed me approved, and in all of them I endured; for endurance is a mighty charm, and patience giveth many good things.

C.27 It is well written of Abraham in the Book of Jubilees that he endured '10 severe temptations' from the hand of God Himself during his life. Tests that he endured and prevailed over because of his faith. (**See my Book of Jubilees Insights**)

Luke 21.19 In your patience, possess ye your soul.

Romans 5:3-4 And not only so, but we glory in tribulations also: knowing that tribulation worketh patience And patience, experience; and experience, hope.

> 25 How often did the Egyptian woman threaten me with death!

C.28 Potiphar's wife was given over to some terrible and very evil spirit of temptation in the form of lust. If Joseph had given into that spirit it could have destroyed him. Potiphar's wife would have used Joseph for a season and then gotten rid of him. Joseph wasn't taken any chances with a bad spirit like that as he did not want to be 'cursed'.

> 26 How often did she give me over to punishment, and then call me back and threaten me, and when I was unwilling to company with her, she said to me:
>
> 27 Thou shalt be lord of me, and all that is in my house, if thou wilt give thyself unto me, and thou shalt be as our master.

C.29 This verse reminds of when Satan was talking to Jesus, trying to tempt him when Jesus had fasted 40 days and nights whilst in the wilderness just before He started his ministry:

Matthew 4.8-11 Again, the devil taketh him up into an exceeding high mountain, and shewed him all the kingdoms of the world, and the glory of them;

[9] And saith unto him, All these things will I give thee, if thou wilt fall down and

worship me.

[10] Then saith Jesus unto him, Get thee hence, Satan: 'Nothing doing' - for it is written, Thou shalt worship the Lord thy God, and him only shalt thou serve.

[11] Then the devil left him, and, behold, angels came and ministered unto him.

C.30 This story with Potiphar's wife begs the question: Why would Satan appear in person so strongly? If Satan is wandering around in his usurped kingdom of earth as he claimed to Jesus that he was then to choose a role to play for himself that he didn't give to those under his command which role would he play?

Luke 4.5-7 And the devil, taking him up into an high mountain, shewed unto him all the kingdoms of the world in a moment of time.

[6] And the devil said unto him, All this power will I give thee, and the glory of them: for that is delivered unto me; and to whomsoever I will I give it.

[7] If thou therefore wilt worship me, all shall be thine. ****29/06/2022

C.31 In the case of Joseph, Satan tried everything he could do to destroy Joseph or to trick and beguile him. Why? If Satan could get rid of Joseph or alternatively get Joseph to disobey God's laws such as 'Do not to commit adultery', then Joseph would never have fulfilled his great destiny to watch over and care for Israel, which he did when he became ruler over Egypt. As a result, God's promises to Abraham never would have been fulfilled. That was clearly Satan's thinking, so he personally got into the situation with Potiphar's wife, because of her arrogance, lust and refusal to stop trying to force herself on Joseph. That is how Satan gets into people either to possess them or influence them in their minds from without.

---

28 But I remembered the words of my father, and going into my chamber, I wept and prayed unto the Lord.

29 And I fasted in those seven years, and I appeared to the Egyptians as one living delicately, for they that fast for God's sake receive beauty of face.

30 And if my lord were away from home, I drank no wine; nor for three days did I take my food, but I gave it to the poor and sick.

31 And I sought the Lord early, and I wept for the Egyptian woman of Memphis, for very unceasingly did she trouble me, for also at night she came to me under pretence of visiting me.

---

32 And because she had no male child she pretended to regard me as a son.

33 And for a time she embraced me as a son, and I knew it not; but later, she sought to draw me into fornication.

34 And when I perceived it I sorrowed unto death; and when she had gone out, I came to myself, and lamented for her many days, because I recognized her guile and her deceit.

35 And I declared unto her the words of the Most High, if haply she would turn from her evil lust.

36 Often, therefore, did she flatter me with words as a holy man, and guilefully in her talk praise my chastity before her husband, while desiring to ensnare me when we were alone.

C.32 Potiphar's wife sounds like the beguiling evil snake in the Garden of Eden who tempted Adam and Eve. Just like the anaconda in the Disney cartoon of Mowgli in 'Jungle Book', where Kaa the snake tried to hypnotize Mowgli and then lure him into a trance and finally devour him whole. Well, that was the snake's intent! Fortunately, in this story it did not happen to Joseph any more than it did to Mowgli.

37 For she lauded me openly as chaste, and in secret she said unto me: Fear not my husband; for he is persuaded concerning thy chastity: for even should one tell him concerning us, he would not believe.

38 Owing to all these things I lay upon the ground, and besought God that the Lord would deliver me from her deceit.

39 And when she had prevailed nothing thereby, she came again to me under the plea of instruction, that she might learn the word of God.

40 And she said unto me: If thou will that I should leave my idols, lie with me, and I will persuade my husband to depart from his idols, and we will walk in the law by thy Lord.

41 And I said unto her: The Lord will not. that those who reverence Him should be in uncleanness, nor doth He take pleasure in them that commit adultery, but in those that approach Him with a pure heart and

undefiled lips.

42 But she held her peace, longing to accomplish her evil desire.

43 And I gave myself yet more to fasting and prayer, that the Lord might deliver me from her.

44 And again, at another time she said unto me: If thou wilt not commit adultery, I will kill my husband by poison; and take thee to be my husband.

C.33 Here we can clearly see that the woman is totally obsessed with Joseph to the point that she is now threatening to poison her husband if she can't get her way. What utter insanity! What is obsession, in spiritual terms? It starts with a temptation. Giving into temptation one sins against God. God's Spirit tries to patiently encourage the person to change and to not keep committing this sin so that the person can regain their contact with God and His Love. If the person persists in their wantonness to sin then that is opening the door to demons and even to Lucifer himself if the sins continue.

Ephesians 4.27 'Neither give place to the devil'.

Matthew 12:45-50 Then he, (the evil spirit) goes and taketh with himself seven other spirits more wicked than himself, and they enter into the person) and dwell there: and the last state of that man is worse than the first. Even so shall it be also unto this wicked generation.

C.34 It would seem that in the case of Potiphar's wife she ended up yielding to a very strong demon and very bad spirit which would probably end up destroying her, as Satan often ends up destroying his victims.

C.35 Her behaviour was totally irrational. She was a very beautiful woman and very rich and powerful. She could have had any man as even her husband was afraid of her. When she saw that Joseph didn't want to be with her, she could have found another guy that was willing. But no, it had to be Joseph and that against his will. When she could not get what she wanted she became totally obsessed, and blamed Joseph to her husband for attempted rape, had him beaten, being innocent, and thrown into prison. Even whilst he was in the prison, she tormented him with her obsession. Her obsession being her lust for Joseph. Those who are obsessed can become very dangerous people and violent and even murderous.

45 I therefore, when I heard this, rent my garments, and said unto her:

46 Woman, reverence God, and do not this evil deed, lest thou be destroyed; for know indeed that I will declare this thy device unto all

men.

47 She therefore, being afraid, besought that I would not declare this device.

48 And she departed soothing me with gifts and sending to me every delight of the sons of men.

49 And afterwards she sent me food mingled with enchantments.

C.36 It would seem that Potiphar's wife had contact with a Satanic priest who could make enchantments of seduction like unto the effects of the aphrodisiac plant and place in Joseph's food.

50 And when the eunuch who brought it came, I looked up and beheld a terrible man giving me with the dish a sword, and I perceived that her scheme was to beguile me.

C.37 God gave Joseph a vision to warn him not to be tempted by her craft devices. There is a story in the Bible that when Israel was in the process of wiping out the Canaanites as an obedience to God's command to Abraham and to Jacob and the 12 Patriarchs, that in one country, the men of that country were very smart and, they put their wives and daughters in the doors of their houses looking alluring and half naked. They said the only way we can defeat Israel is to get them to disobey their God. Sure enough, many of the Israelites gave in to the temptation of the sexy Canaanite or Moabite women, and God slaughtered the Israelite soldiers whom were involved in the sin, as a direct result. What a lure of Satan! It would appear that Satan was trying doing the exact same thing against Joseph. Fortunately for the future of the budding nation of Israel Satan failed in the case of Joseph.

Book of Jasher 85.54-56,61 And the children of Moab were afraid of the children of Israel, and the children of Moab took their daughters and wives of beautiful aspect and comely appearance and dressed them in gold and silver and costly garments. 55 And the children of Moab seated these women at the door of their tents, in order that the children of Israel might not fight against them. 56 And the children of Israel turned to the daughters of Moab and coveted them and they went to them. 61 And the anger of the Lord was kindled against Israel on account of this matter, and he sent a pestilence amongst them and there died of the Israelites 20,000 men. [**See the whole story in Jasher 85.54-63**]

51 And when he had gone out, I wept, nor did I taste that or any other of her food.

52 So then after one day she came to me and observed the food, and

said unto me: Why is it that thou hast not eaten of the food?

53 And I said unto her: It is because thou hast filled it with deadly enchantments; and how thou said: I come not near to idols but to the Lord alone.

54 Now therefore know that the God of my father hath revealed unto me by His angel thy wickedness, and I have kept it to convict thee, if haply thou mayst see and repent.

55 But that thou mayst learn that the wickedness of the ungodly hath no power over them that worship God with chastity behold I will take of it and eat before thee.

56 And having so said, I prayed thus: The God of my fathers and the angel of Abraham, be with me; and ate.

57, And when she saw this she fell upon her face at my feet, weeping; and I raised her up and admonished her.

58 And she promised to do this iniquity no more.

59 But her heart was still set upon evil, and she looked around how to ensnare me, and sighing deeply she became downcast, though she was not sick.

C.38 It seems that with some people if they can't get what they want they become sullen and bored and down-hearted and even crest-fallen. What does that all mean? Spiritually speaking it means surrendering to a spirit of depression. A spirit which makes 'mountains out of mole-hills' in your mind. If you give in to such a spirit it could lead you to worse spirits which cause you to take action or even revenge or worse yet be given over to violent retaliation. Such is the case with Potiphar's wife. I think the real problem with her, was that she was a spoilt rich brat, who was accustomed to getting everything she wanted, and she was not used to others saying 'No' to her. That, she could not handle, because it humbled her pride and arrogance.

60 And when her husband saw her, he said unto her: Why is thy countenance fallen?

61 And she said unto him: I have a pain at my heart, and the groanings

of my spirit oppress me; and so he comforted her who was not sick.

62 Then, accordingly seizing an opportunity, she rushed unto me while her husband was yet without, and said unto me: I will hang myself, or cast myself over a cliff, if thou wilt not lie with me.

63 And when I saw the spirit of Beliar was troubling her, I prayed unto the Lord, and said unto her:

C.39 Satan often ends up killing his victims such as tempting them to throw themselves off a cliff or a bridge even in modern times. So, Satan certainly does exist. Look how he tempted Jesus in the wilderness just before He started His great ministry.

Matthew 4.5-7 Then the devil taketh him up into the holy city, and sets him on a pinnacle of the temple, And saith unto Him, If thou e the Son of God, cast thyself down: for it is written, He shall give his angels charge over thee: and their hands shall bear thee up, lest at any time thou dash thy foot against a stone.

Jesus said unto him, 'It is written again, Thou shalt not tempt the Lord thy God'.

64 Why, wretched woman, art thou troubled and disturbed, blinded through sins?

65 Remember that if thou kill thyself, Asteho, the concubine of thy husband, thy rival, will beat thy children, and thou wilt destroy thy memorial from off the earth.

66 And she said unto me: Lo, then thou love me; let this suffice me: only strive for my life and my children, and I expect that I shall enjoy my desire also.

67 But she knew not that because of my lord I spake thus, and not because of her.

68 For if a man hath fallen before the passion of a wicked desire and become enslaved by it, even as she, whatever good thing he may hear with regard to that passion, he receives it with a view to his wicked desire.

69 I declare, therefore, unto you, my children, that it was about the sixth hour when she departed from me; and I knelt before the Lord all

day, and all the night; and about dawn I rose up, weeping the while and praying for a release from her.

70 At last, then, she laid hold of my garments, forcibly dragging me to have connexion with her.

71 When, therefore, I saw that in her madness she was holding fast to my garment, I left it behind, and fled away naked.

C.40 In this last verse it states that the woman was mad. Another definition of mad is insane or demon possessed.

72 And holding fast to the garment she falsely accused me, and when her husband came he cast me into prison in his house; and on the morrow he scourged me and sent me into Pharaoh's prison.

73 And when I was in bonds, the Egyptian woman was oppressed with grief, and she came and heard how I gave thanks unto the Lord and sang praises in the abode of darkness, and with glad voice rejoiced, glorifying my God that I was delivered from the lustful desire of the Egyptian woman.

74 And often hath she sent unto me saying: Consent to fulfil my desire, and I will release thee from thy bonds, and I will free thee from the darkness.

75 And not even in thought did I incline unto her.

76 For God loveth him who in a den of wickedness combines fasting with chastity, rather than the man who in kings' chambers combines luxury with license.

C.41 It would seem that there is a time and place to fast and pray and avoid sexual relationships at least for a time or season as in the case of Joseph. Abstaining from marrying however is not normally God's will or the average man as God has stated that the 1st commandment is to 'Be fruitful and multiply'. How can a man do that without a woman? Better to get married, I think. Of course, if you were put to disadvantage such as the situation young Joseph was in with a sexy beautiful lusty wife of a powerful man like Potiphar, then you better do as Joseph did and try to avoid such a person.

C.42 I must admit that even Jesus did state that some people have been made eunuchs by man and others have made themselves eunuchs for the

Kingdom of Heaven's sake. Chastity long term is for the few. For most of us, getting married and having children and having a normal sex life is what God intended for us according to the Bible.

Matthew 19.12 For there are some eunuchs, which were so born from their mother's womb: and there are some eunuchs, which were made eunuchs of men: and there be eunuchs, which have made themselves eunuchs for the kingdom of heaven's sake. He that is able to receive it, let him receive it.

C.43 Paul was undoubtedly the most dedicated of Jesus's disciples. Paul was chaste as far as we know and did not marry. It is true that he was very dedicated to the Lord. Even he, however stated that it is better for people to 'marry rather than to burn' Meaning to burn in desire for sex.

1 Corinthians 7.9 For if they cannot contain, then let them marry, it is better that they marry than to burn

C.44 Let's face it in the times of Paul doing what he was doing you practically had to be a martyr for the cause. Paul probably looked to the sample of Jesus, who only lasted 3 years in his ministry, before being crucified.

C.45 It is true that the apostle Peter was married and the leader of the church. Paul with the amount of persecution he attracted from the Pharisees for betraying them and going to the side of the Nazarene, simply did not have time to either marry or have a family and he was martyred in 66 AD. Peter was also martyred around the same time.

C.46 Paul mentions that marriage is a good thing, but he also gives a warning to those of us who are married and living in the times of trouble such as in the time of the End:

1 Cor 7.1-2 Now concerning he things whereof ye wrote unto me: It is good for a man not to look on a woman. Nevertheless, *to avoid* fornication, let every man have his own wife, and let every woman have her own husband.

1 Cor 7.29 But this I say, brethren, the time is short: it remains, that both thy that have wives be as though they had none:

C.47 There is time to have sex or to even get married and a time to refrain from getting married or even having sexual relationships. The Patriarch Joseph was especially talking to the 'young men' in his family, and warning them of some of the dangers, such as he himself faced when he was but 17-18 years old.

> 77 And if a man lives in chastity, and desires also glory, and the Most High knows that it is expedient for him, He bestows this also upon me.

C.48 It has been mentioned by the translators of 'The Testaments of the 12 Patriarchs' that Paul the Apostle who was celibate, kept a copy of the Testament of the 12 Patriarchs with him. I would imagine that he obtained a copy of that when he was still a Pharisee.

78 How often, though she were sick, did she come down to me at unlooked for times, and listened to my voice as I prayed!

79 And when I heard her groanings I held my peace.

80 For when I was in her house she was wont to bare her arms, and breasts, and legs, that I might lie with her; for she was very beautiful, splendidly adorned in order to beguile me.

C.49 Joseph was very strong to resist the wiles of a very beautiful and sexy woman. Most men would not have been so strong and determined to resist this woman's wiles and attractions. He was very strong because he walked in the fear of God and knew what had happened to his eldest brother Reuben who had raped his father Jacob's concubine Bilhah and was thereafter very sick unto death for 7 months according to the Testament of Reuben himself. He also was warned by his mother Rachel that it was god's will for him to go down with his Ishmaelite captors. Joseph knew from the amazing dreams that God had given him whilst he was still 17 and living with his father Jacob, that he himself was supposed to fulfil a very great destiny, and he wasn't about to fail both God and the 'budding' tribe of Israel. So, Joseph was strong to resist the temptations and attractions of Potiphar's wife even though she was very voluptuous and beautiful.

81 And the Lord guarded me from her devices.

C.50 It was the Lord that gave Joseph the grace to endure the very difficult and trying situation that he that he had found himself in, concerning the woman of Memphis

C.51 Joseph was chaste or celibate whilst in this very difficult situation with Potiphar's wife. He had to be for the safety of his own life.

C.52 Joseph did not become totally celibate, as he later went on to get married and have two children with Asenath the daughter of the High Priest of On.

Genesis 41.45 And Pharaoh called Joseph's name Zaphnathpaaneah; and he gave him to wife Asenath the daughter of Potipherah priest of On. And Joseph went out over all the land of Egypt.

CHAP. II.

> YE see, therefore, my children, how great things patience worketh, and prayer with fasting.

C.1 It is stating that patience is a Virtue and a quality to be sought after. It is also stating that there is great personal profit I prayer and fasting. Fasting can certainly help to cleanse the physical body. Prayer can change the circumstance in which we find ourselves. When things are not going as we would like or even as they should be going then patience is essential in order not to give up on a difficult situation That is when endurance is essential

2 Timothy 2:3-4 Thou therefore endure hardness, as a good soldier of Jesus Christ. No man that goes to war entangles himself with the affairs of this life; that he may please him who hath chosen him to be a soldier.

> 2 So ye too, if ye follow after chastity and purity with patience and prayer, with fasting in humility of heart, the Lord will dwell among you because He loveth chastity.
>
> 3 And wheresoever the Most High dwelleth, even though envy, or slavery, or slander befalls a man, the Lord who dwelleth in him, for the sake of his chastity not only delivers him from evil, but also exalts him even as me.

C.2 I don't think that there is any spiritual merit in abiding in chastity indefinity. However, we could find ourselves in a situation, where being chase for a season would be very wise. Normally, and in most cases, God would prefer people to marry and have children as that was His 1st commandment to Adam and Eve, and also to Noah and his family, right after the Great Flood.

Genesis 1:28: And God blessed them (Adam and Eve), and God said unto them, Be fruitful, and multiply, and replenish the earth, and subdue it: and have dominion over the fish of the sea, and over the fowl of the air, and over every living thing that moves upon the earth.

Genesis 9:1: And God blessed Noah and his sons, and said unto them, 'Be fruitful, and multiply, and replenish the earth.'

> 4 For in every way the man is lifted up, whether in deed, or in word, or in thought.
>
> 5 My brethren knew how my father loved me, and yet I did not exalt myself in my mind: although I was a child, I had the fear of God in my heart; for I knew that all things would pass away.

C.3 I don't think that Joseph was so perfect as he never would have gotten into trouble in the first place if he hadn't been boasting to his brethren how superior he was and he caused his brethren to hate him because of his dreams of grandeur.

C.4 Why did Joseph's brethren hate him so much when he was only 17-years -old? He was a typical spoilt brat whom Jacob had spoilt because he was the child of Rachel his favourite wife and the child of his old age.

C.5 His father showed favouritism unto Joseph in making him a coat of many colours

C.6 Joseph annoyed his brethren with his 'superior' airs. I think he was practically poking his tongue out at his brethren and saying how superior he was. However, he was only 17 and did not deserve to be murdered or thrown into a pit or sold to the Ishmaelites.

C.7 Why do the 'religionists' try to make the patriarchs or even their fathers seem to be perfect when they themselves never claimed that they were perfect and admitted countless times like King David in the Psalms that he was a sinner.

C.8 The original story content of the Testament of the Patriarchs is very good but in some places it has been 'doctored' to conform with too 'religious' views as held in 100 BC.

C.9 Over emphasis on both chastity and fasting was a thing that was the doctrine of the Essenes Jewish sect in 100 BC who allegedly re-wrote the Testament of the Patriarchs in 100 BC. That sect didn't even believe in marriage but in celibacy and fasting and it is reflected in the 'Testaments of the 12 Patriarchs' trying to make some of the Patriarchs such as Joseph seem to be absolutely perfect without a flaw, but it just was not true. Nobody is perfect and neither can they be by mere 'works' of trying to be good using ascetics, chastity and fasting or other seeming good works. Those 'good works' do not give any spiritual merit before God. What gives merit before God is the humility that Joseph had in forgiving his brethren despite the cruel way they had treated him, and sold him into slavery and not even knowing what would befall him.

C.10 There are reasons why Joseph had a strong conviction in resisting Potiphar's wife with her trying to entice him to commit adultery with her. It is stated in this very Testament of Joseph that she was very beautiful to look at.

C.11 Firstly, Joseph knew about his oldest brother Reuben who went and committed adultery with Bilhah the handmaiden of Rachel who had become Jacob his father's wife. It was stated in the Testament of Reuben that he suffered a 'loathsome disease' unto death for a long time from committing adultery with his father's concubine wife.

C.12 Rachel's grave at Ephrah: Another factor is that on the way down to Egypt when Joseph was a slave of the Ishmaelites according to the **Book of Jasher**, he passed by the grave of his mother Rachel and wept at her grave, and she spoke to him, and told him that in effect it was God's will for him to continue down to Egypt.

C.13 Rachel speaking from the grave - *continued*: At first, Joseph seemed not to like her advice, but later once he was down in Egypt, this would explain why in this Testament of Joseph he stated that he was a slave and *didn't want to incriminate **his** brethren.* Why? Because putting all the above factors into prospective, as well as his past *'dreams of grandeur'* and being *'lord over his brethren'*, he must have finally realised that God 'had a plan' for the budding nation of Israel, and that God was going to realize that plan through Joseph himself sooner or later. So, Joseph endured the suffering that came his way until his brethren had come down to Egypt and he had practically become Pharaoh of Egypt.

> 6 And I did not raise myself against them with evil intent, but I honoured my brethren; and out of respect for them, even when I was being sold, I refrained from telling the Ishmaelites that I was a son of Jacob, a great man and a mighty.

C.14 Joseph didn't tell the truth to the Ishmaelites and that he was the son of Jacob. Joseph knew that God had promised that He would do a great miracle for Jacob and his family and that his tribe would become a great nation according to what God had originally said unto Abraham. He therefore endured and trusted God and he waited patiently. His mother Rachel had also told him to go down to Egypt together with his captures the Ishmaelites as it was part of God's will.

Hebrews 11.3 These all died in faith, not having received the promises, but having seen them afar off, and were persuaded of them, and embraced them, and confessed that they were strangers and pilgrims on the earth.

> 7 Do ye also, my children, have the fear of God in all your works before your eyes, and honour your brethren.
>
> 8 For everyone who doeth the law of the Lord shall be loved by Him.
>
> 9 And when I came to the Indocolpitae with the Ishmaelites, they asked me, saying:
>
> 10 Art thou a slave? And I said that I was a home-born slave, that I might not put my brethren to shame.

C.15 Joseph refuses to admit that he was not a slave but free-born and the son of a powerful lord, his father Jacob. At first, verse 10 would seem to be a strange reaction, but was it? As they say in the military, it was a brave unselfish 'act of camouflage', because Joseph knew that God had a purpose in his going done to Egypt. Joseph also knew that His word to Abraham would be fulfilled.

C.16 God's purpose was not fulfilled until Joseph became the right hand of Pharoah and helped his family with grain during the famine. Then, after testing his brothers to see if they had changed from the 'monsters' they had been, Joseph saw that his brothers had changed, and had become concerned and sacrificial, he revealed himself to them. From that point on Joseph took care of Jacob and his family for the next 80 years and Israel both budded and grew strong in Egypt in the land of Goshen.

---

11 And the eldest of them said unto me: Thou art not a slave, for even thy appearance doth make it manifest.

12 But I said that I was their slave.

13 Now when we came into Egypt they strove concerning me, which of them should buy me and take me.

14 Therefore it seemed good to all that I should remain in Egypt with the merchant of their trade, until they should return bringing merchandise.

15 And the Lord gave me favour in the eyes of the merchant, and he entrusted unto me his house.

16 And God blessed him by my means, and increased him in gold and silver and in household servants.

17 And I was with him three months and five days.

18 And about that time the Memphian woman, the wife of Pentephris came down in a chariot, with great pomp, because she had heard from her eunuchs concerning me.

19 And she told her husband that the merchant had become rich by means of a young Hebrew, and they say that he had assuredly been stolen out of the land of Canaan.

20 Now, therefore, render justice unto him, and take away the youth to thy house; so shall the God of the Hebrews bless thee, for grace from heaven is upon him.

C.17 If Joseph was not 'letting on' that he himself was Jacob's son and insisted to the Ishmaelites that he was a slave to 'protect his brethren', then how did Potiphar's wife know that Joseph was a Hebrew. Was it using 'dark arts' and some type of sorcery, such as Laban had used many years preciously, in 'discerning' where young Jacob had suddenly disappeared to?

> 21 And Pentephris was persuaded by her words, and commanded the merchant to be brought, and said unto him:

C.18 It sounds like Potiphar's wife had Potiphar under her spell as he seemed to believe everything that his wife stated even if wasn't true. In this case though she was correct - Joseph was indeed a Hebrew. Was Potiphar's wife a witch?

> 22 What is this that I hear concerning thee, that thou steal persons out of the land of Canaan, and sell them for slaves?
>
> 23 But the merchant fell at his feet, and besought him, saying: I beseech thee, my lord, I know not what thou sayest.
>
> 24 And Pentephris said unto him: Whence, then, is the Hebrew slave?
>
> 25 And he said: The Ishmaelites entrusted him unto me until they should return.
>
> 26 But he believed him not, but commanded him to be stripped and beaten.
>
> 27 And when he persisted in this statement, Pentephris said: Let the youth be brought.
>
> 28 And when I was brought in, I did obeisance to Pentephris for he was third in rank of the officers of Pharaoh.
>
> 29 And he took me apart from him, and said unto me: Art thou a slave or free?
>
> 30 And I said: A slave.
>
> 31 And he said: Whose?
>
> 32 And I said: The Ishmaelites'.

33 And he said: How didst thou become their slave?

34 And I said: They bought me out of the land of Canaan.

35 And he said unto me: Truly you are lying; and straightway he commanded me to be stripped and beaten.

36 Now, the Memphian woman was looking through a window at me while I was being beaten, for her house was near, and she sent unto him saying:

37 Thy judgement is unjust; for thou dost punish a free man who hath been stolen, as though he were a transgressor.

C.19 Potiphar's wife - (The Memphian woman), seems to know a lot about Joseph. Did she use sorcery? Or had she been very interested in Joseph the slave from the time he had arrived in the slave market, as her house was just next door and over-looking the place. It sounds like she had already shown an interest in Joseph and had had her eunuchs finding out exactly who he was, and why such a good-looking well-attired young person of 17-year-old, was a slave. She had her eyes on him as she had 'something else' in, more than just him being a mere slave!

38 And when I made no change in my statement, though I was beaten, he ordered me to be imprisoned, until, he said, the owners of the boy should come.

39 And the woman said unto her husband: Wherefore dost thou detain the captive and wellborn lad in bonds, who ought rather to be set at liberty, and be waited upon?

40 For she wished to see me out of a desire of sin, but I was ignorant concerning all these things.

41 And he said to her: It is not the custom of the Egyptians to take that which belongs to others before proof is given.

42 This, therefore, he said concerning the merchant; but as for the lad, he must be imprisoned.

43 Now after four and twenty days came the Ishmaelites; for they had

heard that Jacob my father was mourning much concerning me.

44 And they came and said unto me: How is it that thou said that thou was a slave? and lo, we have learnt that thou art the son of a mighty man in the land of Canaan, and thy father still mourns for thee in sackcloth and ashes.

45 When I heard this my bowels were dissolved and my heart melted, and I desired greatly to weep, but I restrained myself that I should not put my brethren to shame.

C.20 That was exceedingly hard decision for Joseph as he probably could have been set free. Pharoah and his people had been afraid of Abraham in his time and if they had assuredly known that Joseph was the great grandson of Abraham, I am sure they would have made sure that he was returned to his father Jacob. Joseph denying that he was of noble birth and was, but a slave kept the Egyptians from doing this. Joseph must have realized that if he told the truth about himself at that particular time, that he would have been returned to his father Jacob and God's word would not be concerned concerning himself.

46 And I said unto them, I know not, I am a slave.

47 Then, therefore, they took counsel to sell me, that I should not be found in their hands.

48 For they feared my father, lest he should come and execute upon them a grievous vengeance.

49 For they had heard that he was mighty with God and with men.

50 Then said the merchant unto them: Release me from the judgement of Pentiphri.

51 And they came and requested me, saying: Say that thou was bought by us with money, and he will set us free.

52 Now the Memphian woman said to her husband: Buy the youth; for I hear, said she, that they are selling him.

53 And straightway she sent a eunuch to the Ishmaelites and asked

them to sell me.

54 But since the eunuch would not agree to buy me at their price he returned, having made trial of them, and he made known to his mistress that they asked a large price for their slave.

55 And she sent another eunuch, saying: Even though they demand two minas, give them, do not spare the gold; only buy the boy, and bring him to me.

56 The eunuch therefore went and gave them eighty pieces of gold, and he received me; but to the Egyptian woman he said I have given a hundred.

57 And though I knew this I held my peace, lest the eunuch should be put to shame.

58 Ye see, therefore, my children, what great things I endured that I should not put my brethren to shame.

59 Do ye also, therefore, love one another, and with long-suffering hide ye one another's faults.

60 For God delights in the unity of brethren, and in the purpose of a heart that takes pleasure in love.

61 And when my brethren came into Egypt they learnt that I had returned their money unto them, and upbraided them not, and comforted them.

62 And after the death of Jacob my father I loved them more abundantly, and all things whatsoever he commanded I did very abundantly for them.

63 And I suffered them not to be afflicted in the smallest matter; and all that was in my hand I gave unto them.

64 And their children were my children, and my children as their servants; and their life was my life, and all their suffering was my suffering,

and all their sickness was my infirmity.

65 My land was their land, and their counsel my counsel.

66 And I exalted not myself among them in arrogance because of my worldly glory, but I was among them as one of the least.

67 If ye also, therefore, walk in the commandments of the Lord, my children, He will exalt you there, and will bless you with good things for ever and ever.

68 And if anyone seeks to do evil unto you, do well unto him, and pray for him, and ye shall be redeemed of the Lord from all evil.

69 For, behold, ye see that out of my humility and longsuffering I took unto wife the daughter of the priest of Heliopolis.

70 And a hundred talents of gold were given me with her, and the Lord made them to serve me.

71 And He gave me also beauty as a flower beyond the beautiful ones of Israel; and He preserved me unto old age in strength and in beauty, because I was like in all things to Jacob.

72 And hear ye, my children, also the vision which I saw.

73 There were twelve harts feeding: and the nine were first dispersed over all the earth, and likewise also the three.

74 And I saw that from Judah was born a virgin wearing a linen garment, and from her, was born a lamb, without spot; and on his left hand there was as it were a lion; and all the beasts rushed against him, and the lamb overcame them, and destroyed them and trod them under foot.

C.21 A prophecy about the birth of Jesus born from the tribe of Judah, born of a virgin. Jesus was the Lamb of God, a lamb without spot or blemish meaning he was sinless. He was also symbolised by a Lion - the Lion of Judah. When Jesus returns in the 2nd Coming he will destroy all the bestial and monstrous rulers of the earth. These beasts are known as the merchants in the Book of Revelation chapter 18 as well as the demonic spirits behind them will be locked up in the Bottomless Pit.

Isaiah 7.14 "The Lord himself shall give you a sign; behold, a virgin shall conceive and bear a son, and shall call his name Emmanuel."-

John 1.29 The next day John saw Jesus coming unto him and he said 'behold the **Lamb** of God which taketh away all the sins of the world

Revelation 5:5-6 And one of the elders said unto me, 'Weep not: behold, the **LION** of the tribe of **Judah,** the root of David, hath prevailed to open the book, and to loose the 7 seals thereof. 6And **I** beheld, and, lo, in the midst of the throne and of the four beasts, and in the midst of the elders, stood a **Lamb** as it had been slain, having seven horns and seven eyes, which are the seven Spirits of God sent forth into all the earth.

1 Peter 1.19 But with the precious blood of Christ, like that of a **lamb** without blemish or spot.

Revelation 13.8 And all who dwell on earth will worship it, everyone whose name has not been written before the foundation of the world in the book of life of the **Lamb** who was slain.

Revelation 7.17 For the **Lamb** in the midst of the throne will be their shepherd, and he will guide them to springs of living water, and God will wipe away every tear from their eyes."

Revelation 5.13 And every creature which is in heaven, and on the earth, and under the earth, and such as are in the sea, and all that are in them, heard I saying, Blessing, and honour, and glory, and power, be unto him that sits upon the throne, and unto the **Lamb** for ever and ever.

Revelation 14.1 And I looked, and, lo, a **Lamb** stood on the mount Sion, and with him an hundred forty and four thousand, having his Father's name written in their foreheads

Revelations 19.15-16 And out of his mouth goes a sharp sword, that with it he should smite the nations: and he shall rule them with a rod of iron: and he treads the winepress of the fierceness and wrath of Almighty God. And he hath on his vesture and on his thigh a name written, KING OF KINGS, AND LORD OF LORDS.

---

75 And because of him the angels and men rejoiced, and all the land.

76 And these things shall come to pass in their season, in the last days.

C.22 Joseph is mentioning that many things that he is predicting will come to pass in the Last Days. The Last Days is generally defined as being from the time of Christ's 1st Coming 2000 years ago unto His 2nd Coming and the final Wrath of God led by the Lamb of God in Revelation chapters14 and 19.

Revelation14.1,4-5,14-15. And I looked, and, lo, a Lamb stood on the mount Sion, and with him an hundred forty and four thousand, having his Father's name written in their foreheads.

These are they which follow the Lamb whithersoever he goes. These were redeemed from among men, being the first fruits unto God and to the Lamb.

And in their mouth was found no guile: for they are without fault before the throne of God. And I looked, and behold a white cloud, and upon the cloud one sat like unto the Son of man, having on his head a golden crown, and in his hand a sharp sickle.

And another angel came out of the temple, crying with a loud voice to him that sat on the cloud, 'Thrust in thy sickle, and reap: for the time is come for thee to reap; for the harvest of the earth is ripe'.

Revelation 19.7-9, 11-13,15-16 'Let us be glad and rejoice and give honour to him: for the marriage of the Lamb is come, and his wife hath made herself ready'.

And to her was granted that she should be arrayed in fine linen, clean and white: for the fine linen is the righteousness of saints.

And he saith unto me, 'Write, Blessed are they which are called unto the marriage supper of the Lamb. And he saith unto me, 'These are the true sayings of God'.

And I saw heaven opened and behold a white horse; and he that sat upon him was called Faithful and True, and in righteousness he doth judge and make war. His eyes were as a flame of fire, and on his head were many crowns; and he had a name written, that no man knew, but he himself. And he was clothed with a vesture dipped in blood: and his name is called The Word of God.

> 77 Do ye therefore, my children, observe the commandments of the Lord, and honour Levi and Judah; for from them shall arise unto you the Lamb of God, who taketh away the sin of the world, one who saves all the Gentiles and Israel.

John 1.29 The next day John sees Jesus coming towards him and said' Behold the Lamb of God who takes away the sins of the whole world.

John 1.36 And looking at Jesus as He walked, he said, "Behold the Lamb of God!"

C.23 In the Old Testament with the Laws of Moses, it was required to make a sacrifice of a lamb to symbolize the real Lamb of God who would take away the sins of the whole world when the Messiah arrived to give his life as a ransom for all.

Exodus 12:3 Speak to all the congregation of Israel, saying: "On the tenth of this month every man shall take for...

Exodus 12:5-6 Your lamb shall be without blemish, a male of the first year. You may take it from the sheep or from the...

Isaiah 53:7 He was oppressed and He was afflicted, Yet He opened not His mouth; He was led as a lamb to the slaughter...

Revelation 13.8 All who dwell on the earth will worship him, whose names have not been written in the Book of Life of the Lamb slain from the foundation of the world.

> 78 For His kingdom is an everlasting kingdom, which shall not pass away; but my kingdom among you shall come to an end as a watcher's hammock, which after the summer disappears.

Daniel 7.27 And the kingdom and dominion, and the greatness of the kingdom under the whole heaven shall be given to the people of the saints of the Most High whose kingdom is an everlasting kingdom, and all dominions shall serve and obey Him.

> 79 For I know that after my death the Egyptians will afflict you, but God will avenge you, and will bring you into that which He promised to your fathers.

Genesis 50.24 And Joseph said unto his brethren, I die: and God will surely visit you and bring you out of this land unto the land which he swore to Abraham, to Isaac and to Jacob.

C.24 It happened exactly as Joseph had prophesied. Jacob and his sons went down into Egypt where they were nourished by Joseph who had become the right hand of Pharoah until the original 70 souls that went down into Egypt became 3,000,000 souls by the time of Moses. God sent Moses to deliver their descendants the Israelites from their oppressors the Egyptians some 150 years after the death of Joseph and his brethren.

> 80 But ye shall carry up my bones with you; for when my bones are being taken up thither, the Lord shall be with you in light, and Beliar shall be in darkness with the Egyptians.
>
> 81 And carry ye up Asenath your mother to the Hippodrome, and near Rachel your mother bury her.
>
> 82 And when he had said these things he stretched out his feet, and died at a good old age.

Genesis 50.26 So Joseph died, being an hundred and ten years old: and they embalmed him, and he was put in a coffin in Egypt.

> 83 And all Israel mourned for him, and all Egypt, with a great mourning.

Book of Jasher 59.25-26 And it came to pass after this that Joseph did in that year, the seventy-first year of the Israelites going down to Egypt. And Joseph was one hundred and ten years old when he died in the land of Egypt, and all his brethren and his servants rose up, and they embalmed Joseph, as was their custom, and his brethren and all Egypt mourned over him for seventy days.

Genesis 50.26 So Joseph died, being an hundred and ten years old; and they embalmed him, and he was put in a coffin in Egypt.

Jubilees 46.3 And Joseph died being an hundred and ten years old; seventeen years he lived in the land of Canaan, and ten years he was a servant, and three years he was in prison, and eighty years he was under the king, ruling all of the land of Egypt.

> 84 And when the children of Israel went out of Egypt, they took with them the bones of Joseph, and they buried him in Hebron with his fathers, and the years of his life were one hundred and ten years.

Genesis 50.25 And Joseph took an oath of the children of Israel, saying God will surely visit you, and you shall carry up my bones from hence.

Jubilees 46.6 And he made them swore concerning his bones, for he knew that the Egyptians would not bring him forth.

THE TESTAMENT OF BENJAMIN

The Twelfth Son of Jacob and Rachel.

CHAP. I.

THE copy of the words of Benjamin, which he commanded his sons to observe, after he had lived a hundred and twenty-five years.

2 And he kissed them and said: As Isaac was born to Abraham in his old age, so also was I to Jacob.

3 And since Rachel my mother died in giving me birth, I had no milk; therefore, I was suckled by Bilhah her handmaid.

4 For Rachel remained barren for twelve years after she had borne Joseph; and she prayed the Lord with fasting twelve days, and she conceived and bare Me.

C.1 A new detail was that there was a gap of 12 years between the birth of Joseph and the birth of Benjamin. Why did God allow this gap in time? It is interesting that it states that Rachel also fasted for 12 days, and then conceived. Jacob also ended up with a total of 12 sons. They were also of the 12 different star signs and months of the year. It was stated by Jacob that he and Leah were like the sun and the moon and their 12 sons as the stars of the ZodiaC. The number 12 is a special biblical number. 12 Patriarchs. 12 Apostles of Jesus the Messiah. In fact the number is so important to God that the New Jerusalem has a foundation wall which had 12 foundations, and 12 Gates, and 12 angels at those gates. The 12 foundation stones are named after the 12 apostles of Jesus and the 12 pearly gates have the names of the 12 Patriarchs written on them. Jesus was 12 years old when he was talking with the wise men in the temple, and they were amazed at his knowledge and wisdom at so young an age.

Luke 2.41-42,46-47 Now his parents went to Jerusalem every year at the feast of the Passover.

[42] And when he was **twelve** years old, they went up to Jerusalem after the custom of the feast. [46] And it came to pass, that after three days they found him in the temple, sitting in the midst of the doctors, both hearing them, and asking them questions.

[47] And all that heard him were astonished at his understanding and answers.

C.2 Why am I mentioning the above biblical numerology? Because things that happen are not merely rdkandom or coincidence, but everything that is to happen is thoroughly planned by God in advance including numbers. Bible numerology proves there are absolutes: * See 'There are Absolutes':

5 For my father loved Rachel dearly and prayed that he might see two sons born from her.

> 6 Therefore was I called Benjamin, that is, a son of days.

C.3 Why was Benjamin called the 'son of days'. This probably means that Benjamin was the son of Jacob's old age.

> 7 And when I went into Egypt, to Joseph, and my brother recognized me, he said unto me: What did they tell my father when they sold me?
>
> 8 And I said unto him, 'They dabbled thy coat with blood and sent it and said: Know whether this be thy son's coat.'

Genesis 37.31-34 And they took Joseph's coat, and killed a kid of the goats, and dipped the coat in the blood;

[32] And they sent the coat of many colours, and they brought it to their father; and said, This have we found: know now whether it be thy son's coat or no.

[33] And he knew it, and said, It is my son's coat; an evil beast hath devoured him; Joseph is without doubt rent in pieces.

[34] And Jacob rent his clothes, and put sackcloth upon his loins, and mourned for his son many days.

> 9 And he said unto me: Even so, brother, when they had stripped me of my coat they gave me to the Ishmaelites, and they gave me a loin cloth, and scourged me, and bade me run.

Genesis 37.27 Come, and let us sell him to the Ishmaelites, and let not our hand be upon him; for he is our brother and our flesh. And his brethren were content.

> 10 And as for one of them that had beaten me with a rod, a lion met him and slew him.
>
> 11 And so his associates were affrighted.
>
> 12 Do ye also, therefore, my children, love the Lord God of heaven and earth, and keep His commandments, following the example of the good and holy man Joseph.
>
> 13 And let your mind be unto good, even as ye know me; for he that hath his mind right sees all things rightly.
>
> 14 Fear ye the Lord and love your neighbour; and even though the spirits of Beliar claim you to afflict you with every evil, yet shall they not

> have dominion over you, even as they had not over Joseph my brother.
>
> 15 How many men wished to slay him, and God shielded him!
>
> 16 For he that fears God and loveth his neighbour cannot be smitten by the spirit of Beliar, being shielded by the fear of God.

C.4 This is indeed the whole essence of the commandments given by God to Moses in the Old Testament and through Jesus in the New Testament. To love God and your neighbour as yourself.

Deuteronomy 6.5 "And thou shalt love the LORD thy God with all thine heart, and with all thy soul, and with all thy might."

Leviticus 19.17b 'Thou shall love your neighbour as yourself': I am the LORD.

Matthew 22.36-39 Master, which is the great commandment in the law? Jesus said unto him, thou shalt love the Lord thy God with all thy heart, and with all thy soul, and with all thy mind. This is the first and great commandment. And the second is like unto it, thou shalt love thy neighbour as thyself. On these two commandments hang all the law and the prophets.

> 17 Nor can he be ruled over by the device of men or beasts, for he is helped by the Lord
>
> through the love which he hath towards his neighbour.
>
> 18 For Joseph also besought our father that he would pray for his brethren, that the Lord would not impute to them as sin whatever evil they had done unto him.
>
> 19 And thus Jacob cried out: My good child, thou hast prevailed over the bowels of thy father Jacob.

C.5 What exactly does Jacob mean by *'thou hast prevailed over the bowels of thy father Jacob'*? In modern lingo, it does not sound right, as today bowels means intestines. In the New Testament there is an unsavoury story of a wicked person who fell and it states and all his bowels gushed out. Jacob is obviously not talking about physical bowels, so what is he talking about?

Colossians 3:12 Put on therefore, as the elect of God, holy and beloved, bowels of mercies, kindness, humbleness of mind, meekness, longsuffering.

Genesis 43:30 "And Joseph made haste; for his bowels did yearn upon his brother

C.6 It is said that 'The seat of the spirit is in the belly': For more on this topic:

Jeremiah 4:19 "[The LORD says] My bowels, my bowels! I am pained at my very heart; my heart makes a noise in me;"

Lamentations 1:20 "Behold, O LORD; for I am in distress: my bowels are troubled"

C.7 In conclusion concerning 'bowels of mercies' it is talking about spiritual emotions rather than talking about the physical bowels.

John 7.38 He that believes on Me as the scripture hath said out of his belly shall flow rivers of living waters

> 20 And he embraced him, and kissed him for two hours, saying:

C.8 This last verse is talking about Jacob meeting his long lost son Joseph after 20 sad lonely years. Jacob then prophesies over his son Joseph:

C.9 Jacob is explaining that his long-lost son Joseph being the most obedient of his sons in spite of great affliction, imprisonment, privation, great temptations, persecution and immense difficulty still stayed true to God and to his father and therefore Jacob compares him to the Christ or the Messiah that was to come.

> 21 In thee shall be fulfilled the prophecy of heaven concerning the Lamb of God, and Saviour of the world, and that a blameless one shall be delivered up for lawless men, and a sinless one shall die for ungodly men in the blood of the covenant, for the salvation of the Gentiles and of Israel, and shall destroy Beliar and his servants.

C.10 What an amazing prophecy given by Jacob when he met his long lost son Joseph whom he hadn't seen for 20 years and he both embraced him and wept for him he thought was dead, and his emotions spilled out to such a degree that he received an amazing prophecy, which is backed up by the book of Isaiah the prophet in the Old Testament and also by the New Testament. Here is another similar prophecy about Jesus the Messiah.

C.11 Jacob was also saying that without Joseph the future of the budding nation of Israel and the resultant coming of the Messiah never would have happened.

Isaiah 53.3-5 He is despised and rejected of men; a man of sorrows and acquainted with grief: and we hid as it were our faces from him; he was despised, and we esteemed him not. Surely, he hath borne our griefs, and carried our sorrows: yet we did esteem him stricken, smitten of God, and afflicted. But he was wounded for our transgressions, he was bruised for our iniquities: the chastisement of our peace was upon him; and with his stripes we are healed.

Isaiah 49:6 "And he said, It is a light thing that thou shouldest be my servant to raise up the tribes of Jacob, and to restore the preserved of Israel: I will also give thee for a light to the Gentiles, that thou mayest be my salvation unto the end of the earth."

Isaiah 62:1-4 For Zion's sake will I not hold my peace, and for Jerusalem's sake I will not rest, until the righteousness thereof go forth as brightness, and the salvation thereof as a lamp that burns. And the Gentiles shall see thy righteousness, and all kings thy glory: and thou shalt be called by a new name, which the mouth of the LORD shall name. Thou shalt also be a crown of glory in the hand of the LORD, and a royal diadem in the hand of thy God. Thou shalt no more be termed Forsaken; neither shall thy land any more be termed Desolate: but thou shalt be called Hephzi-bah, and thy land Beulah: for the LORD delights in thee, and thy land shall be married. Hephzi-bah: that is, My delight is in her.

John 1.29 The next day John sees Jesus coming unto him, and saith, Behold the Lamb of God, which taketh away the sin of the world.

1 John 4:14 - And we have seen and do testify that the Father sent the Son to be the Saviour of the world.

Luke 1.47 "And my spirit hath rejoiced in God my Saviour."

1 John 2.2 And he is the propitiation for our sins: and not for ours only, but also for the sins of the whole world.

Romans 5.8,12 But God commended his love toward us, in that, while we were yet sinners, Christ died for us. "Wherefore, as by one man sin entered into the world, and death by sin; and so death passed upon all men, for that all have sinned:"

Revelation 20.10 And the Devil (Beliar) that deceived them was cast into the lake of fire and brimstone, where the beast and the false prophet are, and shall be tormented day and night for ever and ever.

---

22 See ye, therefore, my children, the end of the good man?

23 Be followers of his compassion, therefore, with a good mind, that ye also may wear crowns of glory.

Isaiah 62.3 Thou shalt also be a crown of glory in the hand of the LORD, and a royal diadem in the hand of thy God.

---

24 For the good man hath not a dark eye; for he shows mercy to all men, even though they be sinners.

25 And though they devise with evil intent. concerning him, by doing good he overcomes evil, being shielded by God; and he loveth the righteous as his own soul.

---

26 If anyone is glorified, he envies him not; if anyone is enriched, he is not jealous; if anyone is valiant, he praises him; the virtuous man he lauds; on the poor man he hath mercy; on the weak he hath compassion; unto God he sings praises.

27 And him that hath the grace of a good spirit he loveth as his own soul.

28 If therefore, ye also have a good mind, then will both wicked men be at peace with you, and the profligate will reverence you and turn unto good; and the covetous will not only cease from their inordinate desire, but even give the objects of their covetousness to them that are afflicted.

Proverbs 16.7 When a man's ways please the Lord, he makes even his enemies to be at peace with him.

C.12 Benjamin is stating that if you are strong in God's Word and obey Him and his commandments, then others will not harm you, but by your good example will be encouraged to do good, and even change their ways.

C.13 In more modern lingo: It pays to be good to others as you never know how far that good influence will go. How does one learn to be kind, loving and humble and to have all the fruits of the Spirit of God? Only, by spending time daily with the Lord in prayer and meditating upon his word.

Galatians 5.22-23 For the fruit of the spirit is love, joy, peace, longsuffering, gentleness, goodness, faith, meekness, temperance, against such there is no law.

29 If ye do well, even the unclean spirits will flee from you; and the beasts will dread you.

Isaiah 59.19 When the enemy shall come in like a flood. The Spirit of the Lord shall raise up a standard against him.

30 For where there is reverence for good works and light in the mind, even darkness flees away from him.

31 For if anyone does violence to a holy man, he repents; for the holy man is merciful to his reviler and holds his peace.

32 And if anyone betrays a righteous man, the righteous man prays: though for a little he be humbled, yet not long after he appears far more glorious, as was Joseph my brother.

> 33 The inclination of the good man is not in the power of the deceit of the spirit of Beliar (Satan), for the angel of peace guides his soul.

John 14.27 "Peace I leave with you, my peace I give unto you: not as the world giveth, give I unto you. Let not your heart be troubled, neither let it be afraid.

> 34 And he gazes not passionately upon corruptible things, nor gathers together riches through a desire of pleasure.
>
> 35 He delights not in pleasure, he grieves not his neighbour, he satiates not himself with luxuries, he errs not in the uplifting of the eyes, for the Lord is his portion.

1 John 2.15 Love not the world nor the things that are in the world. If any man love the world, the love of the Father is not in him.

Luke 16.33 No man can serve two masters. For either he will love the one and hate the other, or else he will hold to the one and despise the other. You cannot serve both God and Mammon (material world)

> 36 The good inclination receives not glory nor dishonour from men, and it knows not any guile, or lie, or fighting or reviling; for the Lord dwelleth in him and lights up his soul, and he rejoices towards all men always.

C.14 Positive thinking. Here is an early discourse on being positive, and on not being deceptive for the sake of gain. Notice that the love of money often brings fighting and contention. As it is said today 'The love of money is the root of all evil' but the Lord lights up the soul of the one who is truly dedicated to both Him and His Word.

> 37 The good mind hath not two tongues, of blessing and of cursing, of contumely and of honour, of sorrow and of joy, of quietness and of confusion, of hypocrisy and of truth, of poverty and of wealth; but it hath one disposition, incorrupt and pure, concerning all men.

C.15 Definition of the archaic word: 'contumely': - insolent or insulting language or treatment.

> 38 It hath no double sight, nor double hearing; for in everything which he doeth, or speaks, or sees he knows that the Lord looks on his soul.

James 1.8 A double-minded man is unstable in all of his ways.

39 And he cleanses his mind that he may not be condemned by men as well as by God.

40 And in like manner the works of Beliar are twofold, and there is no singleness in them.

41 Therefore, my children, I tell you, flee the malice of Beliar; for he giveth a sword to them that obey him.

42 And the sword is the mother of seven evils. First the mind conceives through Beliar, and first there is bloodshed; secondly ruin; thirdly, tribulation; fourthly, exile; fifthly, dearth; sixthly, panic; seventhly, destruction.

43 'Therefore was Cain also delivered over to seven vengeances by God, for in every hundred years the Lord brought one plague upon him.

C.16 New information about Cain and the 7 vengeances of God. See below for more information.

44 And when he was two hundred years old he began to suffer, and in the nine-hundredth year he was destroyed.

45 For on account of Abel, his brother, with - all the evils was he judged, but Lamech with seventy times seven.

C.17 Read my book Eden Insights which is based on 'The Lost Books of Adam and Eve', as it clearly shows these 70 x 7 curses which came upon mankind through the sons and daughters of 'Lamech the Blind'. This was a much earlier Lamech than the father of Noah. The first Lamech was the great great-grandson of Cain.

C.18 Lamech killed Cain his relative by accident, thinking that he was an animal whilst out hunting with his young son Tubal Cain. Lamech was having problems with his eyesight and the last thing that he should have been doing was shooting a bow. Something was bound to go wrong, and it did.

C.19 It was as though Lamech in killing Cain inherited all the evil of Cain's spirit upon his household and it was his sons and daughters that led mankind totally away from God and faith in Him. Lamech's household was indeed cursed 7- fold or even 70 x 7- fold in his descendants.

C.20 Lamech's son Jubal, who was the inventor of many musical instruments, was said to have been possessed by Satan from a very young age according to the Lost Books of Adam and Eve - book 2.

C.21 His brother Jabal, was the inventor of all kinds of weapons for killing mankind. Between those two brothers the world descended into anarchy, drunkenness, lawlessness like unto Sodom and Gomorrah.

> 46 Because for ever those, who are like Cain in envy and hatred of brethren, shall be punished with the same judgement.

CHAP. II.

AND do ye, my children, flee evil-doing, envy, and hatred of brethren and cleave to goodness and love.

2 He that hath a pure mind in love, looks not after a woman with a view to fornication; for he hath no defilement in his heart, because the Spirit of God rests upon him.

C.1 You might wonder why the Patriarchs keep hammering the point home about not lusting after women when most people go about their work in modern times too busy to think about such things so why the seeming fuss? First of all, he is talking to a young audience and perhaps back then often the young people did not see the opposite sex very often. Under those circumstances teenagers can go wild when they do meet young women. The more restrictive the society, the more likely going hog wild is likely to happen especially when young through lack of experience.

3 For as the sun is not defiled by shining on dung and mire, but rather dries up both and drives away the evil smell; so, also the pure mind, though encompassed by the defilements of earth, rather cleanses them and is not itself defiled

C.2 A very different way at looking at things in the time of the Patriarchs, or in comparing to natural events that happen around people if they are observant. Of course, the Patriarchs did take care of cattle. In modern times most people don't generally live in the country and probably do not see cattle all the time or ever work with them. Another thing is that in modern times people in general are offended by unsavoury comparisons and would find this last verse to be exactly that - and yet it is in reality actually a good comparison between good and evil.

Conclusion: the evil dung is dried up by the good sunshine, but the sun is no worse off for doing so. Even so a righteous person does not get besmirched by the evil world all around him because God protects him from the world.

4 And I believe that there will be also evildoings among you, from the words of Enoch the righteous: that ye shall commit fornication with the fornication of Sodom, and shall perish, all save a few, and shall renew wanton deeds with women; and the kingdom of the Lord shall not be among you, for straightway He shall take it away.

C.3 What was the **Book of Enoch** talking about? It mentioned not just the Fallen angels but also about the '**fallen** human women' of the daughters of Cain, who were known as the licentious daughters of Cain. How did the whole house of Cain become evil? It started with Cain going astray and being in direct rebellion against God.

C.4 Benjamin is stating that the nation of Israel that would descend from him and his 11 brethren would become like the descendants of Cain or as Sodom and Gomorrah. A nation ready to be destroyed. [See my book **Eden Insights & Enoch Insights**]

> 5 Nevertheless the temple of God shall be in your portion, and the last temple shall be more glorious than the first.

C.5 In summary of all the following points about man's temples verses God's temple: The first temple represents the temples of man and that which is of the flesh and worldly. The last temple is talking about Christ the Messiah. The connection between the physical and the spiritual is shown so well by Jesus in his dissertation to the Pharisees, when he said while standing in front of their fancy temple in Jerusalem:

John 2.19-21 "Jesus answered and said unto them, "Destroy this temple, and in three days I will raise it up." "Then said the Jews, Forty and six years was this temple in building, and wilt thou rear it up in three days?" "But he spake of the temple of his body."

C.6 Jesus made this point to the Jewish leaders, to try and show them that physical temples were of little value. What was valuable, was knowing the Messiah and being saved by believing in Him.

John 3.36 He that believes on the Son has everlasting life and he that believes not on Him shall not see life, but the wrath of God abides on him.

C.7 What is the point of building religious temples of any religion if you are not saved and not going to heaven? Most temples are idols in the sight of God and will be destroyed in the 'Wrath of God' when all of man's cities are totally destroyed along with all of his idols such as the temples of man.

Revelation 16.13 And the great city (Jerusalem) was divided into three parts, and the cities of the nations fell: and great Babylon came in remembrance before God, to give unto her the wine of the fierceness of his wrath.

C.8 The 1st temple built in Jerusalem in Israel, was the temple of Solomon, which was built around 1000 BC. This 1st temple was destroyed by king Nebuchadnezzar and the Babylonian world empire around 589 BC.

C.9 The 2nd temple was built in the 5th century BC in the time of Ezra and Nehemiah under Artaxerxes the emperor of the Medio-Persian world empire. The 2nd temple was totally destroyed by the Romans in 70 AD.

C.10 The 3rd temple, it is prophesied, that it will be built in the time of the coming Anti-Christ.

*Revelation 11:8 And their dead bodies (The 2 End-time prophets) shall lie in the street of the great city (**Jerusalem**), which spiritually is called **Sodom** and **Egypt**, where also our Lord was crucified.

C.11 There is a very large temple, and its magnificence is described in the book of Ezekiel. Where does that vision fit in the picture of the 3rd temple?

C.12 The famous and 'yet to be-build' 3rd physical temple is mentioned in the Book of Revelation chapter 11, as being under siege by the Anti-Christ world government – the 7th world empire of man and the last one.

C.13 The Jews state that the 3rd Temple can only be built when the Messiah arrives or in the time of the Messiah. Since they have already rejected the true Messiah – Jesus, when the Anti-Christ comes on the scene, they will flock to him. Eventually they will realize to their absolute horror, that he is a false Messiah, and Great Tribulation will follow for 3 and a half years according to both the book of Daniel and the book of Revelation. A time when the False Christ or Anti-Christ will seek to destroy all religions except for the worship of himself as he will state that he is god.

C.14 The Anti-Christ will set up an Image of himself in the newly soon to be build 3 Temple in Jerusalem known in Revelation chapter 13 as The Image of the Beast. He will set out to brand every human-being with a 'mark' in their hands or their foreheads. All the world will be seemingly forced to bow down and worship this Image of the Beast. It is now becoming apparent that transhumanism has a lot to do with this future technology of the Beast.

> 6 And the twelve tribes shall be gathered together there, and all the Gentiles, until the Most High shall send forth His salvation in the visitation of an only-begotten prophet.

C.15 Who is the Patriarch talking about in this verse? It sounds like the Messiah at the 2nd Coming and his rescuing all of his people - the saints of the Most High, but why does the Patriarch Benjamin call him: only-begotten prophet and not Son?

C.16 The key is the word 'only-begotten'. The Greek term translated "only begotten" is *monogenes*, a word used nine times in the New Testament that can mean one of a kind or unique. For example, Luke uses the term three times to refer to an only child (Luke 7:12; 8:42; 9:38). The writer of Hebrews uses the term to refer to Isaac, the only son of Abraham and Sarah, the son of the promise (Hebrews 11:17). Modern translations generally translate *monogenes* in John 3:16 as «one and only Son» or «only Son» to reflect this definition. **SOURCE**: What does 'only begotten Son' mean? How is Jesus God's only begotten Son? (compellingtruth.org)

Definition: Only begotten Son of God - born of a woman, unique because Jesus was born of a woman but did not have a physical father but God was His Father.

C.17 Was Jesus a prophet? Yes, he certainly was, and he prophesied that their temple would be destroyed because of the Jews rejection of Him the Only begotten Son. The temple *was* totally destroyed some 40 years after the Jews crucified their own Messiah.

251

> 7 And He shall enter into the first temple, and there shall the Lord be treated with outrage, and He shall be lifted up upon a tree.

C.18 Was Jesus lifted up upon a tree? He was crucified upon a wooden cross which by definition came from a tree.

C.19 By the time of the birth of Christ, the 2nd physical Temple was the one in existence, so if this book had been written by the Pharisees in 100 BC they would have certainly have corrected the last verse about it being the 1st temple.

C.20 Alternatively, if the last verse was added in Christian times, it certainly was done very clumsily, which does not make any sense at all.

C.21 What if the last verse about the 1st temple was originally written by Benjamin? Why did he state the 1st temple and not the 2nd which was rebuilt in 5th century BC? Is it just possible that the 1st temple being the original one, was the origin of the Jewish nation as to holy temples. This temple was destroyed by their enemies around 589 BC and was rebuilt in 520 BC Perhaps in the eyes of God, Israel was just rebuilding the 1st temple.

C.22 The 1st temple being a physical temple. The 2ND temple must be a spiritual one.

'For I shall soon put off this physical tabernacle'.

2 Corinthians 5.1 'For we know that if our earthly house of *this* tabernacle were dissolved, we have a building of God, an house not made with hands, eternal in the heavens."

1 Corinthians 3:16-18 Know ye not that ye are the temple of God, and that the Spirit of God dwelleth in you? If any man defile the temple of God, him shall God destroy; for the temple of God is holy, which temple ye are.

BIBLE VERSES ABOUT YOUR BODY IS A TEMPLE (kingjamesbibleonline.org)

C.23 TEMPLE: definition from verses in the KJV of the Bible: "First used of the tabernacle, which is called "the temple of the" "Lord" (1 Sam. 1:9). In the New Testament the word is used" "figuratively of **Christ's human body** (John 2:19, 21). Believers" "are called "the temple of God"** (1 Cor. 3:16, 17). The Church is" "designated "an holy temple in the Lord" (Eph. 2:21). Heaven is" also called a temple (Rev. 7:5). We read also of the heathen temple of the great goddess Diana (Acts 19:27). "This word is generally used in Scripture of the sacred house erected on the summit of Mount Moriah for the worship of God. It "is called "the temple" (1 Kings 6:17); "the temple [R.V.," "'house'] of the Lord" (2 Kings 11:10); "thy holy temple" (Ps." "79:1); "the house of the Lord" (2 Chr. 23:5, 12); "the house of" "the God of Jacob" (Isa. 2:3); "the house of my glory" (60:7); an" "house of prayer (56:7; Matt. 21:13); "an house of sacrifice" "(2 Chr. 7:12); "the house of their sanctuary" (2 Chr. 36:17);" "the mountain of the Lord's house (Isa. 2:2); "our holy and our" "beautiful house" (64:11); "the holy mount" (27:13); "the palace" "for the Lord God" (1 Chr. 29:1); "the tabernacle of witness" (2" "Chr. 24:6); "Zion" (Ps. 74:2;

84:7). Christ calls it "my" "Father's house" (John 2:16).": TEMPLE (kingjames-bibleonline.org)

C.24 I would also mention that the scriptures clearly state that God simply does not abide in temples built by man! A house of cement sand stones and wood is not a temple of God or a house of the Lord. Jesus even made a point of driving the moneychangers out of the temple in Jerusalem with a whip. Why? Because of the corruption of the rich merchants turning the temple into an unholy place of mammon worship instead of the worship of God.

John 2.13-17 And the Jews' Passover was at hand, and Jesus went up to Jerusalem. And found in the temple those that sold oxen and sheep and doves, and the changers of money sitting: And when he had made a scourge of small cords, he drove them all out of the temple, and the sheep, and the oxen; and poured out the changers' money, and overthrew the tables; And said unto them that sold doves, Take these things hence; make not my Father's house an house of merchandise. And his disciples remembered that it was written, The zeal of thine house hath eaten me up.

C.25 The *zeal of thine house hath eaten me up'* is also mentioned in the Psalms - prophesising about the Messiah. What does this verse about Jesus the Messiah actually mean? It means that Jesus was very angry when he saw that those who claimed to be religious, were in practice, a bunch of hypocrites who were making money inside God's Temple, instead of using it for its correct purpose of 'dedication to God'. So, in his zeal for God and righteousness, he whipped the hypocrites out of the temple.

Ps 69.9 "For the zeal of thine house hath eaten me up; and the reproaches of them that reproached thee are fallen upon me."

Acts 7:47-49: But Solomon built Him a house. However, the Most High does not dwell in temples made with hands, as the prophet says, Heaven is my throne, and earth is my footstool: what house will build for Me? says the Lord: or what is the place of My rest?

C.26 In the famous book 'Within the Gates' which was about Heaven, by Rebecca Springer and written around 1900: she talks about her going on a long spirit trip or Life After Death experience whilst she was very sick in hospital. One of the things that she mentioned was that she was shocked to see that there were no temples in heaven.

Revelation 21.22 And I saw no temple therein for the Lord God almighty and the Lamb are the temple of it.

C.27 Perhaps the Patriarch was only given the information by God about Christ coming during the **1ˢᵗ Temple** because the **1ˢᵗ temple represented man** and his **false religions,** which would all soon crumble and fall. The true temple came with Jesus Christ, not as a building or religion, but as a holy and **spiritual house.**

---

8 And the veil of the temple shall be rent, and the Spirit of God shall pass on to the Gentiles as fire poured forth.

C.28 '*Spirit of God shall pass onto the Gentiles as fire poured forth.*' This is clearly talking about what happened in the **Book of Acts** when the 'fire' of the '**Holy Spirit**' came upon the gentiles and they also became powerful witnesses of the Christ as their Jewish brethren the apostles.

C.29 The 'veil of the temple' in Jerusalem was rent by God Himself, to show everyone that the Ark or the Shekinah Glory had departed from the Holy of Holies and been taken up to heaven. Israel murdered their own Messiah Jesus and as a result their whole religion was destroyed in 70 AD and most of the people slaughtered by the Romans just 40 years after they had crucified their own Saviour, as predicted by the Patriarchs including Benjamin.

C.30 The 'Shekinah Glory'. It appears that according to Jewish teachings that the Spirit of prophecy left Israel in the time of the last minor prophet Malachi around 390 BC [Note: The life of the prophet Malachi is an important turning point in Jewish history, as it marks the close of the glorious era of Jewish prophecy. The Talmud teaches, "After the last prophets Chaggai, Zechariah, and Malachi died, the Divine Spirit of prophetic revelation departed from the Jewish people."]

> 9 And He shall ascend from Hades and shall pass from earth into heaven.

Matthew 12.40 For as Jonah was 3 days and nights in the heart of the whale so the Son of man shall be three days and nights in the heart of the earth (Hades)

1 Peter 3:18-20 [18]For Christ also hath once suffered for sins, the just for the unjust, that he might bring us to God, being put to death in the flesh, but quickened by the Spirit: [19]By which also he went and preached unto the spirits in prison; [20]Which sometime were disobedient, when once the longsuffering of God waited in the days of Noah, while the ark was a preparing, wherein few, that is, eight souls were saved by water.

> 10 And I know how lowly He shall be upon earth, and how glorious in heaven.

C.31 Fulfilled prophecy in both the Old Testament and then the New Testament.

Zechariah 9.9 Rejoice greatly, O daughter of Zion; shout, O daughter of Jerusalem: behold, thy King cometh unto thee: he *is* just, and having salvation; lowly, and riding upon an ass, and upon a colt the foal of an ass.

Matthew 21.5 Say to the Daughter of Zion, 'See, your King comes to you, gentle and riding on a donkey, on a colt, the foal of a donkey.'" *

C.32 Meaning that Jesus rode on the mother animal and sometimes on the colt or otherwise known as the foal of that donkey, so the mother donkey would not get too tired. The colt was probably almost an adult or grown up.

11 Now when Joseph was in Egypt, I longed to see his figure and the form of his countenance; and through the prayers of Jacob my father I saw him, while awake in the daytime, even his entire figure exactly as he was.

C.33 The patriarch Benjamin had the gift of visions and could see Joseph his older brother and having the same mother as himself -Rachel. He could see his long lost brother Joseph over there in Egypt as he now was fully grown up. When Benjamin went down to Egypt he would have been the only one who recognized Joseph, but Joseph told him to remain quiet, according to the Book of Jasher about this until he could 'test' his brothers.

12 And when he had said these things, he said unto them: Know ye, therefore, my children, that I am dying.

13 Do ye, therefore, truth each one to his neighbour, and keep the law of the Lord and His commandments.

14 For these things do I leave you instead of inheritance.

C.34 Notice how this world counts the value of a man in the wealth he has accumulated in his lifetime which is a very poor way to judge a person and certainly not God's way. That is because this physical world has been usurped by Satan and his demons like Pan and Mammon so that people worship not God in general but the mind of man and money.

C.35 In contrast to the above-mentioned thoughts of man, Benjamin in his wisdom states to his sons and descendants, that the most important thing that he can bequeath to them is God's Word, His Truth and Commandments.

15 Do ye also, therefore, give them to your children for an everlasting possession; for so did both Abraham, and Isaac, and Jacob.

16 For all these things they gave us for an inheritance, saying: Keep the commandments of God, until the Lord shall reveal His salvation to all Gentiles.

C.36 It is interesting how many times that the Patriarchs mention the Lord bringing Salvation to the Gentiles.

Isaiah 49.6 "And he said, It is a light thing that thou shouldest be my servant to raise up the tribes of Jacob, and to restore the preserved of Israel: I will also give thee for a light to the <u>Gentiles</u>, that thou mayest be my salvation unto the end of the earth."

17 And then shall ye see Enoch, Noah, and Shem, and Abraham, and

> Isaac, and Jacob, rising on the right hand in gladness,
>
> 18 Then shall we also rise, each one over our tribe, worshipping the King of heaven, who appeared upon earth in the form of a man in humility.

C.37 Here again it is clearly showing the coming of the Messiah and all the great men of the Bible rising up in the resurrection in great joy to meet their Saviour the King of Kings.

> 19 And as many as believe on Him on the earth shall rejoice with Him.

John 3.36 He that believes on the Son has everlasting life and he that believes not the Son shall not see life, but the wrath of God abides on him.

> 20 Then also all men shall rise, some unto glory and some unto shame.

Daniel 12.3 And they that be wise shall shine as the brightness of the firmament, and they that instruct many as the stars forever.

Daniel 12.2 And many of them that sleep in the dust of the earth shall awake, some to everlasting life, and some to shame and everlasting contempt.

> 21 And the Lord shall judge Israel first, for their unrighteousness; for when He appeared as God in the flesh to deliver them they believed Him not.

Ezekiel 18.30 "Therefore I will judge you, O house of Israel, everyone according to his ways, saith the Lord GOD. Repent, and turn *yourselves* from all your transgressions; so, iniquity shall not be your ruin."

> 22 And then shall He judge all the Gentiles, as many as believed Him not when He appeared upon earth.

Ecclesiastes 3.17 "I said in mine heart, God shall judge the righteous and the wicked: for *there is* a time there for every purpose and for every work."

> 23 And He shall convict Israel through the chosen ones of the Gentiles, even as He reproved Esau through the Midianites, who deceived their brethren, so that they fell into fornication, and idolatry; and they were alienated from God, becoming therefore children in the portion of them that fear the Lord.

C.38 This could be have been talking about Jesus' *'chosen ones of the Gentiles'* serving him as disciples, but it did not happen in Jesus time as he personally mostly witnessed only to the lost sheep of the house of Israel. It was his disciples and in particular Paul the apostle who first reached the Gentiles and then Peter.

C.39 The verse above seems to have been altered. Instead of the preposition 'of', it should say 'to' in order to make any sense. This last verse in talking about *'He shall convict Israel through the chosen ones (to) the Gentiles'* could be talking about someone like the apostle Paul who was certainly Jewish and had been a Pharisee but he became very dedicated to the cause of Christ the Saviour, to the point that he spent most of his time preaching unto the Gentiles and I suppose that the Gentiles (non-Jewish) peoples felt that Paul was one of them because he reached more of the Gentiles in preaching the Gospel of Jesus Christ than did all the other apostles. Well, at least in his day he certainly evangelized a lot of the Roman world. Paul won many Gentiles including the governor of Cyprus who used his position and influence to allow the apostles to more freely preach the Gospel to the whole island. This is why Cyprus become of the first Christian nation howbeit a relatively small island.

C.40 The history of the 300 years of the decline of Israel prior to the birth of Christ from the book of Malachi unto the Pharisees and Sadducees. Were the Maccabee brothers as described in the Apocryphal book called Maccabees really working for God, or were they in fact Israel rebelling against their enemies at a time when God had departed from Israel? Jesus came to earth when Israel's capital is described as 'Sodom and Egypt'.

Revelation 11.8 "And their dead bodies *shall lie* in the street of the great city (**Jerusalem**), which spiritually is called Sodom and Egypt, where also our Lord was crucified."

Acts 9.15 "But the Lord said unto him, Go thy way: for he is a chosen vessel unto me, to bear my name before the Gentiles, and kings, and the children of Israel:"

> 24 If ye therefore, my children, walk in holiness according to the commandments of the Lord, ye shall again dwell securely with me, and all Israel shall be gathered unto the Lord.
>
> 25 And I shall no longer be called a ravening wolf on account of your ravages, but a worker of the Lord distributing food to them that work what is good.

C.41 It sounds like Benjamin is prophesying that the tribe of Benjamin which would descend from him, would get into a lot of trouble and be called a 'ravening wolf'. He is also prophesying that Benjamin will turn good again. Did this happen in history? Yes, it did happen. At one time in history, the whole tribe of Benjamin was almost completely destroyed by the other tribes, because of its vicious nature as shown in the Bible.

Judges 20.48 And the men of Israel turned again upon the children of Benjamin, and smote them with the edge of the sword as well as the men of every city as the beast, and all that came to hand: and they set fire to all the cities that they came to.

C.42 Why were the Benjaminites destroyed? Read Judges 19 for the horrific and graphic story. They were as Sodom.

C.43 The men of Israel after obliterating the whole tribe of Benjamin except for 600 young men who had escaped, suddenly realised that it was not good if the whole tribe of Benjamin was destroyed:

Judges 21.17 "And they said, '*There must be* an inheritance for them that be escaped of Benjamin', that a tribe be not destroyed out of Israel."

---

26 And there shall arise in the latter days one beloved of the Lord, of the tribe of Judah and Levi, a doer of His good pleasure in his mouth, with new knowledge enlightening the Gentiles.

C.44 Here again Benjamin is clearly prophesying about the Messiah.

---

27 Until the consummation of the age shall he be in the synagogues of the Gentiles, and among their rulers, as a strain of music in the mouth of all.

28 And he shall be inscribed in the holy books, both his work and his word, and he shall be a chosen one of God for ever.

C.45 Has this proven to be true? Absolutely! Jesus the Saviour and Messiah is the Word of God and the Creator of the world and the universe. More books have been written about Him than anyone in history and that is as it should be.

C.46 Why does the verse state with 'And through them' Who is this talking about?

---

29 And through them he shall go to and fro as Jacob my father, saying: He shall fill up that which lacks of thy tribe. Is it talking about the heavily depleted tribe of Benjamin or is it talking in general about Israel?

C.47 God certainly had hoped that the Jews would be a special people unto God who would tell the nations about his laws in the Old Testament times and to give his words of Salvation about Jesus the Messiah in the New Testament times. It is a fact that all the prophets of God were Jewish, as were all of the early disciples of Jesus Himself.

C.48 I take my hat off to all the believing Jews and the prophets and the disciples of Jesus for their dedication to God and His word, as well as the thousands of faithful scribes who wrote down the law and the Word of God and His truth. Without all of them along with the Jewish prophets, we all never would have found Salvation in Jesus Christ or as in Hebrew, Yeshua.*

Yeshua Hamashiach means "Jesus the Messiah." The name *Jesus* is the Greek form of the Hebrew name *Yeshua*, which is the shortened form of the name *Yehoshua*. From this Hebrew word we also get the name *Joshua* (Joshua 5:15) or *Hoshea* (Numbers 13:8; Deuteronomy 32:44). The name means "salvation" and is found more than often throughout the Old Testament. This is the name from which we get the Greek word *Iesous*, pronounced "yay-sus," or as we say it, "Jesus." - Is Yeshua Hamashiach the proper Hebrew name/title for Jesus Christ? | GotQuestions.org

---

30 And when he had said these things he stretched out his feet.

31 And died in a beautiful and good sleep.

32 And his sons did as he had enjoined them, and they took up his body and buried it in Hebron with his fathers.

33 And the number of the days of his life was a hundred and twenty-five years.

THE END OF THE TESTAMENTS OF THE TWELVE PATRIARCHS

SALVATION

Finally, I challenge you, that if you have not already prayed to receive Jesus into your heart, so that you can have eternal life, & be guaranteed an eternal place in Heaven, then please do so immediately, to keep you safe from what is soon coming upon the earth!

If we confess our sins, God will save us from our sins and mistakes.

1 John 1:9 If we confess our sins, He is faithful and just to forgive us our sins and to cleanse us from all unrighteousness.

Jesus stated in **Revelations 3.20** "Behold, I stand at the door and knock, if any man hear my voice, and open the door, I will come in to him and live with him and him with me".

"He who believes on the Son of God has eternal life." John 3.36. That means right now!

PRAYER: Once saved, you are eternally saved, and here is a very simple prayer to help you to get saved:

"Dear Jesus, please come into my heart, forgive me all of my sins, give me eternal life, and fill me with your Holy Spirit. Please help me to love others and to read the Word of God in Jesus name, Amen".

Once you've prayed that little prayer sincerely, then you are guaranteed a wonderful future in Heaven for eternity with your creator and loved ones. "For God is Love" **(1 John 4.16)**

As I mentioned earlier in this book, your Salvation does not depend on you going to church, and your good works.

Titus 3.5 states "Not by works of righteousness which we have done, but according to His mercy he saved us".

Your salvation only depends on receiving Christ as your saviour, not on church or religion!

(If I could get saved having been an atheist and an evolutionist whilst at university, then anyone can get saved! Just challenge God to prove He exists & ask Him into your heart! He will show up in your life & teach you the truth!) **(John 14.6)**

"He that comes unto Me I will in no wise cast out"- Jesus

Jesus explained that unless you become as a child you won't even understand the Kingdom of Heaven. **(John 3.3)**

[How I Personally Got Saved When I Was 20 Years Old - By S N Strutt] **http://www.outofthebottomlesspit.co.uk/413469553]**

APPENDIX 1: More 'Credits' details:

R.H.Charles translated the 'Testaments of the Twelve Patriarchs' from Latin into English in 1917] Robert Charles (scholar) - Wikipedia

The original Hebrew version was translated into Latin in the 13th century by the bishop of Lincoln - Robert Grosseteste, who stated that he believed that the Testaments were a genuine work written by the Twelve Patriarchs - the sons of Jacob. Robert Grosseteste - Wikipedia

'The Testaments of the Twelve Patriarchs on which this Testaments of the Twelve Patriarchs -'*Insights*' book is based, was translated into English from Latin by R.H.Charles in 1917 and was part of the Apocrypha and Pseudepigrapha.

The Hebrew original of this text was translated from Hebrew into Latin in the 13th century by the bishop of Lincoln, Robert Grosseteste. According to Canon R.H. Charles in translating this book from Latin into English in 1917 he stated that: 'The bishop of Lincoln in translating the book of the Testaments of the Twelve Patriarchs into Latin in the 13th century also accused the Jews of hiding this important book because it spoke in such derogatory terms about the Levites and what would become known as the Pharisees and Sadducees in the 30 years leading up to the birth of the Messiah'. He also believed that the Christian interpolations were the genuine product of Jewish Prophecy.

APPENDIX II Meaning of the word Israel:

'Israel' is the Hebrew name Yisrael, meaning God contends, or one who 'struggles with God'.

Genesis 32.24-28 'And Jacob was left alone and wrestled with a man (angel) until the breaking of day; and he said, 'Thy name shall no longer be Jacob but Israel for as a prince thou hast power with God and with men and hast prevailed.'

This verse showed that Jacob had to keep wrestling with the angel until he got the blessing and so is it with all of us in this life, we must all keep fighting spiritually until we prevail.

Those identified with the name Israel are God's people, chosen for a purpose. And that is what Israel ultimately means: God's people.

APPENDIX III

It is stated that Moses was born in 1571 BC according to Exodus 2 in my Thomson chain ref Bible, which is around 94 years after the death of the Patriarchs.

APPENDIX IV

Abraham was the first to learn Hebrew which was the language of Creation according to the Book of Jubilees.

APPENDIX V

A Pharisee was the last Maccabee king/priest of Israel. The Pharisees were a political party in 70 BCE along with the Sadducees. Like the Zealots that Judas was part of, the Pharisees could not stand Jesus the Messiah's doctrine of 'love your enemies' as they wanted to kick out the Romans from Israel. The 'Powers that be did not like Jesus' doctrine of Love. They then committed the crowning crime of all of history is crucifying their own Messiah, and as a direct result as Jesus said very clearly directly to their faces in Matthew 23 'Your House is left to you desolate.

APPENDIX VI

There were Warrior King Priests mentioned along with the Maccabee King/ Priests around 100 BCE by Canon Charles in his commentary on the TESTAMENT of the 12 Patriarchs in 1917. -From the 'Antiquities of the Jews' by Josephus in 100 AD.

APPENDIX VII

Apart from the High Priests at the time of the crucifixion of Christ, many of the priests did believe in Jesus and a large portion of the people heard Jesus gladly. It would appear that only the very powerful and rich rejected Jesus and wanted Him killed. A large amount of Jewish Christians were warned by a prophet of God not to stay in Jerusalem in 66 AD. So, the Christians went to live up in the hills, and fled to other places, and as a result were not massacred by the Romans under general Titus in 70 AD.

When the Jews returned to the land of Israel in 1947 there were 50,000 Palestinians living there who were largely Christians...but that is another story.

APPENDIX VIII

In the Book of Jubilees it is brought out how Israel was cultivated originally by Isaac, Jacob and then his 12 sons. As Abraham, Isaac, Jacob and the 12 Patriarchs lived in tents and kept travelling around the country they actually irrigated the land of Israel. Israel normally looks like a baren land. Fortunately, there are many underground streams and rivers right under the land of Israel. All that Abraham and then Isaac had to do was to dig wells. Then fountains would spring up and then oases would form to feed the people and animals. Truly amazing. Isaac one time in digging a well also talked about 'Living Waters' just as Jesus the Messiah did in the New Testament. 'He that believeth on Me as the scripture hath said out of his belly shall flow rivers of living waters'. -Jn 7.37 See the Story of Jesus and the woman at the well which was one of Jacob's wells dug 2000 years before his time.

APPENDIX IX

How long do books last? All books made of paper and papyrus disintegrate within 200 years, so there have been many faithful scribes keeping the scriptures alive.

APPENDIX X - THE HISTORY OF THE WARRIOR KINGS OF ISRAEL

The last Maccabee was a Pharisee and was both Warrior Priest and King. Although, I would agree that the Maccabee brothers could have fit the description given in the Testaments of the Twelve Patriarchs - so could also many of kings of Israel who had gone before – King David, and other Kings of Israel. King David was known as a king and also a prophet of God and he was also a mighty warrior.

The point here is that God had made a distinction between the Tribe of Judah for the Kings and Levi for the Priesthood. How could someone be from both tribes at the same time? Mother was from Judah and father from Levi? Jewish custom was to marry from the same tribe normally.

Only man and historians twist the truth to fit their particular fancy of history and make it come out the way that makes them and their political parties look good.

One of the Apocryphal books that I am simply am not sure about is the **Books of the Maccabees.** Why do I say that?

In my opinion Israel took matters into their own hands during the times of the Maccabees. Why? Well, I think that a more relevant question would be 'Why didn't God protect the Maccabees, in the same way that he had miraculously protected the 12 Patriarchs during their long and difficult lives as warriors or even Warrior Kings and Priests circa 1650 BCE. God protected King David miraculously, although he was also a Warrior King and Prophet all the days of his life and had many enemies circa 1030 BC. God also protected king Jehoshaphat in battle because he believed in God circa 900 BCE. In the whole history of the state of Israel some kings believed and fully obeyed God's instructions and yet others partly obeyed like king Josiah circa 630 BCE. He was blessed and protected until he pulled a dumb stunt as to go and fight against the king of Egypt when it simply was not God's will and he got killed for his trouble. A sad story of a king who otherwise had been a godly king. It is dangerous for kings to go ahead without God's direction and blessing as the History of Israel clearly shows us. Another example in Jewish History is big old King Saul circa 1100 BCE. He started off well and was humble and God used him for many years to defeat all of Israel's enemies. But one day he thought he knew better than God and as a direct result lost the kingdom which was inherited by King David.

Notice, that all the Maccabee brothers were nearly all eventually killed or murdered. The last Maccabee was a Pharisee Priest and King from circa105 BCE to 72 BCE. (Antiquities of the Jews-Josephus)

APPENDIX XI

Jesus the Messiah was born in circa 4 BCE and died in 30 AD. He also was the King of Kings and a High Priest after the order of Melchizedek.

Hebrews 7.1-7 For this Melchisedec, king of Salem, priest of the most high God, who met Abraham returning from the slaughter of the kings, and blessed him; ² To whom also Abraham gave a tenth part of all; first being by interpretation King of righteousness, and after that also King of Salem, which is, King of peace;³ Without father, without mother, without descent, having neither beginning of days, nor end of life; **but made like unto the Son of God; abideth a priest continually.**⁴ Now consider how great this man was, unto whom even the patriarch Abraham gave the tenth of the spoils.⁵ And verily they that are of the sons of Levi, who receive the office of the priesthood, have a commandment to take tithes of the people according to the law, that is, of their brethren, though they come out of the loins of Abraham:⁶ But he whose descent is not counted from them received tithes of Abraham, and blessed him that had the promises.⁷ And without all contradiction the less is blessed of the better.

The Pharisees could not stand the teachings of Jesus or accept that he was the Messiah because He taught about love and loving your enemies instead of slaughtering them on the spot if at all possible, which did not fit into the Pharisee political 'control mechanism'.

The truth is that the Pharisees hated Jesus their own Messiah because Israel had become satanic in nature at least in its leadership in the years leading up to Christ.

Paul also warned people in his writings about not being 'under the letter of the law' –

John 1.17 The Law came by Moses, but Grace and truth by Jesus Christ.

Christ is the one who brought in dire change and kicked out the old law of an 'Eye for an Eye' and a 'Tooth for a Tooth' and replaced it with God's original commandment of 'Love the Lord your God with all of your heart and soul mind and 2ndly to Love your neighbour as yourself',

APPENDIX XII Who was the Author of the Twelve Testaments of the Patriarchs?

According to R.H. Charles, who translated the Testaments of the 12 Patriarchs from Latin into English in 1917, the Pharisees, which were a political party of priests in 100 BCE, were trying to take the credit for the writing of the Testaments of the 12 Patriarchs, as they thought that those manuscripts mentioned 'warrior king-priests'. as they had one warrior King-Priest, the last Maccabee brother from 100 BCE until 70 BCE who himself happened to be a Pharisee. **Robert Henry (R. H.) Charles:** Robert Henry Charles (scholar) - Wikipedia

In my opinion the Pharisees were simply trying to twist the narrative to try and make themselves popular - but the truth is that the people did not like them according to R.H. Charles article about that time period.

Contrary to what others have suggested, I believe that The Testaments of the 12 Patriarchs could **not** have been originally written in 100 BCE! Why?

1) Because some odd things that they stated were not written in the Bible or even the Book of Jubilees known as Little Genesis to the Jews.

2) Even a Pharisee would not get away with corrupting the scriptures and writing a random story that made him popular.

3) Another important point is why would a writer who was supposedly a Pharisee write in very derogatory terms against the Levite Priests meaning themselves in that time period. The Testaments of the Twelve Patriarchs also prophesied that Israel would become progressively very wicked and that Israel would be eventually judged and kicked out of its own lands many times and their land left desolate in the time of the coming Messiah because of their cruel treatment and murder of their own Messiah.

4) From 100 BC forwards Israel was only captured by her enemies one time in 70 AD by the Romans. If the Testaments of the Twelve Patriarchs was written by the Patriarchs themselves, then the story makes much more sense, as Israel was separated in 722BC into the 10 Northern Tribes and the Southern 2 tribes. The 10 Northern tribes were taken away captive into Assyria. Then in 589 BC the Babylonians through Nebuchadnezzar took Jerusalem and the Southern two tribes captive to Babylon. Israel was totally thrown out of Israel altogether in 70 AD by the Romans, exactly 40 years after Jesus prophesied that the land of Israel would be made desolate in Matthew 23 because Israel did not receive the truth of her own Messiah -Jesus and crucified Him. The Jews were crucified by the Romans some 40 years after the death of Christ because of their rebellion against God Himself.

The Twelve Patriarchs actually warned that this would happen to Israel. It does not make sense therefore for a Pharisee of all people – the ones who killed their own Messiah to write a book that was so condemning of the Pharisees in particular. The Pharisees and the Sadducees were like two warring political religious parties in 100 BCE. It is possible that a faithful scribe re-wrote the old Testaments of the 12 Patriarchs in 100 BC, but certainly he could not have been the original author because of the specific details written in the Original Testaments.

5) The reason that these Twelve Testaments could not have been written in 70-100 BC is simple. Back in those times the largest Library in the world at Alexandria would pay lots of money to get a hold or original documents and would copy them and put them into their Library. The older the manuscripts the more money was paid. It is very likely therefore that those putting together the Testaments of the 12 Patriarchs were merely re-assembling older manuscripts. Another fact is that the 12 Testaments contain a lot of anti-Israel material which is very unusual for Israel. Only if the 12 Patriarchs had written the original documents would Israel take notice to them as the documents would be regarded as sacred and not to be interfered with or altered.

APPENDIX XIII: THE ANCIENT LIBRARY AT ALEXANDRIA IN NORTHERN AFRICA:

It was built in the time of Alexander the Great, and the Grecian World Empire.

Here is a YOUTUBE VIDEO that I recently made: (13) 'INSIGHTS BOOKS' by S N Strutt: ALEXANDRIAN LIBRARY, THE SEPTUAGUINT & THE APOCRYPHA BOOKS - YouTube

Here is a written summary of some of the above video content: '**HIDING THE TRUTH':** Someone or someone with authority, has deliberately tried to hide the truth from everybody about past biblical History. The truth is always being hidden away when it suits the purposes of the rulers of the world. We know that they did not like the **BOOK OF ENOCH** and banned it for 1000 years under the Catholic church inquisition, people were burned at the stake for possessing the Book of Enoch for 1000 years. Why? What were the 'powers that rule' afraid of in the Book of Enoch? If the powers that be can't exactly totally hide something away that is inconvenient for their 'paradigm of truth' which is really a lie such as Evolution or the lie of Global Warming' they have so much money and control all the main media in modern times that they spend their time discrediting the truth in many areas from science to history to true medicine. The far past biblical history proves that God exists and Satan and his crowd don't want people to believe in God and especially not in Jesus, as they might get genuinely saved and escape the fangs and claws of the Devil in a fiery hell.

One pivotal point or nugget of true wisdom and knowledge is to know why the SEPTUAGINT and in fact many of the Ancient Jewish books were supposedly written in around 300 BCE to 100 BCE including many of the Apocryphal books. Why?

Sometimes ancient Hebrew books like the ancient Book of Enoch has been explained away as having been written by a pseudepigraphal writer in 300 BCE. Pseudepigraphal writer just means someone wrote it other than the original writer. See also the APPENDIX of my books JASHER INSIGHTS & ENOCH INSIGHTS for a lot more on this topiC.

Some 'controllers' have tried to explain away important books that were in fact written in Pre-Flood times, such as THE BOOK OF ENOCH, THE TESTAMENTS OF THE TWELVE PATRIARCHS, which is the book I have just completed, which is called '**THE TESTAMENTS OF THE TWELVE PATRIARCHS-***INSIGHTS'.*

Why was the Septuagint version of the Bible written in 300 BC and who ordered it to be translated from Hebrew into Greek. Did they alter something in the biblical time-line to please the Pharoah Ptolemy?

As many of you know who have read my 'INSIGHTS' books now 7 in number are all based on Apocryphal books. What I have discovered is incredible. That these books were not written between 300 to 100 BCE.

SEE MY BOOKS JASHER INSIGHTS & ENOCH INSIGHTS for more this topic.

More info: [Library of Alexandria - Wikipedia
The library of Alexandria (3): The Library of Alexandria acquired books in a curious way (antiquitatem.com)]

APPENDIX XIV: The Patriarchs and The Heavenly City – The Crystalline 'Foundation Stones' and The 'Pearly Gates' - Revelations: 21.

Revelation 21.12 'And had a wall great and high, and had twelve gates, and at the gates twelve angels, and names written thereon, which are the names of the twelve tribes of Israel.

Revelation 21.14 And the wall of the city had twelve foundations and in them the names of the twelve apostles of the Lamb.

C.1 Have you ever wondered why did God call the Foundations of the Wall after the names of His 12 Apostles and the 12 Pearly Gates after the names of the 12 Patriarchs?

C.2 It would seem that the Pearly Gates represent SALVATION and all have to go through the Gates of Salvation in order to get into Heaven through the Saviour Jesus Christ. It is very interesting that most of the 12 Patriarchs prophesied about the coming Messiah 1650 years before it happened. The Patriarchs in effect pointed the way to the Messiah and thus by inference SALVATION. Somewhere it is written that 'SALVATION' is written above the Gates of the Heavenly City.

C.3 In the case of the Apostles, they were chosen by the Messiah himself to teach others the New Testament teachings of Love for God and for your neighbour and even for your enemies.

C.4 The coming of the Messiah was a total break from the Old Jewish law of an 'Eye for and Eye' and a 'Tooth for a Tooth'. I believe that the Creator built the Heavenly city with the new law of Love in mind when the called the colourful FOUNDATION STONES after the 12 Apostles. Each level is made of a different Crystal which has a different colour. The New Testament made worshiping God much more 'colourful' and 'varied' and not so restrictive as the harsh laws of Moses.

John 1.17 The law came by Moses but Grace and Truth by Jesus Christ

John 4.23-24 'The hour cometh and now is when the true worshippers shall worship God the Father in spirit and in Truth'. For the Father seeks such to worship Him. God is a Spirit and they that worship Him must worship Him in spirit and truth.

When one thinks of the 12 Gates all being made of the same material - PEARLS. What comes to mind is that the 12 PATRIARCHS were all precious in the sight of God in their own and colourful ways. However, they were all the same as regards to their worship of God under the Old rigid Laws of Abraham and Noah. *Pearls are known to reflect many different colours of the rainbow

267

- green and purple and other colours. Related: The healing powers of crystals.

I originally thought that perhaps it had been more suitable for the 12 FOUNDATION STONES to be called after the 12 PATRIARCHS and the 12 GATES after the 12 APOSTLES, but with the above presented argument, I am sure that our Creator got it exactly right, as in calling the 12 Gates after the names of the 12 Patriarchs and the 12 Foundation Stones of the Wall of the City after the 12 Apostles.

Overall thinking about these ideas, one has the impression that the OLD PATRIARCHS pointed the way to Salvation and the 12 Apostles of Jesus the Messiah led the way into the new age of religious freedom where eventually God will not need any religions or temples at all. Jesus is Love, caring, sharing and mercy and healing and His ways of Eternity are reflected in the building of the Heavenly City.

Acts 7.48 Howbeit the Most High abides not in temples made by hands as saith the prophet.

APPENDIX XV The Throne of God

REVELATION Ch 4.4 And around the throne were four and twenty seats: and upon the seats I saw four and twenty elders sitting, clothed in white raiment, and they had on their heads crowns of gold.

Interestingly enough 24 = 2 x 12. What if the 24 ELDERS around the THRONE of GOD mentioned in Revelations 4.4 are 12 PATRIARCHS + 12 APOSTLES which would made a perfect union of the Old and New Testament beliefs. Of course, we can all think of even greater souls such as Enoch, Noah, Abraham, Moses, David, and probably many other wise leaders and kings of Israel down through the annuls of Jewish history which spanned 2000 years. In thinking about this topic my wife mentioned what makes you think that the 24 Elders are permanent positions rather than 'rotating' positions? This brought up the topic of learning. God is always teaching us His children new things. God is anything but stuffy, religious or boring. He likes all of His children to have fun and to enjoy learning His secrets howbeit little by little and not all at once. What if the 24 Elders before the Throne of God changes all the time in order for God to counsel with many different peoples about a whole host of topics. I think that that makes a lot more sense. Also, who is to say that all the elders are men? I doubt that very much! In the Old Testament there were many wise women and also in the New Testament. There were many prophets and prophetesses after the outpouring of the Holy Spirit in the Book of Acts. Notice how this present world belittles great women like Mother Theresa for example, not to mention nurses like Florence Nightingale. Motherhood is minimized in the West. All mothers should be encouraged and helped and certainly not belittled. Without the wonderful mothers throughout history of Israel there would not have been any kings or prophets. After all, it is the hand that rocks the cradle, that rules the world.

APPENDIX XVI

What does the Bible tell us about the future as of from 2022 onwards? I personally believe that very soon after the CONFUSION of 2020-2022, we will see the 'Rise of the Anti-Christ' as mentioned so clearly in 2 Thessalonians Ch 2 and in Daniel 11 as well as Matthew 24. There will be the Last 7 years as mentioned in Daniel 9.27 as the Last week or The Last 7- years of man's history. The first three and a half years the Anti-Christ will be doing many signs and wonders and also fulfilling his promises to the peoples of the earth, and thus winning them over to his side where the CONFUSION of FORCE of MANDATES of 2020-2022 have failed miserably because the 'Elite rulers' simply don't understand people and their emotions. Why? Because many politicians are guided and even in some cases controlled by non-human entities or demons/devils. In the middle of the Last 7 years Satan will possess the Anti-Christ and rule over the world. That's when the real trouble begins with the setting-up of the Image of the Beast and the Mark of the Beast. Then the peoples of the earth will all be branded with the Mark of the Beast and be forced to worship the Devil or DIE! It all sounds so silly and childish in a way, but sadly like for the persecution of the Jews in Nazi Germany in the 2nd world war these things can happen, as long as Satan still exists. This is also the time of Jacob's trouble and Matthew 24.

Thus, the Great Tribulation will begin. After three and a half years of that then comes the RAPTURE of the SAINTS.

75 Days Later - the Millennium Begins which will be The Golden Age of Peace.

Apart from Jesus our Saviour, all of the resurrected saints will be ruling and reigning along with the help of God's angels.

APPENDIX XVII THE 'FEMALE' HOLY SPIRIT

I believe that the Holy Spirit, who became much more evident at the time of the apostles and thus from Jesus time onwards, she being female according to Proverbs 8 and many other scriptures throughout Holy texts will send her maidens (spirits) down to earth to influence mankind much more in the future and there will be much more feminine traits appreciated such as Love, Kindness, Mercy, Forgiveness and a mothering spirit.

The problem with our present world is that it is too satanic and governed by force and war and trickery and certainly not by love and humility.

In the Kingdom of God, what really counts is humility and having all the fruits of the Spirit. The Feminine Holy Spirit: *The earliest Christians – all of whom were Jews – spoke of the Holy Spirit as a feminine figure. The present article discusses the main proof texts, ranging from the 'Gospel according to the Hebrews' to a number of testimonies from the second century. The ancient tradition was, in particular, kept alive in East and West Syria, up to and including the fourth century Makarios and/or Symeon, who even influenced 'modern' Protestants such as John Wesley and the Moravian leader Count von Zinzendorf. It is concluded that, in the image of the Holy Spirit as woman and mother, one may attain a better appreciation of the fullness of the Divine.* http:www.hts.org.za/index.php/HTS/article/view/3225/html

& The Holy Spirit: The Feminine Aspect Of the Godhead | Pistis Sophia

Women to Rule much more in the future: The real feminine values will be much more appreciated in the future. So, summing up, women will be much more appreciated as leaders and counsellors in the future. There will be a perfect balance of male and female in the future world.

There will be no more religious narrow-minded statements such as 'Let the women keep silent in the church' made the apostle Paul who was a eunuch. Those days will be over, along with all the 'letter of the Law' religious rules, as God's only Law will be Love.

'There is no male of female in Christ Jesus.'

Matthew 22.37- 40 'Thou shalt love the Lord thy God with all thy heart and all thy mind and with all thy spirit' & secondly, 'Thou shall love thy neighbour as thyself.' On these two commandments hang all the 'Law and the Prophets'.

APPENDIX XVIII – Prophecies Fulfilled In The Messiah Jesus Christ

In the first books of the Bible, known as the "Old Testament," over 300 such predictions about the "Messiah" or "Saviour" can be found. The discovery of hundreds of ancient Old Testament manuscripts by archaeologists during this century has proven without a doubt that these prophecies were indeed written centuries and even thousands of years before this man called Jesus was born.

Here is a small sampling of the kind of specific predictions we're talking about:

In **750 B.C.**, the prophet Isaiah made the astounding prediction that:

"The Lord Himself Shall Give You A Sign; Behold, A Virgin Shall Conceive And Bear A Son, And Shall Call His Name Emmanuel."- ISAIAH 7:14.

Seven and a half centuries later, a young virgin girl in Israel named Mary was visited by the angel Gabriel, who announced to her that she would bear a Son Who would be called Emmanuel, which means "God with us." The books of the Bible which were written after Jesus came to Earth, the "New Testament," tell us that, "Mary said to the angel, 'How can this be, seeing I have not lain with any man?' And the angel answered, 'The Spirit of God shall come upon you, and the power of the Almighty shall overshadow you! Therefore, that Holy One which shall be born of you shall be called the Son of God!'"-**Luke 1:26-35**.

So, even the very beginning of His life on Earth - His conception and birth were not only unique, but miraculous, in that the simple and humble young girl who became His mother had never slept with a man! In fact, the Bible tells us that the news of her pregnancy was so shocking to the young man to whom she was engaged to be married, Joseph, that when he learned about it he promptly decided to break off the engagement and call off the wedding! - Until the angel of the Lord appeared to him also, and instructed him to stay with her and rear and protect the very special child that she was carrying.

A full **800 YEARS** before Jesus was born, the prophet **Micah** foretold the exact village where the Messiah would be born:

"You, Bethlehem, Though You Are Small Among the Clans of Judah, Yet Out of You Shall He Come Forth Unto Me Who Is To Be Ruler Over Israel; Whose Goings Forth Have Been of Old, From Days of Eternity."- MICAH 5:2

Although His earthly parents lived in the town of Nazareth, 100 miles to the north of Bethlehem, a decree from Rome demanded that all families return to their ancestral homes to register for a worldwide census. The decree came just as Mary's child was due to be born.

Thus, God used a Roman emperor, Caesar Augustus, to help bring about the fulfilment of Micah's prophecy. Joseph and Mary journeyed to Bethlehem, and upon their arrival, Mary went into labour, and as the Gospels inform us, "Jesus was born in **Bethlehem** of Judea" (**Matthew 2:1**), just as the prophet Micah predicted.

Micah's prophecy also tells us that the Messiah "Has been of old, from days of Eternity." Jesus Himself said, "Before Abraham was (around 2000 B.C.), I Am."-**John 8:58**.

Abraham was the forefather of the Jews and Arabs, who lived about 2,000 YEARS before Jesus was born to Mary. So, Jesus was referring here to His **pre-existence with God** before His life on Earth in the form of a man.

Though born in Bethlehem, Jesus grew up in Nazareth. In His first recorded public address there, He openly declared that He indeed *was* the fulfilment of the Old Testament prophecies regarding the Messiah.

While attending the local house of worship, He stood up before the crowd and read a prophecy from the book of the prophet Isaiah. In the passage, Isaiah predicted that the Messiah would be anointed with the Spirit of God to "preach Good News to the poor, to heal the broken hearted, to give freedom to the captives, recovering of sight to the blind and to set at liberty those who are oppressed, to proclaim the acceptable year of the Lord."

Isaiah 61:1,2.

The New Testament tells us that after He read this prophecy aloud to the congregation, Jesus told them, "Today is this Scripture fulfilled in your ears!"- **Luke 4:18-21**.

Another outstanding prophecy regarding the Messiah was made by Israel's King David around the year **1000 B.C.**, or over **10 centuries** before Jesus was born. In his prophecy, David gave details of a cruel and agonising death which he himself never suffered:

"I am poured out like water, and all my bones are out of joint. My heart is like wax, it has melted within me...Like a pack of dogs, they have surrounded me; a company of evil doers has encircled me. They have pierced my hands and my feet. They divide my clothing among them and cast lots for my garment."- **Psalm 22:14-18.**

King David died a peaceful, natural death, so we know he was not talking about himself in this passage of Scripture. But being a prophet, he predicted with unerring accuracy the circumstances surrounding the cruel death on the cross of the Messiah, the Christ that was to come. Let's examine some of the details outlined in the above prophecy:

"I am poured out like water...my heart is melted within me." Jesus not only poured out His life for us spiritually, but the New Testament tells us that shortly after He died, while He was still hanging on the cross, "one of the soldiers pierced His side with a spear, and immediately 'blood and water flowed out'."-**John 19:34**.

Modern medical authorities have affirmed that in the case of heart rupture-- when a human heart literally bursts open under extreme stress and trauma-- the blood collects in the pericardium, the membranous sac that encloses the heart and the roots of the main blood vessels. This blood then separates into a sort of bloody clot and a watery serum, thus when the soldier pierced His side, His life was literally, "poured forth like water."

(Unwittingly, this Roman soldier fulfilled another prophecy, "They will look upon Me whom they have **pierced**," a prophecy given by the Prophet Zechariah around **500 B.C.**--**Zechariah 12:10**.)

"All my bones are out of joint."--This is one of the horrors of death by crucifixion; the weight of the victim's body literally pulls his arms out of their sockets.

"Like a pack of dogs...a company of evil doers has encircled me."

The New Testament tells us that Jesus' wicked and vengeful religious enemies, the Scribes and the Pharisees, gathered around Him as He was nailed on the cross, mocking and reviling Him. - **Matthew 27:39-44.**

"They have pierced my hands and my feet." This is probably the most astounding prediction within this prophecy. Crucifixion was not practiced by the Jews of David's time.

Their religious laws demanded that criminals be executed by *stoning*.

But God showed His Prophet, David, how the Messiah would die 10 centuries later, executed at the hands of an empire that did not even exist in David's day, Rome, whose principal means of executing criminals was crucifixion!

"They divide my clothing among them and cast lots for my garment." In the Gospels of the New Testament we find the almost incredible fulfilment of this prophecy: "When the soldiers had crucified Jesus, they took His clothes, and divided them into four shares, one for each of them, with the undergarment (a long robe-like tunic) remaining. This garment was seamless, woven in one piece from top to bottom. So they said one to another, 'Let us not tear it, but let us cast lots to decide whose it shall be.'"--**John 19:23,24.**

In **487 B.C.**, the prophet **Zechariah** predicted: "And I said unto them, if you

272

think well, give me my price; and if not, keep it. So they paid me **30 pieces of silver."--Zechariah 11:12.**

On the night that Jesus was arrested by His enemies, the New Testament tells us that, "One of the twelve Apostles, Judas Iscariot, went to the chief priests and said to them, 'What will you give me if I deliver Him to you?', and they counted out for him 30 pieces of silver."-**Matthew 26:14,15.**

Imagine! Over five hundred years before the event took place, God's Prophet, Zechariah, predicted the exact "price" that Jesus' enemies would pay to His traitorous disciple, Judas! In the next verse of Zechariah's prophecy, he goes into even more astounding details:

"And the Lord said, 'Cast it unto the potter--the handsome price at which they priced Me!' So, the 30 pieces of silver were taken and cast to the potter in the House of the Lord."-**Zechariah 11:13.**

The New Testament tells us that, "When Judas saw that Jesus was condemned, he repented, and returned the 30 pieces of silver to the chief priests of the Jews, and he cast down the pieces of silver in the Temple. Then the chief priests picked up the silver pieces and said, 'It is against our law to put it into our treasury because it is blood-money.' So they used the money to buy a potter's field, to bury foreigners in."-

Matthew 27:3-6. The 30 pieces of silver were literally "Cast to the potter in the House of the Lord"!-Just as Zechariah predicted 500 years earlier!

In 712 B.C., the prophet Isaiah predicted that the Son of God would "be given a grave with the wicked, and with the rich in his death."-**Isaiah 53:9.**

Jesus' bitter religious enemies condemned Him as a criminal, as a wicked man, thus as he died, the Bible tells us "there were two robbers crucified with Him."-**Matthew 27:38**. After His body was removed from the cross, "a rich man named joseph of Arimathea went to Pilate and pleaded for the body of Jesus, and when joseph had taken the body, he laid it in his own new tomb."-**Matthew 27:57-60**.-A "Grave with the rich!"

1,000 YEARS before Jesus was born, the Spirit of God prophesied through **King David** that the **Saviour would be resurrected from the dead**: "God will not leave His soul in the grave, neither will He suffer His Holy One to see corruption or decay."-**Psa.16:10.**

King David died and was buried in a grave, and HIS flesh saw corruption and decay. But Jesus was raised from the grave three days after His death! - As the Angel said to the mourners who came to Jesus' tomb, "He is not here, but is risen! Why do you seek the living among the dead?"-**Lk.24:5,6.**

APPENDIX XIX - Can Self Works Save Us?

Many Religions Teach That It Is Necessary For Us To Suffer In Order To Truly Please And Draw Close To God.- Is This True?

No!- God is love, and He loves you very much and wants you to be happy! This is why he's placed you here in this beautiful world in the first place! He intended for you to enjoy living, and has given you the ability, the senses and the environment to do so. he created you to enjoy the life he's given you, and to love and enjoy him forever!

But sad to say, a lot of people do not realise that God wants them to be happy. their concept of religion is like that of the young boy who, while walking home from a religious service that he attended with his strict and ultra-religious grandfather, stopped and spoke to a neighbour's mule. as he stroked the mule's nose he said, "You must be an awfully religious creature, you have such a long, sad face!"

To many, godliness and saintliness are supposed to consist of a denial of all human happiness and general enjoyment of any kind. Some go so far as to believe and teach that any kind of physical pleasure must be sinful or wicked!-And they think that godliness consists of such suffering, pain, self-torture, self-denial and self-crucifixion that you must be in utter misery and agony in order to get close to God! this, thank God, is not the case according to the Bible!

Nevertheless, some poor folks are so obsessed with a fetish for self-denial and self-torture that they actually sit on nails, put skewers through their cheeks, walk barefooted on hot coals, whip themselves and even have themselves nailed to crosses! Purposely suffering all kinds of physical torture because they think that the more they suffer, the more "religious", "holy" or close to god they will become!

It's true that there are times when we may need to sacrifice or suffer, but according to God's Word in the Bible, we do not have to do it on purpose, as some kind of means to gain personal merit or favour with God! If we suffer, it's usually because God allows it for some reason, but it's usually a result of our sacrificing and giving of ourselves in order to help others, not because we necessarily ask for it or want it or think we are gaining any merit or righteousness by it.

IF SELF-DENIAL, SACRIFICE AND SUFFERING ARE NOT THE WAY TO SALVATION, WHAT THEN CAN I DO TO SAVE MYSELF?

Nothing! You can't save yourself! Yet the central belief of almost all of man's religions is that man is basically good & righteous, & he can save himself. In fact, after careful analysis we can safely conclude that there are really only two schools of religious thought & belief in the world: the do-it-yourself religions & the God-alone-can-save-you kind!

Most of the world's religions teach their followers that they can save themselves by their own piety and good works, by their own holiness, by their own sufferings, their own self-denial, or by their own obedience to the laws and traditions of that particular religion! But no man yet has ever been good enough to earn or merit his own Salvation! "For there is not a righteous man upon the earth who always does good and never sins."-Ecclesiastes 7:20.

in the very beginning, God originally intended for each of us to have a close personal relationship and communication with him. he wanted to be our closest friend, someone whose love, faithfulness, concern and care we could always count on.

However, God did not want to make us be friends with him. He could have easily created us all to automatically obey and worship him, like some kind of robots, but he didn't want to force us to love or obey him. This is why he allowed both Good and Evil to be revealed, so that we could each make a personal choice, so we could voluntarily choose to love and obey him, or rebel and go our own way.

Sad to say, each of us has made the wrong choices at some time or another. we have acted selfishly, unkindly and unlovingly, not only hurting others, but even hurting God himself, who as our loving heavenly father, is saddened when he sees we are going the wrong way.

Despite all of our troubles, problems and imperfection, God still loves us and wants to be close to us, to be our nearest and dearest helper and friend. yet no matter how earnestly and sincerely we try by our own piety, good works, suffering etc. To become close to him, to become one with him, to become "enlightened" by him, to attain salvation from him, we will always fall short of reaching this goal. "For all have sinned and come short of the glory of God!" Romans 3:23. No matter how good or righteous we try to be, no matter how severely we discipline ourselves or strive to attain godliness or salvation, it is simply not within man to save himself!

What Then Can I Do To Be Saved? Must I Resign Myself To Remaining Forever Separated From God?

God is so great, so high, so almighty, so beyond our limited human understanding and comprehension, that it is impossible for us to fully understand or grasp him or his ways. He says, "As the heavens are high above the earth, so high are my ways above your ways, and my thoughts than your thoughts!" Isaiah 55:9. But, he so much wanted to help us and to become our close friend that he sent somebody who could show us his love, somebody who could live with us as a man, who could embody and show us what God himself is like.

God loves us so much, He doesn't want us to have to suffer separation from him. When we're without God's love, our hearts can never be truly satisfied, and we will remain spiritually empty and lifeless. So, to bring us his everlasting life and salvation, he sent his own son, Jesus, to earth almost 2,000 years ago.

Jesus was miraculously conceived by the spirit of God and born to a young virgin girl named Mary. He grew up to become, in a sense, a picture of his father, so we could see what the great invisible creator is like. And that picture is a picture of love, for all Jesus did was go about everywhere doing good, helping others and teaching about God's great love for us all.

Finally, Jesus completed his task of proclaiming the good news of salvation to the world, and he gave his life, and was cruelly crucified by his cruel and self-righteous religious enemies. Then three days after his lifeless body was laid to rest in the grave, Jesus arose from the dead, conquering death and hell forever!

The Bible tells us, "God so loved the world (you and me) that he gave his only begotten son (Jesus), that whosoever believes in him, should not perish but have everlasting life." John 3:16. All you have to do now to come into a full and living personal relationship with the God of love is to simply believe on Jesus and accept his free gift of eternal life!

Jesus said, "Greater love has no man than this, that a man lay down his life for his friends." John 15:13. he was the friend who laid down his life for you, so that you would not have to suffer being separated from the God of love who loves you so!

If you would like to personally know God's great love, find the solution to all of your troubles and problems, and be forgiven for all the wrongs that you have ever done, all you have to do is believe on and receive his Son, Jesus, into your heart. Jesus said,

"Come unto me, all you who labour and are heavily burdened, and i will give you rest. ... for I am the way, the truth and the life! no man comes unto the father but by me!"-Matthew 11:28, John 14:6.

Although it may sound so simple or even childlike to you, this is the plan by which the great creator of the universe has chosen to reveal and bring his love, truth and salvation to you and me! He made it so simple that anybody can receive his love. - A young child or an elderly grandparent, a poor peasant or a rich tycoon, an illiterate tribesman or an intellectual scientist, an easterner, westerner, northerner or southerner!-Anybody!-Including you!

in fact, receiving Jesus is so simple that he said, "Unless you humble yourself and become as a little child, you shall not enter into the kingdom of heaven!"-Mark 10:15. will you humble yourself and receive God's love, joy, peace of mind, contentment of heart and eternal life through Jesus as a free gift to you, his child?

Jesus loves you and will give you this wonderful gift right now if you will simply and sincerely pray this little prayer and ask him to personally come into your heart:

"Dear Jesus, I know that I need help and that I can't save myself. I have heard that you are the Son of God, and that through you I can personally find and know the God of love. Jesus, I need your love to cleanse me from all fear and hate. I need your light to drive away all darkness. and I need your peace to fill and satisfy my heart. So, I now open the door of my heart and I ask you, Jesus, to please come in and give me your free gift of eternal life! thank you, Jesus, for suffering for all of the wrong I have done and for forgiving me and hearing my prayer! in Jesus' name, amen."

Now that you have asked Jesus to come into your heart, a wonderful new life has begun for you! The Bible says, "If anyone be in Christ, he is a new creation. old things are passed away, behold, all things are become new!"-2 Corinthians 5:17.

My 7 Insights books:

These books are all based on Jewish apocryphal books or Hebrew books including 1) 'Enoch Insights' is based on the Book of Enoch.

2) 'Ezdras Insights' is based on the Book 2nd Esdras

3)'Jubilees Insights' is based on the 'Book of Jubilees'.

4) 'Jasher Insights' Book 1 is based on the Book of Jasher

5) Jasher Insights Book 2 is based on the Book of Jasher.

6) Eden Insights is based on the Lost Books of Adam and Eve.

7) 'The Testaments of the 12 Patriarchs' "*Insights*" is based on 'The Testaments of the 12 Patriarchs'.

All these books can be found at Amazon.com

My 1st book or the 'eighth book' is called '**OUT OF THE BOTTOMLESS PIT**' and is about the paranormal, as related to scriptures and the above-mentioned '*Insights*' books, which are based on the apocryphal books. Amazon. co.uk

See my class of the **Coming of the 3rd TEMPLE in Jerusalem:** MY ARTICLES 2 - www.outofthebottomlesspit.co.uk

Feel free to write me – Steve, at: strangetruths@outofthebottomlesspit. co.uk